Corporate Communications

Corporate Communications

A 21st Century Primer

Joseph Fernandez

Response Books
A division of Sage Publications
New Delhi / Thousand Oaks / London

659
F36c

First published in 2004 by

Response Books
A division of Sage Publications India Pvt Ltd
B-42, Panchsheel Enclave
New Delhi 110 017

Sage Publications Inc
2455 Teller Road
Thousand Oaks, California 91320

Sage Publications Ltd
1 Oliver's Yard, 55 City Road
London EC1Y 1SP

Published by Tejeshwar Singh for Response Books, typeset in 11/13 pts Baskerville MT by Innovative Processors, New Delhi, and printed at Chaman Enterprises, New Delhi.

Library of Congress Cataloging-in-Publication Data

Fernandez, Jospeh, 1968-
    Corporate communications : a 21st century primer/Joseph Fernandez.
        p. cm.
    Includes bibliographical references and index.
    1. Business communication. 2. Advertising. 3. Public relations. I. Title.

HF5718.F47   659—dc22   2004   2004019688

ISBN: 0–7619–9746–6 (PB)   81–7829–424–9 (India–PB)

Production Team: Geetanjali Minhas, R.A.M. Brown and Santosh Rawat

For my Mother
Grace Fernandez
(1938-2002),
who walked this earth
with Love, Life & Laughter

Contents

List of Figures

List of Boxes

Acknowledgements

CORPORATE *Communications: A 21st Century Primer* is, in many ways, the chronicle of a personal journey through the worlds of advertising, journalism and corporate communications. And, its acknowledgements span associations made over a decade. In terms of academics, I remember with gratitude, the following people: Professor Francis Jose of Loyola College, Madras; Jacob C. Varghese of Madras Christian College; Marie Gillespie, Thor Ekevall and late Geoff Mungham of the School of Journalism Studies at Cardiff University, Britain. A special thought for Steve Sawyer, Giovanni Facchini, Ursual Zerle-Facchini, Lana Nowatschek, Karen Sands, Robert Cheung, Fabienne Cotte and Gerald Kochappan: all friends from a very special time in Wales.

I acknowledge the men and women who have constituted my media experience. George Jacob of Anugraha Communications; Abraham Eraly, Janaki Venkataraman and the feisty team at Aside—India's first city magazine—it was here that I learned to write. S. Muthiah the doyen of Madras Publishing and Editor of Madras Musings, K.S. Ramakrishnan and Vincent D'Souza, founders of Chennai's neighbour newspapers and Aubrey and Maria Sequeira of Goldwire Communications, whose organization unveiled for me, the potential of the Information Age.

This book has been made a new era reality, thanks to friends and the gentle folk at Median, who contributed centrally to its form. They are the royal 'We' in this book. For their insights, inputs and inspiration, I acknowledge R. Sreedhar, Fern Pereira, Pricilla Victor, Vandana Vishwanath, Anna Preetha Jacob, Lincoln Victor and Snathos Malliah. And, our friends in the media: Jonathan and Deepika Davidar, Visalakshi and CT Ramasamy, Ramkumar

Singaram, Arup Kavan and Vanaja Pillai of Ogilvy PR Worldwide. For their presence at crucial stages of this book, I thank Dr. Varaprasad Rau, R.K. Dastur and Harry Davidar. The Jambotkar family—Anil, Birdie, Shanta and Raj—whose love, and support continue to be an abiding presence in my life.

For the spiritual guidance that shaped the soul of this book, my immeasurable gratitude to Joe Mannath SDB, Francis Gonsalvez SJ, and Thomas George MSFX. This book is in your hands today, thanks to the vision, support and effort of the following people: Tejeshwar Singh and Udaya Kumar at Sage Publications and the determined team I have known at Response Books: Ranjan Kaul, Anil Chandy, Leela Gupta and for his unstinted support, Chapal Mehra.

Beyond its dedication to my beautiful mother, Grace, this book owes its support to my family: my father Frankpet and Manuel, Mark, Marissa and Marinelle and Don. In a special way, I remember Randa Fernandez, whose love completes Life, as I know it. You, the Reader, are the purpose of this book. I hope that it marks for you, the beginning of an eventful journey—full of wondrous learning—in the realm of Corporate Communications. Centuries ago, intrepid old world explorers on their way to a brave new world wished each other 'Godspeed'. As your own journey begins, I leave you with that same wish: *Vaya Con Dios*!

Joseph Fernandez
June 2004, Chennai

Introduction

SOMEWHERE along your journey through this book, you will come across a nugget of corporate wisdom, a passing phrase that might have escaped your attention, if you had not read this. When you do, I invite you to reflect on the measure of its worth for you. The phrase reads: an evolved response to the business realities of the 21st century. Historically, the 'evolved response' triggered meta-leaps of understanding and imagination that transformed human history. The Wright Brothers. Henry Ford. Alexander Graham Bell. Each of them transformed their worlds with evolved responses to their times.

In the business world, corporate communications is precisely that. An evolved response to the communication needs of the modern corporate. *Corporate Communications: A 21st Century Primer* is your pivotal introduction to this emerging world. Are you immersed in the academic study of advertising, public relations, business management, mass/visual communications or corporate communications? Or, are you a management professional in a real-time work environment, grappling with the task of becoming a corporate communicator? If the answer to either of these questions is a resounding yes, then consider this book, written for you—and written by someone like you.

Corporate Communications: A 21st Century Primer offers you a rich lore of contemporary theory, embedded with real-time practice over 10 chapters. It begins with an invitation. And, then accompanies you on the journey through the emergence and evolution of the modern business organization. What makes the 21st century corporate tick? And, how does its management view its presence?

More importantly, how is its essence—its mission, vision and core values—communicated to the world? The Primer brings you the insider-view on these compelling questions of corporate existence. Corporate communications, it then argues, is a key cornerstone for its future growth. The Primer looks at contemporary definitions of corporate communications, and sets the frame of reference for the book. It presents the brand, as the core of a corporate's existence. Corporate communications, in other words, is the way that a Corporate communicates.

And, who exactly does the new era corporate communicate to? Does everyone get the same core messages? Or do different approaches exist? In any case, who are the audiences, communities or publics that today's corporate seek to communicate with? The Primer chances upon those surprising answers in the 'Domains of Influence'. A brand is best built through advertising. Or, is it? As corporate communications and public relations practice move to the fore, the Primer looks into the case for advertising, arguably the most potent tool of brand-building. Public relations has for long, been considered the nurturing ground of Corporate communications. Discover for yourself, how 'PR' functions in our new era, as a Market Strategy, an Image Builder and a Crisis Manager. Read the amazing story of how the Hot Shoe Dance Company became one of India's most desired performing companies—thanks to a nifty PR strategy!

The traditional media and the new media provide technology platforms on which corporate communicators weave brand magic to create lasting brands. The Primer leads you through a corporate communicator's understanding of the traditional and new media—backed with step-by-step case studies that have worked successfully. And, so how does corporate communications really work? Four real-time case studies prove that they do—a beach resort, an heritage village, a classic two-wheeler manufacturer and, India's largest network and e-Commerce services corporation. All organizations with an agenda for brand-building and business growth—with diverse approaches to communicate, survive and thrive. The industry case-studies spotlighted here tracked the concerned organizations over a four-year period. In the process, they tracked the way these organizations dealt with the overwhelming challenge of steering a modern enterprise, through the choppy, often turbulent, waters of the new era.

The learning then comes full circle. A journey that began with the 21st century Corporate, its emergence and growth ends with you. The Primer, in its final analysis, conclusively spells out the individual qualities, traits and skills that corporate communicators today require to get ahead in real-time work environments. When you have made the compelling journey through this Primer, only one thing remains—an evolved response for your time: to become the corporate communicator that the business world is looking for....

1 The 21st Century Corporate: In the Beginning

...And whether or not it is clear to you,
no doubt, the universe is unfolding as it should

—Desiderata (1692)

IMAGINE, for a moment, that you are on a windswept desert in West Asia. Everywhere around you, the wind howls, as the unforgiving desert keeps up a continuous barrage of sand. All that shelters you is your thick desert clothing. It is 1000 BC. You remind yourself that you are in a journey in a caravan from tropical India carrying invaluable pepper and spices to icy Europe. It is an event-filled journey that lasts months—sometimes even years. You were warned that this is one of the most dangerous routes in the world—the only bridge between the East and the West, in a world that has yet to discover sea routes. The environment is hostile, and dangerous. But the treasure you carry is, in the end, worth every step you take through the bleak West Asian terrain. The treasure is pepper. Back in India, a handful of pepper would fetch you a measly one rupee. But sell the same handful in Europe, and it will fetch you a princely 70 rupees!

'Caravan!' a hoarse voice ahead of you shouts into the sandblasted reality. Through the blurred view of your coarse headdress, you turn to acknowledge a trail of silhouetted figures about 500 metres away. A caravan headed for India, you think to yourself (Business is good these days!). The endless trudge of thoughts leads your mind through trade, commerce and myriad routes—all means to make the world a smaller place. These trade routes, you realize, are the world's most powerful trade 'network', driven by ancient communication. You muse over the countless caravans that traverse thousands of miles, bringing with them goods, commodities and that most valuable resource of all—trade information. The world would not be the same without it, you tell yourself as you disappear into the Medes—the land that history remembers as the 'Middle Land'.

So, what does the company of today—the 21st century Corporate—have in common with a caravan in the extreme desert reality of the Medes? Everything. If you really think about it, like the Medes, the new era's business environment is extremely challenging, ruthlessly competitive and dangerously unpredictable. Like its historical predecessor, today's Corporate is a channel of exchange for goods and services across the world. In its modern avatar, it is driven by the exchange of data and information. Most importantly, the unhindered flow of information is central to its smooth working. Interestingly enough, the word 'Media' itself derives its name from the word 'Medes', or Middle land which was the sole channel for goods, services, trade and information between Asia and Europe—the Orient and the Occident. And, it is here that the world first began to realize the benefits of barter trade—and Globalization.

The vantage point of history is a fascinating one. Standing on it, you would be privileged to witness one of the most vibrant sights on earth—the march of human civilization. Five thousand years of recorded human history tell us that for centuries, the world progressed at a steady pace, with the ancient civilizations in Asia, Europe and the Americas being its hub of development. The onset of the Industrial Revolution in the 18th century was to change all that. It changed the way the world went about its business. The whirr and clank of machines in factories across English cities like London and Manchester began to reverberate through the other countries of Europe and, eventually, through the rest of the world. Through it, the world was to discover the matchless advantages of assembly line production. Every nation would realize that the key to its prosperity lay in the mass-production of goods. For countries like Britain and France, already established colonial powers, it marked a new age of prosperity. In the years to follow, the Industrial Revolution would play a key role in America's rise to world leadership.

The Industrial Revolution's greatest contribution was the timely establishment of vibrant global markets. It ushered in an age of economic prosperity that was to alter the course of world history. Political proof of this view lies in the world's latest strategic alliance—The European Union. For centuries, Europe was a clutch of aggressive nations that were steeped in constant conflict. Two ruthless World Wars in the 20th century left the European economy in ruins. At that point, Europe's visionary statesmen saw a powerful economic truth—international trade and commerce would create an economically prosperous Europe, while creating the conditions for political peace. Since 1942, the European nations, battered by their political folly, have worked towards the growth of a single political and economical entity—The European Union. A long time Euro-observer, Giovanni Facchini, Correspondent at the Rome office of Deutsche Presse Agentur observes that the single most important step in this direction was the introduction of the 'Euro' currency. Through the 'Euro' and other economic measures, every member of the European Union has a shared interest in sustaining its growth. War, they realized, is the worst idea for a win-win situation. A view that South Asia's belligerent powers have woken up to!

Thanks to her unique place in history, India has always played host to a vibrant trade and commerce system. A favoured trade hub of the Old World, India had a robust trade in gems, spices, silk, condiments, handicrafts and precious metals. Over the centuries, Indian bazaars would resound with the chatter of the marketplace and the jingle of prosperity. Merchants negotiated in unknown languages to strike the best deals. In every corner of the country, Arab, Chinese and European traders thronged its marketplaces. Ancient India spawned a very sophisticated barter system, in which gold was the standard currency.

For centuries, India's prosperous trade and commerce system was empowered by its indigenous business communities. It typically comprised trade merchants, jewellers, moneylenders and spice traders who formed the hubs of economic prosperity. In time, these communities would become the hub of India's entrepreneurial tradition. As trade expanded, new sea routes opened up between India and Europe, signalling the start of a new era of trade and political ties. With trade, came colonialism. And, the Industrial Revolution that impacted India's trade and commerce systems by the 19th century. India's significant entry into the Industrial Age marked an important moment in that ongoing historic process known as the March of Civilization. In it, we would understand reasons for the emergence of the 21st century Corporate.

The March of Civilization

The five key eras that have made up the march of civilization are the Agricultural Age, the Industrial Age, the Service Industry Age, the Information Age and our era—the Biotechnology Age. In his book, *The Future Manager: A Value Builder for Tomorrow's Organization*, Satish Khanna elaborates on the five 'Waves of Development' that have marked the march of human civilization:

Development in the past through a series of waves:
(a) The Agricultural Age—the first wave of civilizational growth, and the main source of livelihood until around 500 years ago.
(b) The Industrial Age—the second wave, characterized by the emergence of steel, textile, cement and other core industries in the last few centuries.
(c) The Service Industry age—the third wave, signifying the emergence of services like banking, insurance, travel and communications, around a century ago.
(d) The Information age—the fourth wave, structured around computerisation, automation, telecommunications etc. which started in the 1950s.
(e) The Next wave, the project fifth wave, will be based on advanced biotechnology, bio-informatics and Internet applications.

(Khanna, 2000, p. 10)

The five Ages of Human Civilization, outlined above have led to the emergence of the 21st century Corporate, as we know it today. Fortunately, for us, history has immortalized the moment in which corporate India was born. In 1867, a young Indian stood thoughtful and pensive, in a crowded lecture hall, in Manchester, England. He had come to listen to Thomas Carlyle, the legendary Scottish historian speak on the Industrial Revolution and economic prosperity. One of Carlyle's key thoughts in that address had made the young man's day—the nation that controls iron soon acquires control of gold. On that day, the seed of a vision was sowed. Years later, in 1893, it was time for another historic meeting, this time on a steamer ship sailing from Yokohama to India. On it, he met Swami Vivekananda returning from the famous World Religion Congress in Chicago. During their meeting, the Swami wondered why Indians were still buying Japanese matchboxes. He asked the young man whether he could build a matchbox factory in India. The young man, of course, was ahead of his time—thinking far beyond matchboxes. He was dreaming of steel, and ushering the Industrial Revolution into India. Ten years later, in 1903, Jamsetji Nusserwanji Tata laid the foundations of the Tata Steel plant in Sakchi, (now Jamshedpur).

Today the Tata conglomerate that J.N. Tata founded presides over the Indian markets with diversifications in steel, chemicals, consumer goods, automobiles and information technology. Even today, the founder's qualities of thrift, resilience, and home-grown entrepreneurship stand reflected, in its vision for the new era. In its growth from a family business to a multinational conglomerate, you will find the Tata story, a reflection of the evolution of corporates—in India, across Asia and around the world. But what differentiates a group like the Tatas from the thousands of companies in the global marketplace? Why do some companies blaze their way to prosperity? Why do other lesser known companies fade into obscurity?

The Age of the Corporate

In their already classic book, *Built to Last*, the authors James C. Collins and Jerry I. Porras picked some of America's most endearing companies to study the reasons for their longevity and continued market success. Their conclusion was a case of the unique found in the commonplace. The companies that mattered, the companies that succeeded were, in their words, 'visionary companies'. The authors candidly point out that these companies survived in the long run, because their vision—a shared ideology—became a legacy that outlived its founders.

Over the course of their book, they studied American corporate icons like Disney, IBM, Motorola, 3M and highlighted the reasons for their market standing. Their six year research led to one key concept: 'Preserve the Core and Stimulate Progress'. Capturing the spirit of this thought are the words of Thomas Watson Jr. of IBM in his booklet, *A Business and its Beliefs*—'If an organization is to meet the challenges of a changing world, it must be prepared to change everything about itself except [its basic] beliefs as it moves through corporate life...The only sacred cow in an organization should be its basic philosophy of doing business.' (Watson, quoted in Collins and Porras, 2000, p.1).

In each of their case studies, Collins and Porras eloquently point out that while the company's core values remained the same, the drive for progress led it to evolve for market leadership. They go on to outline five specific methods of 'preserving the core and stimulating progress' in their inimitable style:

Big Hairy Audacious Goals (BHAGs):
Commitment to challenging, audacious—and often risky—goals and projects toward which a visionary company channels its efforts (stimulates progress).

Cult-like Cultures:
Great places to work only for those who buy in to the core ideology; those who don't fit with the ideology are ejected like a virus (preserves the core).

Try a Lot of Stuff and Keep What Works:
High levels of action and experimentation—often unplanned and undirected—that produce new and unexpected paths of progress and enables visionary companies to mimic the biological evolution of species (stimulates progress).

Home-grown Management:
Promotion from within, bringing to senior levels only those
who've spent significant time steeped in the core ideology of
the company (preserves the core).

Good Enough Never is:
A continual process of relentless self-improvement with the
aim of doing better and better, forever into the future
(stimulates progress).

(Collins and Porras, 2000, p.90)

From the vantage point of *Built to Last*, there are Corporates
and there are corporates. And, it is against this backdrop that we
begin to view the emergence of the business organization that we
know as the 21st century Corporate.

Building the New Era Corporate

For those who live its reality, the 21st century Corporate is an
adapting, evolving, growing, living entity that is arguably the single
most powerful catalyst of change on our planet today. It radically
influences the way that we think, work and go about the business
of Life. Because of its vast and diversified nature, the term 21st
century Corporate covers businesses, companies, corporations, and
conglomerates—which are large corporations with wide and
diversified interests. In the scale of evolutionary business growth,
we might look at the 21st century Corporate in the following terms:

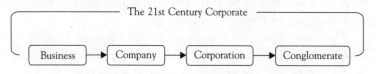

Fig. 1.1: The Evolution of a 21st Century Corporate

Through this approach, you can trace its growth from a
traditional business, to a established company to a transnational
corporation right up to a global conglomerate, seamlessly networked

by strategic alliances. That said, the next key revelation emerges. While the soul of the corporate—its core—remains the same, its character evolves to meet the market needs of its time. At any given point, every Corporate is immersed in three core functions that guarantee its survival—and success:

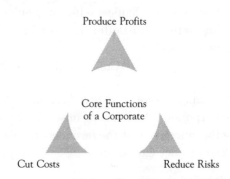

Fig. 1.2: The Time-tested Core Functions of a Corporate

Produce Profits

The key function of the corporate is to create profits. To realize this, it initiates, undertakes and empowers business initiative driven by market strategy. A Corporate's continued existence is assured by its sustained profit-making ability—within the purview of law. The resultant profits are shared among the 'stakeholders' of the corporate i.e., promoters, employees, investors, franchisees and other market partners. Again, in order to 'produce profits', today's corporates look to new and innovative business strategies that build on the synergy of business relationships.

In their book, *The Business of Media: Corporate Media and the Public Interest*, David Croteau and William Hoynes present a compelling example of corporate synergy at work—

> Synergy refers to the dynamic in which components of a company work together to produce benefits that would be impossible for a single, separately operated unit of the company. In the corporate dreams of media giants, synergy

occurs when, for example, a magazine writes about an author, whose book is converted into a movie (the CD soundtrack of which is played on radio stations), which becomes the basis for a television series, which has its own Web site and computer games. Packaging a single idea across all these various media allows corporations to generate multiple revenue systems from a single concept.

(Croteau and Hoynes, 2001, p.74)

Cut Costs

The second key function of a corporate is to cut costs—reducing operational spends, while ensuring that revenues generated are constant or on the increase. While profit making remains the primary function of any corporate, business strategy demands that costs are reduced by improving efficiency and streamlining processes. Japan's phoenix-like rise, from the ashes of the 2nd World War is a now classic example. A war-devastated nation, Japan quickly adopted quality processes that led to competitive costs in the global market. In the production line, this translated into increasingly efficient manufacturing technologies, streamlined processes and trained workforces. In less than five decades, it was to re-emerge a market leader. Following close on the heels of the Japanese example are the Asian Tigers—Korea, Taiwan and now, China.

India's secure niche in the software and outsourcing fields owes its enviable position to the ability to produce world-class software solutions and services, at a fraction of its cost in the West. The current BPO (Business Process Outsourcing) industry allows its client companies to concentrate on their core processes, while outsourcing non-critical processes, bringing down their running costs. Very simply, lower costs mean higher profits.

Reduce Risks

This third, lesser-known function of the corporate is a natural extension of the first two functions. Ruthlessly competitive market environments demand that a corporate reduces its business risk. In a global market, a corporate achieves this by establishing strategic alliances, market partnerships and distribution networks.

This business synergy builds a corporate's market presence, while reducing the overall risk among all its partners. Authors Croteau and Hoynes use the term 'conglomeration' to explain the reduction of risk:

> ...Conglomeration has enabled companies to pursue various business strategies geared to reducing risks. In seeking to ensure continued profits, companies often try to control the environment in which they operate by reducing uncertainty and minimizing expensive competition. By doing so, they can better ensure lower costs and higher profits.
>
> (Croteau and Hoynes, 2001, p.110)

In their landmark book, *Raising the Corporate Umbrella*, authors Kitchen and Schultz provide us with a sneak preview of the markets of the future:

> By 2010 the manufacturer-driven marketplace, and the distribution-driven marketplace will have been dwarfed in comparison (cited in Schultz and Kitchen, 2000) with the global marketplace, which is characterized by interactivity. The most obvious characteristic of the interactive marketplace is that buyers, customers, consumers and stakeholders will have significantly greater access to information than in any previous phase of economic and social development.
>
> (Kitchen and Schultz, 2001, p.14)

In such a competitive market place, it has become clear that alliances, associations, networks, and partnerships are the way ahead, when it comes to producing profits, cutting costs and reducing risks.

Box 1.1
The Emergence of Brand India...

Professor Bala V. Balachandran is your quintessential global Indian. In his academic avatars, he is the J. L. Kellogg Distinguished Professor in Accounting, Information Systems and Director, Accounting Research Centre, North Western University, Chicago. Month after month, he tours the globe seeking out opportunity to highlight India and her cutting-edge corporate potential in a global environment. His associations with Infosys, Wipro, TCS and Lupin Laboratories have led these Indian corporate icons to new levels of corporate excellence. He is the Founder of the Great Lakes Institute of Management (GLIM) in Chennai. Professor Bala chose to view the 21st century Corporate in the light of the sweeping changes in the Asia-Pacific region. A view, he stressed, that was best reflected on, in endless transatlantic flights at about '30,000 feet above sea level':

In the mid 1950s, Arnold Toynbee, the legendary British historian prophesised that in the 21st century, the 'Yellow' race would rule the world. By this old world term, he was referring to the emerging supremacy of Japan and China. The West, he reasoned, would be concentrating on its nuclear pursuits. Five decades later, I see the uncanny accuracy of his vision, with the emergence of the prosperous Pacific Rim countries and now, the Asia-Pacific region, in which Corporate India plays a pivotal role.

I view the emergence of the 21st century corporate in the light of this sweeping global change. The era of 'Brick & Click' companies is already a part of our lives. Where profit-savvy business models, enabled by technology, drive corporations of our future. This wave of innovation and change has affected sweeping change in India. In this light, I see the emergence of Japan as a world platform for R & D quality and excellence. China will fully occupy its niche as the world platform for manufacturing cost-effective products. And, India will become the IT & BPO platform of world. India's unique strengths of its vast professional trained ranks and its IT competencies will ensure that. Where else in the world would you find Meenakshi, from South India, able to transform herself into Michelle with a New Jersey Jewish Accent, to make a perfect product pitch with a potential client?!

(contd.)

Box 1.1 (contd.)

The other sweeping change, I forsee, is the emergence of biotechnology and nano-technology. By 2005, the patents on several established drugs will lapse. And, generic pharmaceutical products will become the order of the day. India, at that point, will be a world production hub of bulk and generic drugs. This will be followed by the 'nano-technology' phenomenon, where technology will take its reign to a microscopic level to play catalyst to 'miraculous' change. Where 'magic' capsules taken by patients will administer timed doses for the system. Where work clothes do not need to be cleaned or ironed—at all. Technology will continue to be that great enabler in our lives.

Over the next fifty years, China, India and their corporates will capture world attention. The rich cultural heritage of these countries will impact the corporate brands that operate out of it. Stand by for the unveiling of new era corporates that are distinctively global—and uniquely Indian. A generation of corporate professionals in their twenties, obsessed with identifying opportunity, creating global quality and delivering on results. In this brave new world, we can look forward to the emergence of Brand India.

Corporate Catalysts of Growth

The development of communications technologies in the 20th century has helped to create the new era Corporate. The key factors that have led to its emergence are Corporatization, Digitization and Globalization. These three catalysts provide the 21st century Corporate with the impetus that it needs in globalized, new era markets (Fig. 1.3).

Corporatization

On the chequered playing fields of global business, the most enduring victories go to master corporate strategists. Their grandmaster-like vision builds on the business learnings of the past,

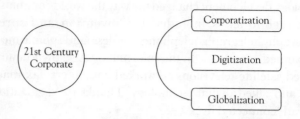

Fig. 1.3: The 21st Century Corporate and its Catalysts of Growth

seizes market opportunity of the present, and rides the crest of future growth. 'Corporatization' is the planned use of business growth strategy in a corporate to radically improve its efficiency and profitability. Based on the 'Produce Profits—Cut Costs—Reduce Risks' paradigm, it implements quantitative measures to produce qualitative growth in Corporates. Corporatization is the stuff that economic miracles are made of. The rise of the Asian tigers—Japan, Korea and Taiwan—stand testimony to that fact.

In the 1940s and 1950s, these countries adopted quality processes that turned them from also-ran imitation-good producers to world leaders in quality manufactured goods. The Japanese industrial juggernaut gave birth to quality concepts like the PDCA cycle (Plan-Do-Check-Act), JIT (Just-In-Time) Management, Poka Yoke, Kaizen (Gradual Change), Kaikaku (Radical Change) and later, TQM (Total Quality Management). In more recent times, quality processes concepts like the BVQI, ISO 9000 certifications, Business Re-engineering Processes, are seen as tools of corporate success in global markets. Ironically today, 'non-profit' organizations are among the strongest supporters of 'corporatization' as a way to survive in the new era.

Digitization

For two decades now, global companies have embraced digital technologies of the new era to become global entities. Historically, this process was a spin-off of the Industrial Age. From the mid 19th century onwards, a series of quantum leaps in communications technology development changed the way the world communicated. These techno-leaps included the invention and spread of photography, telegraph, telephone, wireless, and submarine cables that spanned continents. In the Information Age, their new avatars included satellite television, networked computers, fax machines, ISDN and allied digital technology. Thanks to 'digitization', we now lead 'connected lives'.

Digitization has led to, what media academic Hamid Mowlana terms, 'the growth of dependency on international flows of specialised financial and scientific information'. We are all 'knowledge-workers' in the Information Age. Moreover, Digitization has led us to what communication scholars Arvind Singhal and Everett M. Rogers term 'Informatization'—'the process through which communication technologies are used as strategies for furthering socio-economic development.' (Singhal, A. and Rogers E. M., 2001 p. 278). Informatization refers to communication technologies that offer us an environment where information is gathered, processed and distributed. More importantly for today's corporate communicators, Digitization offers a powerful realm of interaction—a place where the traditional and new media meet.

Globalization

In the early 1960s, Marshal McLuhan, the Canadian media prophet broadcast his vision of the future to a largely puzzled community. He foresaw a single world community—connected by modern telecommunications—in which, countries would be dependent on each other, economically, socially and politically. He called it the Global Village. In the decades to follow, the emergence of the Arab oil states, the Pacific Rim Countries and notably the European Union were to prove his vision accurate. In the early 1990s, yet another term found its way into our collective vocabularies— 'Glocal'. Expanded in its full form, Glocal meant 'think global, act local'. An approach that corporate communicators the world over have put to powerful use.

In its larger interpretation, 'Think Global, Act Local' provides direction to both profit and non-profit organizations that are attempting assiduously to build their presence. For corporates, the term implies the real-time challenge of building a brand, while offering products/services in a dynamic global marketplace. That translates into setting up global quality standards, adopting digital technologies and very simply, building global presence.

Box 1.2
Learn, Evolve, Develop…

As the sluice gates of globalization unleashed their power in India of the early 1990s, Sumanth Sharma returned home after an MS in Industrial Engineering from Purdue University, to consider business opportunities in the era to come. A four month stint at Taiwan led him to the then emerging field of LED (Light Emitting Diodes) manufacture. Today, Sangeetha Enterprises is one of the five LED manufacturers in India. As Sangeetha Enterprises charts new territory in India's burgeoning LED markets, Sumanth spelt out the challenges to business success for a new era enterprise like his:

A 21st Century Corporate, to my mind, is one that has woken up to the realisation that it is doing business in the vibrant marketplace of the Global Village. As entrepreneurs in India, Asia and around the world have discovered, this is a sure-fire way to ensure peak production, distribution and marketing of our brands. The new era will belong to flexible enterprises that are able to evolve to the changing needs of the global marketplace.

For a manufacture-based enterprise like ours, globalization has meant new and wondrous insights into the planning of product cycles to coincide with those of international markets. A decade ago, we operated in a protected environment, hemmed in by legislation. Today, all that has changed. India's new era companies survive and thrive in a gritty environment. And, in ways that even surprise us. Our own company has a product range of over 45 types of LEDs that it offers in the Indian market. However, to get ahead of the competition from China and South East Asia, we need to coincide our product launches with the Chinese New Year!

(contd.)

Box 1.2 (contd.)

The two business organizations that I believe, are conducive to the challenges of the new era market are large corporates and ironically, sole proprietorships. Large corporates—multinationals and transnationals—are naturally globalised and therefore capable of taking on market challenges. In tandem, one must also consider a nimble enterprise like a sole proprietorship that is flexible, able to match the quality of the market leader—and sell the product cheaper.

Enterprises like these reflect the business spirit of the times—evolving their business models, as they go along. Recognizing new products or new ways to manufacture them is one such challenge. Finding new applications for existing product lines is another one. Let me illustrate. India has followed the US early in its initiative to convert traffic signals to more cost-effective LED lights. After all, who would not want lights with an operation life of 11 years?! We were successful in getting the traffic police force in a city like Chennai to use an unique 'Traffic Light Baton' that changed colours from red to green and was especially useful at night. Like I said, new applications for an existing product.

Market awareness and sensitivity has to be factored in, when it comes to a 21st Century Corporate. Though we are a B2B enterprise that deals with Original Equipment Manufacturers (OEMs) of electronic equipment, we need to be tuned in to the market customers' needs. It is the only way ahead. Finally, the 21st Century Corporate will continue to evolve as a flexible, globally aware business organization committed to change, in every sense of the word. I see new era enterprises embarking on the continuous three-step process of 'Learn, Evolve, Develop" to attain market leadership. Perhaps, it is a coincidence that those three words finally read 'LED'!

Corporate Citizenship

Every corporate today, by virtue of its existence in society, is considered a living entity and a corporate citizen in the eyes of law. It is called to affirm its presence by becoming a valid, law-abiding and contributing force in the society that nurtures it. David Appasamy, Chief Communications Officer, SIFY Corporation, speaks of the 'psychological legitimacy' that every corporate today needs to gain in the eyes of its communities. In the new era, a corporate must contribute to its community. By extension, it follows that the community must be kept aware of its contribution to it. 'Corporate Citizenship' represents a complete U-turn from an admittedly exploitative mindset that drove the Industrial Revolution. In Charles Dickens' England, wealth and power lay concentrated with a cartel of industrialists who capitalised on it. Corporate citizenship liberates today's business organizations from that Scrooge-like reputation, born of the Industrial Revolution.

Beyond largesse and charity, corporate citizenship looks at the well-being and diversity of the societies in which organizations function. One can find this vision expressed in the Shell Company's green efforts around the globe, in the TATA Group's schools across the country and the Malayala Manorama Group's initiative to rebuild an earthquake-devastated village in Latur, Maharashtra. In innumerable companies across India, corporate citizenship has translated into local citizenship initiatives, spawning creditable projects in education, empowerment, employment, healthcare and people's welfare.

Taking a cue from this global trend, Philip J. Kitchen and Don E. Schultz, in their seminal work, *Raising the Corporate Umbrella*, dwell on the need for corporate citizenship among 21st century Corporates:

> Even for those firms which maintain a branded approach, many publics (including consumers) are more and more interested in what a company is, where it is coming from, who is managing it, whether there are problems created of an environmental nature because of business processes, and how and in what way the organization as a whole is acting as a solid corporate citizen.
>
> (Kitchen and Schultz, 2001, p.106)

Corporate citizenship begins with vision translated into action, that is then disseminated to society at large, through a corporate voice. In the eyes of society, it bestows a psychological legitimacy on the corporate behind the effort. This, in turn, enables the corporate to ride a crest of goodwill, that further empowers its business and profit-making capabilities. In a larger sense, it gives the corporate a sense of belonging to the larger world community by being 'glocal'—thinking global and acting local. When it comes to corporate citizenship, one of the most respected aphorisms in our popular culture says it all: 'With Power comes Responsibility'.

Wired for Success

It is one of the most compelling success stories of our time. And, it begins at 6 p.m. on 23rd September, 1988, when a starving Indian student arrived at the Los Angeles International Airport from Bangalore. He was there on a scholarship offered by the California Institute of Technology. All of 19 years, he had $400 in his pocket and did not know a single person in America. By 1992, he was a graduate student at Stanford University, attentively listening to America's tech-icons, Scott McNealy of Sun Microsystems and Apple Computers' Steve Wozniak. And, like Jamsetji Nusserwanji Tata at Manchester more than a century ago, young Sabeer Bhatia was already dreaming—of business ideas that lay unexplored in cyberspace. After university, Sabeer worked with FirePower Systems, (a start-up in Silicon Valley) and Apple Computers. Soon an idea emerged—a random, crazy idea from his colleague Jack Smith. And, it changed the way the world communicated. The idea? Free e-mail accounts that could be accessed anonymously, over the Web. It was time now to 'corporatize' the idea.

On 4th July 1996—US Independence Day—Sabeer Bhatia and Jack Smith began Hotmail, the company that provided e-mail services for free. (They had envisioned a new era generation of advertisers who would pay to reach audiences through emerging forms of web advertising.) Po Bronson in his article, *The Man who E-mailed the World*, speaks of the magic of digital technology at work. Hotmail's first users found it by themselves. Then, they e-mailed their friends. There were a 100 users in the first hour; 200 users in the second and 250 users in the third hour. Soon enough, Hotmail had 1,00,000 subscribers and was valued at $18 million. What

Hotmail demonstrated through its strategic use of digital technology was that technology could be used by the widest number of people, at a rate unmatched in human history. Eighteen months later, in December 1997, when Bhatia and his co-founders sold Hotmail to Microsoft, there were 12 million subscribers and at that point, over 1,50,000 Internet users were signing up for new Hotmail accounts everyday.

By January 2000, Hotmail—now a Microsoft subsidiary—was a truly global phenomenon with over 50 million users. A figure that was more than the combined population of 202 countries worldwide. Today, over 200 million computers serve a global population of six billion people. The global Internet community, of which you are part, today numbers 500 million. Every day, 6.1 billion e-mail messages get sent (That is approximately one message for every human being on the planet!). In mid 2004, as this book goes to print, there are over 220 million active Hotmail users. The Hotmail story is yet another maverick story, told with staggering success. Look closely at the tapestry of its worldwide success, you will find the threads of Corporatization, Digitization and Globalization playing catalyst to its awesome growth.

From Here to Posterity

Standing at the threshold of the 20th century, Jamsetji Nusserwanji Tata may have scarcely foreseen the tech-savvy world that Sabeer Bhatia lives in. But his Tata Group continues to straddle the Indian and global markets with a vision and drive that are inspired by its doughty founder. In this first chapter, we have looked at the forces and factors that have shaped the modern Corporate. In it, we learned of the march of human civilization—and its five Ages. We presided over its gritty origins in the Industrial Age and oversaw the evolution of the company in the 20th century. In our time—the Information Age—we were introduced to the 21st century Corporate. We found that its core business principles (produce profits, cut costs, reduce risks) are alive and thriving in new avatars—for the new era.

There was more to it, too. The trajectory of the new era Corporate, we discovered, has three powerful catalysts of business growth empowering it in the global marketplace: Corporatization, Digitization and Globalization. While at it, we struck a lode of corporate wisdom while watching America's most endearing corporation 'preserve the core and stimulate progress'. Here, it was revealed that the soul of a corporate remains the same, but its character evolves to take on the challenges of a competitive, global environment.

Amidst the static, bustle and chatter of the great global marketplace, every corporate, in the words of Kitchen and Schultz, looks to 'a single global corporate voice irrespective of geographies, cultures and nation states'. In this dynamic scenario, the single global corporate voice becomes a time-tested tool of market success. As we will find out in the next two chapters, this implies that every corporate needs to communicate its mission, purpose and capabilities to a diverse group of 'audiences'. Today, in a world criss-crossed by digital networks, every corporate is charting new territory, treading a delicate path in an intensely competitive environment. In this searingly competitive realm, corporates use their formidable market presence to highlight company products and services that need to create a niche for themselves. Now, think about it. And, you will realize that it is not very different from the extreme reality that surrounds you in that trade caravan in 1000 BC.

Signposts

- The 21st century Corporate is a result of the natural evolution of the march of civilization through the Agricultural Age, the Industrial Age, the Service Industry Age, the Information Age and the Biotech Age.
- In the order of growth, businesses become companies, companies evolve into corporations, and corporations become conglomerates. Each of them typifies the 21st century Corporate.
- The traditional business—the forefather of the 21st century Corporate—has worked on the time-tested economic principles of producing profits, cutting costs and reducing risks.

- The 21st century Corporate, as we know it today, is being driven by three catalysts of growth: Corporatization, Digitization and Globalization.
- Corporate citizenship is an integral cornerstone of the 21st century Corporate. Through it, a corporate becomes a productive contributing member of its community.
- The 21st century Corporate is the single most powerful catalyst of change on the planet today.

Media Initiative

You have just been on a whirlwind tour of the 21st century Corporate and the factors that have led to its inception. The Corporate, as you know it today, traces its origins to the very traditional businesses that existed centuries ago. The corporate odyssey has been an event-filled one. And today, the best of this journey is exemplified in the fact that a business, a company or a corporation aspires to become a 'solid corporate citizen'.

This is where theory turns into practice. It is your turn now, to choose a 21st century Corporate. Carefully pick the reasons for your choice. The Corporate could be of Indian or global origin— with an established track record for business excellence and a cast-iron reputation for corporate citizenship. Now, trace its growth from its origins to the successful Corporate that it is today. And, interactively analyse the reasons for its gradual, beacon-like climb to success.

This initiative involves your whole group—either as individual presentations or as groups of fiercely competitive presenters. So, take the opportunity to make your presentation as creative and interactive as possible. Think digital. Consider the use of a PC with a PowerPoint presentation, slide projectors, music systems— practically any gizmo you can lay your hands on. Remember the more creative it is, the more your presentation will impact your audience.

It is time then to build your case for your favourite Corporate's strategy. And, while you are at it, here is a suggested format for the written script that you will use as the basis of your presentation.

Work out an introduction stating your premise about the 21st century Corporate; describe the business environment, and then zero in on your Corporate of the moment. Give your audience the reasons for your choice, amidst the slew of global corporates. Focus on a brief presentation, clearly detailing reasons for the emergence of your chosen Corporate. Bear in mind the fact, that this is the place where you give your argument the impetus it needs. Rely on the use of definitions, concepts, and future corporate scenarios. Conclude rather dramatically with a finale that leads you to the conclusions that you have drawn from your presentation. Restate your premise and the reasons for your choice. Feel free to break every rule of a traditional presentation!

Sources

Publications

Croteau, D., Hoynes, W. (2001). *The Business of Media: Corporate Media and the Public Interest.* Pine Forge Press, Thousand Oaks.

Baker, Stephen. (1979). *Systematic Approach to Advertising Creativity.* McGraw-Hill Book Company Inc., New York.

Gunaratne, S.A.(Ed.).(2000). *Handbook of the Media in Asia.* Sage Publications, New Delhi.

Khanna, Satish. (2000). *The Future Manager: A Value Builder for Tomorrow's Organization.* Tata McGraw-Hill, New Delhi.

Kitchen, Philip J. and Schultz, Don E. (2001). *Raising the Corporate Umbrella: Corporate Communications in the 21st Century.* Palgrave, New York.

Mowlana, Hamid. (1996). *Global Communication in Transition: The End of Diversity?.* Sage Publications, Thousand Oaks, California.

Quintant (2003). *Corporate Brochure.* Quintant Corporation Limited, Bangalore, India.

Schramm, Wilbur in (Eds. Steven H. Chaffee and Everett M. Rogers). (1997). *The Beginnings of Communication Study in America: A Personal Memoir.* Sage Publications, Thousand Oaks, California.

Singhal, A. and Rogers, E. M. (2001). *India's Communication Revolution: From Bullock Carts to Cyber Marts.* Sage Publications, New Delhi.

Periodicals

Akbar, M.J. 'A Man called Jamsetji Tata and his Love Affair with Bombay', (Centenary Issue 2003), Vol. 32, No. 1, Mumbai.

Bronson, Po. (November 2000). 'The Man Who E-mailed the World', *Reader's Digest*, Mumbai.

Fernandez, Joseph. (June 2000). 'Corporate Communications', *Business Mandate*, Madras Management Association (MMA), Chennai.

———— (January 2000). 'Millennial Management', *Business Mandate*, Madras Management Association (MMA), Chennai.

Malliah, Santhosh. (July 2000). 'TQM Unlimited: A Millennial Retrospect', *Business Mandate*, Madras Management Association (MMA), Chennai.

Websites

www.online-pr.com
www.communicationsmgmt.org
www.melcrum.com
www.medianonline.com

Interviews

Prof. Bala V. Balachandran,
Kellogg School of Management, North Western University, Chicago

Giovanni Facchini,
Correspondent
Deutsche Presse Agentur, Rome

Sumanth Sharma,
CEO and Managing Director
Sangeetha Enterprises, Chennai

---

2 Corporate Communications: A Brand New World

When I bestir, I can't help the sensation
that I disturb the stars in their station.

—Fernando Pessoa

IT is the opportunity of a lifetime. A career move that will launch you into the firmament of corporate India's Achievers. You are about to be appointed the corporate communications head of India's top software company. And, you have been handpicked by its visionary CEO, for the task ahead. Your imaginatively written resume first caught his attention, then your work experience comprising chosen years in advertising, journalism and public relations. Then endless interviews followed. And, finally, you stand in front of him. One of the most famous faces of the land. A man whom the Forbes magazine listed among the top 10 Asian corporate thinkers of the 21st century. In his soft, measured tones, he spells out his vision for the company, tells you about the early struggling days, times when salaries were nearly not paid, and how far the company has come with its affiliate offices in the Asia-Pacific region, in North America and in Europe.

And, then he points to the road ahead of you. The challenge is to create and co-ordinate a compelling corporate communications strategy, that will serve as a point of reference primarily for the employees of the company, whose backgrounds and work cultures are as diverse as the world's largest democracy. The market strategy is in place, its economics, meticulously researched. The countrywide team is on stand-by. All that remains is for you to initiate the corporate communications section—a swank new wing in the technopolis of the metro that you live in. iMacs adorn the desks of your team members in the office. A separate conference room, a catalogued library and 24-hour access to the Internet are some tools available to you to craft your strategic success.

One step before you make up your mind. It is time for an India-reality check—a one billion population; 1651 languages; four densely populated metros; 12 major cities; hundreds of small towns and thousands of unnamed villages. And yes, a four million strong Internet community—whose numbers are growing. In the turbulent 10 years to come, this will be your uneven playing field—the arena in which your company will make its stand—in the great global marketplace. Its software solutions will notch up new successes, chart new territories, not to mention, change the way the world looks at India.

Beyond every instinct of corporate survival in the global arena, you will hold the singular weapon of corporate warfare—a corporate communications strategy. You will wield it silently amidst the din and clatter of the marketplace, to network with your constituents and your customer. And, while you and your team are at it, here's wishing you all the luck you will need with your corporate communications strategy. Your Yes, a brave affirmation, will create your destiny or seal your fate. But you are far too busy to think about it. Right now, with that click of your computer's ENTER button—you enter the realm of corporate communications...

The First among Equals

In the 1960s—the most revolutionary decade of the last era—Ted Levitt, a Professor at the Harvard Business School prophesized that brands and branding will be the essence of competitive advantage in the 21st century. Well, it is the 21st century and it turns out, Levitt was right. Today, he stands tall among his peers, for his accurate foresight of our age. The 'Brand' is indeed the core reality of the 21st century Corporate and our globalized lives. And, communicating the 'brand essence' is today an art, craft and science—all rolled into one. And you might ask what is the nature of this communication process? Corporate communicators recognize the following characteristics of communication processes within corporates and organizations:

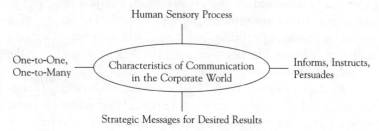

Fig. 2.1: The Organizational Communication Process

- Communication is a sensory human process that involves the five human senses. In the corporate context, sight and sound are the primary senses around which communication should seek to cater to.
- Every communication process begins with the sender and ends with the receiver. Core messages may be interactive (one-to-one) or influential (one-to-many). Digital technology has added a whole new dimension to the field of communication.
- Communication must inform, instruct or persuade. Every core message has a sender, a receiver and an intended result. Every communicator knows that 'it is not what you send, but what "they" receive' that really matters.
- All communication processes are shaped by the corporate culture and group dynamics within which they operate. Every communication strategy must be crafted to effectively achieve measurable results within organizational settings.

We now move to a core question: what is a brand? The *Collins English Dictionary* reflects an established view of a brand. It describes a brand as 'a particular product or a characteristic that serves to identify a particular product', further defining it as a trade name or trademark. A Brand Image, it will add, refers to the 'attributes of a brand, as perceived by potential and actual customers'. Fast-forward to the 21st century. Kitchen and Schultz in their book *Raising the Corporate Umbrella* offer you this insight: 'A brand, very simply, is a collection of perceptions in the minds of the consumer...A brand is built with consistent consumer experiences delivered by the organization, not just promises in marketing communication or the advertising'. The image of a corporate, they importantly point out, will be created among audiences anyway. The key to creating the desired image lies in the corporate's identity programme.

Raising the Corporate Umbrella also presents a compelling brand-insight by Aldo Papone of American Express: 'A brand is a covenant between a marketer and a consumer. A covenant in this context is an unspoken contract, a package of associations and stipulations that are honored by both marketer and consumer. The product is a thing, but the brand is a promise' (Papone, quoted in Kitchen and Schultz, 2001, p. 120). Importantly, *Raising the Corporate Umbrella* observes that 'a company owns the product, but the customer owns the brand'. In the din and clamour of the global brand bazaar, a brand—aspiring or established—has a focussed mission ahead of it. Croteau and Hoynes, in their book, *The Business of Media* elaborate on a brand strategy's three market thrusts:

1. Distinguishing a product from others via real attributes and/or image creation.
2. Maintaining high-profile marketing campaigns highlighting the brand name.
3. Repeating the brand image and message across different media.

(Croteau and Hoynes, 2001, p. 120)

There are reams of paper (and web pages!) being churned out on the brand concept, and branding practice. In this light, branding is a key issue that needs to be addressed by the corporate.

It embraces the entire corporate, involving all its stakeholders. In the competitive clamour of the global brand bazaar, branding makes the corporate identifiable and recognizable.

The Brand Clan

Here is an irony. The CEO (Chief Executive Officer) and senior management create the brand. But ultimately, the customer owns it. The company owns the product/service. *Raising the Corporate Umbrella* presents a corporate and product brand approach proposed by Thomas Mosser of Burson-Marsteller, the world's largest public relations firm. In brief, every institution has two key assets:

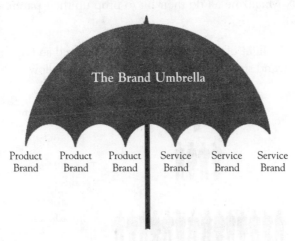

Fig. 2.2: The Corporate Brand Umbrella

- *The Corporate Brand* (by which is meant the institution's image, reputation, financial assets, performance and people). Globally, the Virgin brand implies a maverick corporate that delivers an extraordinary customer experience. In India, the Tata Group built its corporate brand across a spread of product categories: trucks, steel, chemicals, cars, tea, salt, watches, mobile services, information technology and much, much more. Above all these product brands, the Tata corporate brand stands tall, symbolizing the robust Indian qualities of integrity, excellence and corporate citizenship. As the late Shunu Sen put it 'Corporate Brands simply tell us what to expect from the company as a whole.'

- *The Product Brand* refers to the spread of products and services a corporate offers in the market. The corporate brand and product brand have a symbiotic link, i.e., they are dependent on each other. A Reliance product or service in India has its own brand image, in addition to its implied 'corporate heritage' in the form of its parent organization—the Reliance Group. And as we will discover in Chapter 4, ESPN-2, ESPN News, ESPN Classic, ESPN radio, www.espn.com, ESPN Store, the ESPN Zone and ESPN Magazine all do their bit to prop up their parent ESPN brand!

In the light of the brand concepts discussed so far, comprehensive brand strategy must be characterized as follows:

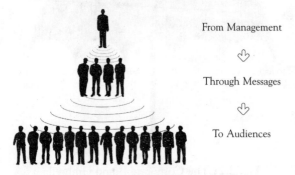

From Management

⇩

Through Messages

⇩

To Audiences

Fig. 2.3: Top-down Brand Communication in Corporate Environments

1. It is a 'top-down' organization process that begins with the CEO and senior management and reaches out to internal and external audiences.
2. All brand communication—with its core messages—needs to be clear, concise and strategically executed. A key understanding of corporate and product brands is central to the success of any brand strategy.

3. All brand communication should be planned and evaluated in measurable terms, taking into account the intended audience, its message and the desired result.

Box 2.1
Corporate Communication for our New Era

Nicholas Marvin's multi-faceted career trajectory has spanned many milestones in the Australian media. He has worked in areas as diverse as journalism, web advertising and marketing communications. In the 1990s, he co-founded TaborVision, a Melbourne-based web advertising agency. Nicholas presents a world-view of corporate communication from Down Under:

The corporate world over the last ten years has witnessed, in many ways an evolution and a revolution. The consumer has matured from demanding a product or service to now wanting an 'experience', and the post dot-com, post-Enron market place in general has transformed requiring greater discourse between the corporation and its stakeholders.

So any corporate communicator that intends to succeed in today's competitive environment must take seriously his responsibility not just to communicate the brand message to its prospects, clients, shareholders and stakeholders, but to also have them experience it.

The Brand Experience

The role of the corporate communicator has expanded from proselytising the company's tag line, to extending the brand experience.

In the past the brand was the product or service...that is no longer good enough. Not long ago, you would extol the global brand that was the BigMac served up exactly the same whether you're in St Petersburg, Sydney, Delhi or Chicago. Now is the entire experience of eating at McDonalds—the golden arches, the internal store layout, the kid's corner and the obligatory 'would you like fries with that'.

Corporate communication of the brand experience is the holistic strategic approach a corporation gives to every message, mode,

(contd.)

Box 2.1 (contd.)

medium and exposure of every facet of its existence and the way it is executed.

It could be performed simply and effectively as in Anita Roddick's The Body Shop, where the brochures, the advertisements, the layout and every single item in the store screams 'natural', 'vegetable products', 'not tested on animals' and the packaging if any is 100% recycled. Not only this, the supply chain usually benefits third world countries and the staff are actively involved in social justice issues. This is true 'brand experience' communication.

In my role as group marketing manager for an educational multimedia company listed on the Australian Stock Exchange, corporate communication starts with the way the phone is answered and ends with the delivery of the annual report. The experience has to be consistent and aligned to the company's raison d'etre. Sending a paper-based annual report to all shareholders and stakeholders is incongruent with the company's purpose to educate using the latest technology—it has to be multimedia.

Stakeholder Communication

Corporate communication must also close the gaping hole in the need for companies to dialogue with their stakeholders. Much has been done in the realm of corporations speaking to shareholders and even more in regards to them dialoguing with clients, but little if any contact exists between companies and stakeholders.

The corporate, political, social and environmental events of recent years have meant that corporate citizens just like their human counterparts can no longer exist as islands. They form part of the society they live in, and must ensure that they act as responsible members as well as communicate their actions and intentions. Transparency is the key!

Effective stakeholder corporate communication mandates going the extra fibre—optic mile. It means talking to the employees, the unions, the governments, the suppliers and sharing not just information about the day-to-day operations, short and medium term plans, but also the corporate vision, mission, purpose and values. It's what I call 360-degree communication.

(contd.)

Box 2.1 (contd.)

Stakeholder corporate communication can be the reason an investor confronted by two comparative stock options chooses your company against another. The frameworks established by effective communication could be the saving grace for a company experiencing an unforseen disaster not unlike Union Carbide in Bhopal, India or BHP in Ok Tedi, Papua New Guinea.

Enter the Matrix

Brands in the 21st century are communicated through corporate communication strategies that begin by creating an identity, then build the brand and manage its reputation. Like the core messages they carry, corporate communication strategies are catalysts of desired action. Having travelled through the realm of brands and understood its totem-like definitions, it is time now to begin our real quest and ask ourselves: what is corporate communications?

Philip Kitchen and Don Schultz offer an insight into the realm of corporate communications in their definitive work, *Raising the Corporate Umbrella*:

> Corporate communication at its simplest is primarily a mechanism for developing and managing a set of relationships with publics or stakeholders who could affect the overall performance. These relationships must be viewed in a long-term strategic fashion.
>
> (Kitchen and Schultz, 2001, p.106)

In their view, corporate communications is a relationship-based initiative between a corporate and its 'publics' in the long term. Implicit in this definition is the need for the corporate to build its 'image' among its audiences with an eye on its overall performance.

The website, www.melcrum.com offers us this definition: 'Corporate Communications is the conscious and systematic communication of an organisation with its internal and external audiences in support of policy'. This definition centres around the use of internal and external communications to disseminate a corporate's organizational policy. It focusses on providing information, directly or through the media, while recognizing that it is a process of permanent dialogue with an organization's spectrum of internal and external audiences.

The nature of the communication is an important facet of our ongoing definition process. Here is one such view:

> Corporate communication is based on the strategic message. The strategic message is an idea that is communicated in depth to achieve fast, coordinated action leading to economic transactions. The strategic message is more a synthesis of a business environment than a concept imposed on it. In the end, a strategic message is an intricate web of understanding, resources and compliance that cannot be repeated precisely in the same way in every case.
>
> (www.pr-online.com).

Internal communications, as the next chapter will reveal, are strategic initiatives for the 'inner circle' that increase the involvement and motivation of the corporate's immediate audiences. Further, they reach out to a corporate's constituents to promote the company's mission and culture. External communications, on the other hand, have the singular objective of establishing and maintaining a proper reputation in support of the 'corporate' policy. This could include information about its commercial, financial and community policies.

Sheik Abdul Taher of Radical Advertising and Consultancy Pvt. Ltd., a Chennai-based brand consultancy takes the 'umbrella' view of the field. According to him, corporate communications encompass the A–Z of the initiatives that an organization (a profit or non-profit organization) adopts to communicate with its constituents and customers. When it comes to parameters of real-time practice, www.online-pr.com has it down to a 'T'. According to it, corporate communications should be:

- *Simple:* The singular focus of messages and media on survival and success of a company.
- *Timely:* Ideal timing delivers information at the exact moment needed to support economic transactions and employees.
- *Open:* The right message reaches the targeted external or internal individual through a proper medium without barriers.
- *Defined:* Defined corporate communication determines who communicates what messages through which media to message receivers individually identified both inside and outside and organization.
- *Flexible:* The organization adapts messages, media and audiences, as necessary, to achieve results.
- *Individual:* In all effective communication, choice and action rest with the individual. Corporate communication does not persuade groups. Rather, it persuades individuals, who accept a definition of self and of group norms.
- *Meaningful:* The intent and purpose of the communication is clear and, as far as possible, without multiple meanings and subtexts.
- *Measurable:* All communication uses resources and competes for attention. Measurement learns what corporate communication works and what does not.

(www.online-pr.com)

Closer home at Median where we work, our collective experience has led us to work with firms in India and around the world. Since 1998, our work has spanned global settings as diverse as Los Angeles, Mauritius and Gloucestershire in Northern England. We discovered, however, that a common thread of insight runs through the global tapestry of corporate communications. In our experience:

'Corporate Communications is the strategic initiative taken by a corporate organization to communicate the corporate brand and its core messages to a spectrum of growing audiences in a globalised market environment. At its core, Corporate Communications is very simply, the way a corporate communicates'.

(www.medianonline.com)

As a strategic initiative, corporate communications is built on the established cornerstones of advertising, journalism and public relations. Beyond the traditional tools of communication, it harnesses the potential of the print, audio-visual and digital media to impact the long-term process of building a company's brand among its target communities. Corporate communications plays three time-specific roles in the evolution of a corporate organization:

Fig. 2.4: The Evolving Roles of Corporate Communications

● Create the Identity

The creation of a brand begins with a corporate identity programme. This includes the creation of the logo, corporate stationery, style guides, internal communication manuals, templates for presentations, annual general meetings, and a truly challenging fact—environmental branding—which involves 'branding' the work environment of the corporate, where innovative ways are found to build a brand presence in the work environment.

● Build the Brand

With the corporate identity programme in place, the brand building process begins. Now, corporate communicators focus their efforts on building the corporate brand, while overseeing the growth of product and service brands, run by the marketing department. Here, the *Built to Last* concept of 'preserve the core and stimulate progress' becomes a worthy indicator of the way to build a brand that lasts.

• Manage its Reputation
When a brand is built, when the corporate's vision and intent have been understood by its audiences, a new communication need comes into play. The corporate's reputation needs to be 'managed'. Paul Holmes, the Editor brings this distinction to the fore in *Raising the Corporate Umbrella:*

> Brand is all the things a company wants you to think and feel when you hear its name, the sum total of its communications while reputation is all the things you really do think and feel, the result of communications plus behaviour. Brand is something you build: reputation is something you earn. Brand is a promise; reputation is the result of keeping that promise.
> (Holmes, quoted in Kitchen and Schultz, 2001, p.181)

Having said that, today's business environment resounds with a war of semantics. There exist emerging approaches, concepts and a terminology battle for acceptance and recognition. In this light, we view corporate communications as an evolved, potent response to the business realities of the 21st century. We see corporate communication as a way to enhance and add impetus to existing communication strategies that build corporate presence.

No quantum of theory is worth its weight without its thriving practice in the real world. Corporate communications is no exception. The best place to begin is the application of real-time corporate communications strategies across the corporate world. The three case studies picked for this chapter are centred around global leaders—that have empowered their market success with a keen understanding of their image and identity—not to mention a sure-fire corporate communications strategy.

Box 2.2
Corporate Communication—Partly Informational,
Partly Promotional

Vijay Menon is General Manager and Head of Corporate Communications and Investor Relations at (SSI) Software Solutions Integrated Limited. SSI (www.ssiworldwide.com) provides consulting and software services mainly in the areas of banking, capital markets, and government services. Vijay has over 18 years experience in IT, media, and engineering, most recently with SSI, Ramco Systems, and *India Today*. Vijay has a masters in engineering from the Indian Institute of Technology, Kanpur, and started his career as a design engineer. He lectures and writes on communication, management, travel, and relationships. Here is his view of corporate communication from the vantage point of SSI:

Think of corporate communication as a part of the 'promotions' P of marketing. The difference is that corporate communication promotes the *company* and not a product or service. It helps define key messages about the company, identifies an audience and sets up processes for dialogue, helps frames disclosure policies, and uses the media, the Internet, meetings, conferences, and other channels to convey the message.

The new corporation is knowledge based and in most cases funded through venture, institutional, or public finance. This automatically imposes an obligation on the part of the company to communicate and discuss its operations and results with investors, regulatory and listing authorities. More so, since the stock price of a company is today often used as currency during mergers and acquisitions. Effective communication aids fair valuation by providing investors comprehensive information about the company, and the reasons for investing in the company. Better valuations translate to a lower cost of capital while raising funds. Therefore, media and financial analysts—the primary audience for corporate communication—become critical channels to market the company to prospective customers and investors.

Unlike product marketing, corporate marketing is a touchy-feely affair involving senior management, the corporate communicator, and media and analysts. The communication is often one-to-one or one-to-few, is between highly knowledgeable and

(contd.)

Box 2.2 (contd.)

often egocentric individuals, and is conducted in a mildly or frankly adversarial environment. Most corporate communication exercises start after the formal press release or company announcement. Companies then engage with the media, analysts or investors to discuss the announcement. These dialogues are potentially confrontational—the reporter or analyst must probe for weaknesses, while companies understandably are keen to spin the story positively. This is why personalities matter in corporate communication—the person is often as important as the message.

In the IT industry at least, the communication practices in India tally closely with international practices. Media and analysts are exposed to best international practices and will expect nothing less from companies. Indeed, research shows that investors are willing to pay a premium for transparency and will punish companies that are secretive about their business. Further, legislation and investor expectation today encourage uniform dissemination of information. The compliance arms of most stock exchanges are quick to rap the knuckles of companies that leak information selectively. The trend is towards detailed press releases and conference calls that are either open to anyone or whose transcripts are published on company websites.

Corporate communication is partly informational and partly promotional. Investors and media expect full and frank disclosure of financial information, warts and all. Having said that, companies have the right to build on that information to present a convincing case for why they are good to invest in or to work with. In other words, corporate communicators have a significant contribution to building the corporate brand.

As a discipline, corporate communication in India is new but is taking root quickly. As opposed to the old 'PR' in the regulated economy that was little more than a cover up to curry favours with influential people in government and the media, corporate communications is coming into its own as a corporate marketing function. In its new avatar, the function combines media relations, investor relations, and corporate branding and works closely with the CEO to articulate and communicate his vision for the company to external and internal stakeholders. In that respect, the corporate communication function is now well aligned with international practices.

The case studies revolve around the world's number one beverage company, the pioneer in personal computers and a global brand leader—The Coca-Cola company, Apple Computer and the Virgin Group. Three examples picked from the thousands that thrive in today's global marketplace. Yet, they serve as beacons of emulation for companies that seek to highlight themselves in the global marketplace. Before we begin, we invite you to understand these case studies in the light of the discoveries we have so far made in the realm of corporate communications—and your own knowledge:

- Corporate communication is a long-term strategic initiative created within a company to communicate its corporate brand and core messages. In a triune process, it creates identity, builds brands and manages the reputation of corporates.
- Corporate communication proceeds from the top management of the company—its senior management—in a credible and informative way to impact every level of the organization. In a larger sense, it aims at internal and external audiences. Each audience group is different and calls for specific communicative approaches, with measurable outcomes.
- Corporate communication is an evolved response to the dynamic communications need of the 21st Century Corporate. As part of its strategic armoury, it uses advertising, public relations, community relations, corporate literature, corporate hospitality, exhibitions, event management, new media, crisis management, lobbying, investor relations, research, sponsorship management, traditional media, and integrated marketing communications. It primarily operates on the platforms of the print, audio-visual and digital media.

The Fizz of Success

The world's number one beverage company began humbly enough—the offbeat initiative of a small-town pharmacist, who hit upon the idea of a fizzy beverage. Founded in 1886 by Dr John Styth Pemberton, Coca-Cola is arguably the best-known name when it comes to beverages. The company, which is headquartered at Atlanta, USA, produces over 230 beverage brands in nearly 200 countries around the world. Although Coca-Cola originated in the United States, it quickly became a global favourite. Its first international bottling plants opened in 1906 in Canada, Cuba and Panama, soon followed by many more. In fact, more than 70 percent of its income comes from outside the US.

Coca-Cola attributes its success to the fact that it celebrates diversity in its tastes—from apricot, coffee, lychee nut, orange and cola mix, to sour cherry beverages. Many of these brands, including soft drinks, fruit juices, bottled waters and sports drinks, are available only in specific regions of the world—sometimes in just a single country. For instance, Limca is specific to South Asia, and not other parts of the world. The reason for this is simple—different people like different beverages at different times, for different reasons. In its own words, Coca-Cola attributes its success to its ability to 'listen to all the voices around the world asking for beverages that span the entire spectrum of tastes and occasions'.

In its website, www.coke.com, 'the Coca-Cola Promise' is reiterated for the benefit of the planet: '…to benefit and refresh everyone who is touched by our business'. The company goes on to make a commitment of corporate citizenship stating that its employees 'strive to be trusted partners and good citizens'. The Coca-Cola company recognizes that these core values are essential to long-term business success and therefore will be reflected in all its relationships and actions—in the marketplace, the workplace, the environment and the community. By way of a statement of mission, the company then spells out its commitment to managing its business around the world with a consistent set of values that represent set standards of corporate integrity and excellence:

Marketplace
We will adhere to the highest ethical standards, knowing that the quality of our products, the integrity of our brands and the dedication of our people build trust and strengthen

relationships. We will serve the people who enjoy our brands through innovation, superb customer service, and respect for the unique customs and cultures in the communities where we do business.

Workplace
We will treat each other with dignity, fairness and respect. We will foster an inclusive environment that encourages all employees to develop and perform to their fullest potential, consistent with a commitment to human rights in our workplace. The Coca-Cola workplace will be a place where everyone's ideas and contributions are valued, and where responsibility and accountability are encouraged and rewarded.

Environment
We will conduct our business in ways that protect and preserve the environment. We will integrate principles of environmental stewardship and sustainable development into our business decisions and processes.

Community
We will contribute our time, expertise and resources to help develop sustainable communities in partnership with local leaders. We will seek to improve the quality of life through locally-relevant initiatives wherever we do business. Responsible corporate citizenship is at the heart of The Coca-Cola Promise. We believe that what is best for our employees, for the community and for the environment is also best for our business...Beyond making great beverages, the Company is also committed to helping communities around the world through 'commitments to education, health, wellness, and diversity'. (Source: www.coke.com)

In a business survey conducted in August 2002 across the globe, it was revealed that Coke is the world's leading brand with an estimated value of over $ 6 billion. The survey revealed that the world over, Coke was perceived as a clear leader in the brand segment, from a slew of product categories. No mean feat for a business pioneer that has had to contend with heated market competition over the last half century. However, the company in the course of its growth to a global beverage conglomerate has assiduously managed its corporate image, changing with time and culture to remain the world's most preferred aerated beverage, while symbolizing a celebrative spirit of life. When you have a potential target audience of over six billion people spread across nearly 200 countries, you cannot get more specific than that!

The Fruit of a Revolution

In the early 1970s, two young men in sunny Cupertino, California dreamed up an idea that would, in their words, 'make a dent in the universe'! The idea was simple enough: a personal computer that could be placed on everyone's table. As ridiculous as it might sound, the idea was trashed in a world that only knew mainframe computers that spread across entire rooms. In fact, Thomas Watson, IBM head in 1958 was once quoted as saying that 'there was a world market for about five computers!'.

The Apple saga began in 1976 with the invention of the now classic Apple II. In the years that followed, the idea took seed. And, then in 1984, in a now classic moment, the Apple Macintosh unleashed a personal computing revolution. It is another matter of course that in the decade and half that followed, Apple Computer experienced the agony and ecstasy of being a pioneer. The company lost out on its brief leadership position. However, it continued to retain a small, fanatically loyal user group, drawn mainly from an achiever-community spread across the globe. Apple Computer is remembered for its ongoing 'Think Different' campaign that has famously used world figures such as Mahatma Gandhi, Dalai Lama and John Lennon.

Since the early 1990s however, Apple Computer has staged a dramatic comeback with the re-emergence of their maverick co-founder Steve Jobs (who was for a while, its iCEO or interim Chief Executive Officer!). Since Jobs took over in the mid 1990s, a world of change swept the Apple Corporation. For one, the radical-looking iMac computer made its appearance. This was complemented by an all out corporate communications initiative to create a new niche for Apple in the minds of the global customer.

And nowhere is this more evident than in its online home: www.apple.com. When you log onto the Apple website, you are introduced to AppleMasters—a select tribe of achievers, ranging from astronauts to rock stars to zoologists, who endorse Apple products (You are told to your disbelief that even a dolphin is using an Apple Computer!). Elsewhere, Apple Computer reaches out to another kind of external audience: future users. The company has hosted a one-of-a-kind programme to nurture future Apple Masters—all drawn from children, who show unusual promise at a young age. All these initiatives coexist on the site, with the latest information on the company's G4 supercomputer series.

In cultivating its internal and external audiences, Apple Computer has left no stone unturned. And, as you log out of the Apple website, you are offered to have an e-newsletter mailed to you regularly—informing you about the latest happenings at the Apple Corporation. It strives at every step to nurture the Apple brand, while encouraging Apple user communities across the world. In the closest that this book comes to a brand endorsement, the first cut of this book saw the light of day, thanks to a trusty Apple Mac Performa 5200 CD!

Apple Computer's resurgence has been a resounding success of our times. Importantly, it has enabled the company to perform where it has mattered the most: profitability. When it came to their corporate communications strategy, the head honchos at Apple got it just right—Think Different.

Virgin Territory

Virgin—the third most recognized brand in Britain—is now on its way to becoming the first global brand name of the 21st century. Virgin, in its three decade mega-profitable existence, has got itself involved in airlines, railways, finance, soft drinks, music, mobile phones, holidays, cars, wines, publishing and bridal wear (In keeping with its quirky brand strategy, the only brand that stays out of the Virgin family is Mates—their leading condom brand!). Virgin values its brand and attitude. The group has created over 200 companies that employ 25,000 people worldwide. In its own words, Virgin stands for 'value for money, quality, innovation, fun and a sense of competitive challenge'.

It is an awareness that dawned on Virgin early in its wild ride to the top. On their mission of breaking every commandment of brand creation, the staff at Virgin make sure they have a whale of a time—thanks to the 'have-fun-while-you-can' attitude of its maverick founder Richard Branson. Remember him doing the *bhangra*, when the first Virgin Atlantic flight landed in New Delhi? Or riding an elephant to remind everyone about the arrival of the Virgin Atlantic Jumbo? Or even that quirky ride in an autorickshaw to prove a point? By assiduously cultivating his brand, Richard Branson has ensured that Virgin stays in the news.

Virgin began quietly enough in England during the 1970s, with its first ventures—a student magazine and small mail order record company. Since then, it has sought out and developed innovative business ideas that have flourished with momentum from excellent management. The Virgin strategy has been pretty much the same—seek out opportunity, offer something better, and let millions of satisfied customers guarantee whopping market success. With this strategy, the Virgin Group made unconventional forays into traditional areas like airlines and railways, and, not without success. As the dotcom revolution took over, Virgin looked to delivering 'old' products and services in newer and more innovative ways.

Globally, the UK-based Virgin Group has created a classic example of a corporate communications strategy. Virgin's delightful blend of irreverence and innovation, fronted by founder Richard Branson's antics, have made it a company to watch out for, the world over. On home territory, the company's growth has been sustained by incredible employee and customer loyalty. In his autobiography, *Losing My Virginity* (Virgin Publications 1999), Branson speaks of the empathy that his group has been able to build with the man on the street. Later, he goes on to state that this innate support has been among Virgin's greatest strengths in its trying hours. If there is any one secret weapon in the Virgin arsenal, it is a sure-fire corporate communications strategy.

Beyond headline-capturing feats by its sprightly CEO, Virgin relies on a intricately planned corporate communications strategy. The individual companies are empowered to run their own affairs, yet all the companies help one another, and solutions to problems come from all quarters. They call themselves a community, with shared ideas, values, interests and goals. Exploring the activities of the Virgin companies, their website demonstrates that 'success is not about having a strong business promise, it is about keeping it!' According to www.virgin.com, 'Once a Virgin company is up and running, several factors contribute to making it a success—The power of the Virgin name; Richard Branson's personal reputation; their unrivalled network of friends, contacts and partners; the Virgin management style; the way talent is empowered to flourish within the group'.

Again, Virgin's ability to reach out to its 'external public' has ensured that it is able to attract the right people for the top jobs. They also draw on talented people from throughout the group. They create partnerships with others to combine skills, knowledge, and market presence. Each successful Virgin venture demonstrates its instinctive skill in picking the right market and the right opportunity. As you read these lines, Virgin continues to chart success after success in the global marketplace.

A Presence for the Planet

Ralph Waldo Emerson, America's most celebrated philosopher, once termed the Institution 'the lengthened shadow of its founder'. In the global marketplace today, corporates build on their business growth with 'the lengthened shadow' of their brand presence. So, whether you are an entrepreneur running your own two-room outfit, a territory manager achieving impossible sales targets or a young CEO, making a bid for posterity, understanding how corporate communication works is crucial to market success. Beyond business acumen, venture capital and financial projections, your understanding of corporate communication and the role it plays in your organization's growth is a vital factor for lasting market success.

To begin with, any corporate communications initiative begins with the premise that you can make a difference to your organization. In its most essential form, corporate communications strategies help companies evolve at two levels: with the internal and external audiences. Advertising, journalism and public relations are tested tools of success for the corporate growth process. These come backed by the 3Cs of corporate communications that drive all initiatives: clarity, consistency and credibility. Having said this, there are two important considerations that must be kept in mind, while affecting a corporate communications strategy. The first is that it calls for an innate understanding of the print, audio-visual and digital media. The second is that both constituents and customers of an organization need radically different approaches of communication.

Corporate communication implies a visionary look at the business's future. No longer is your city or country, your marketplace. Corporate communications in the millennium is about placing your organization, its products and services on a media platform in the great global marketplace. By extension, it also implies that you should be tuned into the potential of planning your organization's presence for the whole world. In the countdown to the 21st century, there is one key challenge that lies ahead of every effective corporate communications initiative—a presence for the planet. You do not have to be the corporate communications Head of India's largest software conglomerate to figure that one out.

Signposts

- Corporate communications is the strategic initiative taken by any corporate organization to communicate its brand and core messages to a spectrum of internal and external audiences in a globalized market environment.

- It is a strategic initiative that draws on the specializations of the media—advertising, journalism and public relations to create and communicate a corporate brand to its internal and external audiences.
- Corporate brand is the qualitative entity that encompasses the corporate's image, reputation, financial assets, performance and people. In today's informed society, the corporate brand is the key to market leadership across a spectrum of sectors. The Tata Group and the Reliance Group are two key examples in India.
- Product brand refers to the products and services the corporate offers in the marketplace. This is the most apparent brand strategy in the market. The corporate brand and product brand, in a symbiotic market relationship, depend on each other. Apple's iMac, the Volkswagen Beetle and the Royal Enfield Bullet are some examples.
- Corporate communications is centred around three time-specific processes in the evolution of a corporate: creating the identity, building the brand, and managing its reputation. In the final analysis, it is simply the way that a corporate communicates.

Concept-Initiative

Remember your appointment as the Corporate Communications Head of India's top software company? Well, your CEO has asked you to present the concept of corporate communications to the Board of Directors of the company. To put it across mildly, they are a cynical lot, who do not see the need for a young upstart (in this case, you) to start this brand new department. Moreover, they believe corporate communication is some new jargon that has been invented to supplant good old advertising and public relations. For the moment, this cynical Board of Directors happens to be your class. So, convince them!

Here is how you get the ball rolling. Introduce corporate communications powerfully. Show them how your corporate communications strategy will work for the first decade of the 21st century, while adding impetus to your company's presence and growth. You need to convince them to adopt your strategy for the company in the year to come. Here are a couple of pointers to help you along the way: the traditional thrusts of old era business, the impetus of Corporatization, Digitization and Globalization and the convergence of the print, audio-visual and digital media.

And, while you are at your presentation, focus on the horizons of potential that this new realm holds for your company. The more creative means you choose to express your ideas, the deeper the concept gets entrenched in the minds of your listeners. You are only limited by your imagination. Make your presentation as creative and interactive as possible. Consider a PowerPoint or Flash animation presentation, make use of slide projectors or even a music system. Remember, that your audience is a sceptical one, so be prepared to stand your ground. Now, go get them!

Sources

Publications

Branson, Richard. (1999). *Losing My Virginity*. Virgin Books, London.

Rice, R.E. and Atkin, C.K. (2001). *Public Communications Campaigns*. Sage Publications, Thousand Oaks.

Choudhury, Pran K. (2001). *Successful Branding*. Universities Press, New Delhi.

Croteau, D., Hoynes, W. (2001). *The Business of Media: Corporate Media and the Public Interest*. Pine Forge Press, Thousand Oaks.

Kitchen, Philip J. and Schultz, Don E. (2001). *Raising the Corporate Umbrella: Corporate Communications in the 21st Century*. Palgrave, New York.

Mohan, Manendra. (1990). *Advertising Management: Concepts and Cases.* Tata McGraw-Hill Publishing Company Limited, New Delhi.

Morrison M., Haley E., Sheehan K.M. and Taylor R.E. (2002). *Using Qualitative Research in Advertising: Strategies, Techniques and Applications.* Sage Publications, Thousand Oaks.

Periodicals

Bhimani, Rita. (18th April 2001). 'Is your Corporate Communication working?', *Catalyst, The Hindu Business Line.*

Bhushan, Ratna. (5th August 1999). 'Advertising is not about Winning Battles, It is War...', *Catalyst, The Hindu Business Line.*

Fernandez, Joseph. (June 2003). 'Corporate Communications', *Business Mandate*, Chennai.

Sen, Shunu. (12th September 2002). 'Consumer Insights Count', *Catalyst, The Hindu Business Line.*

_____ (18th April 2002). 'Advertising is One Element of the Marketing Mix', *Catalyst, The Hindu Business Line.*

Subramaniam, Harsha. (11th April 2002). 'When Media Brands Advertise', *Catalyst, The Hindu Business Line.*

Online References

www.online-pr.com
www.communicationsmgmt.org
www.melcrum.com
www.coke.com
www.virgin.com
www.apple.com

Interviews

Sheik Abdul Taher
Creative Director
Radical Advertising and Consultancy Pvt. Ltd.
Chennai

Nicholas Marvin
Founder, TaborVision,
Melbourne, Australia

David Appasamy,
Chief Communications Officer
Sify Corporation, Chennai

Francis Jose,
Professor, Department of Commerce
Loyola College, Chennai

The Domains of Influence: Audiences, Communities and Publics

3

Who says what to whom via what channel with what effect?

—Harold Laswell, the American
communications guru in 1948

THE man who created India's equity cult began life, humbly enough, as the son of a rural school teacher in Chorwad, a little known village in Gujarat. By his late teens, he found himself at the first crossroad of his life. Unable to continue his education, he decided on the next best thing—to earn a living. All of 17 years old, he made his way to Aden in the Persian Gulf, where he became a petrol pump attendant for A. Beesse and Company, a dealer of Burmah Shell products. From the start, the young man from Chorwad stood out at his place of work. He would tell his co-workers about his dream to start a company like Burmah Shell some day (All this, when he was earning a salary of Rs 300/- per month!). The dream persisted. By 24, he was the General Marketing Manager of the company—honing his acumen and picking up uncanny insights into business. Two years later, his entrepreneurial spirit shone bright and, the young man and his family returned home, to India's throbbing commercial capital Mumbai—to make corporate history.

The world first knew Dhirajlal Hirachand Ambani as the vision-driven proprietor of the Reliance Commercial

Corporation—a fledgeling export firm founded in 1958 that exported commodities and spices to Aden. Even with its Rs 15,000/- investment, the Reliance Commercial Corporation could not afford its own office. So, D.H. Ambani rented desk space for two hours a day. Between long hours at work and life in a cramped two-room Mumbai flat, D.H. Ambani, his wife Kokilaben, his sons Anil and Mukesh, and his daughters Dipti and Nina nurtured the most remarkable corporate saga that independent India has known. The Reliance Group began to chart growth with diversifications into rayon, nylon and polyester exports. By 1966, Reliance opened its first textile mill in Naroda, Ahmedabad. Its next significant milestone was its public issue in 1977—a masterpiece of investor relations strategy at work. The first issue of 28.80 lakh shares of Rs 10 each was oversubscribed seven times over. With its first issue, the Reliance Group created an investor base of historic proportions, catapulting it into the league of India's top players for a long time to come. Two and a half decades later, the same corporate hysteria would be repeated when Reliance Infocomm first built its network of mobile phone dealers.

Dhirubhai as he was popularly known instinctively knew his audiences. And, they iconized him. In his autumnal years, when he received the Lifetime Achievement Award from the *Economic Times*, he celebrated his bond with them—'This award has been earned by the entire Reliance family. It consists of thousands of employees who work with total dedication. Managers who are 'owners of operations under their charge. Business associates who share Reliance's commitment to customers and investors. And, millions of investors who have unshakeable faith in Reliance. They are the pillars of my achievement. They are my family. I am proud of this family.' (Ambani, quoted in *Frozen Thoughts*, September, 2002).

In the 43 years, that Dhirubhai Ambani stood at the helm of the Reliance Group, he created an enviable business empire worth Rs 60,000 crores. In 2002, Reliance's turnover represented nearly three percent of India's Gross Domestic Product. The Reliance industrial conglomerate today holds interests in petrochemicals, textiles, petroleum refining, information technology, telecommunications and life sciences. After his death in July 2002, the corporate world took a solemn moment to celebrate the life and times of one of its greatest icons. And everyone remembered the young petrol pump attendant in Aden and his dream.

As corporates of the 20th century braced themselves for the new era, an exciting and new realization dawned on them—the audiences, communities and publics that they communicated with, had changed forever. This meant new opportunities, new markets and new customers. And yet, importantly, it called for a whole new way of looking at the way they communicated. This new scenario was a direct result of the Corporatization, Digitization and Globalization processes at work in market environments around the world.

In the new era, corporates are taking a 360-degree look around the public domain to find emerging audience-groups to which corporate brands (and mission) need to be communicated. The processes of Corporatization, Digitization and Globalization have lead to quantum leaps in the numbers of audience a corporate addresses. As a clarification, the terms—audiences, communities and publics all refer to the target segments that a corporate will address in the course of its growth. Profit and non-profit organizations today seek communication models that address increasingly diverse audiences. In other words, corporates today address a much wider, growing circle of audiences in the effort to build their brands in competitive marketplaces.

As the first chapter pointed out, the tools of communication for the new era corporate are legion: advertising, public relations, community relations, corporate literature, corporate hospitality, exhibitions, event management, new media, crisis management, lobbying, investor relations, research, sponsorship management, traditional media, and integrated marketing communications. Corporate communications is measurable. It's effectiveness is ably gauged by market studies, customer surveys, viewership ratings and Internet hit-counts.

The term 'corporate communicator' is used to describe a communications professional in a corporate setting. You will know him or her in one of these corporate avatars: public affairs manager, public relations officer, media liaison officer, community relations manager, special events coordinator, publicity officer, political adviser, media adviser, lobbyist/advocate and corporate communications manager. The corporate communicator ensures that his or her corporate connects and communicates with the relevant audience groups to create, build and maintain the corporate brand and its reputation. Thanks to him or her, corporate communications is an 'evolved response to the communication needs of the 21st century Corporate'.

The Audience Spectrum

At the Ogilvy PR Worldwide offices, corporate audiences are always in the spotlight. They come under the incisive scrutiny of global communication professionals, who bring 'PRowess' to their client-companies. One such approach is to 'Influence the Influencer'—a concept that we will be introduced to later, in the PR chapter. It is also interesting to observe that the Ogilvy PR approach forms a key part of the O&M 360 degree branding approach. The two kinds of audiences that a corporate interacts with in the course of its day-to-day operations are its internal and external audiences. So, how do you differentiate between the two audiences?

The distinguishing factor between an internal and external audience is the nature of its relationship with the corporate. Ogilvy PR recognizes a key distinction between these two audiences. An internal audience, almost always, shares a symbiotic relationship with its corporate. It is intrinsically linked with the existence and growth of the corporate. Internal audiences need to have a 'pride of association' with their corporate organization. External audiences are central to the future growth of the corporate. The challenge here is to consistently disseminate information about the corporate's brand and its core messages. Today's corporate recognizes that it must communicate with external audiences for a single, compelling reason—everyone in the public domain is a potential customer. In Ogilvy PR practice, external audiences need to possess a 'value of association' in their perception of and interaction with the corporate.

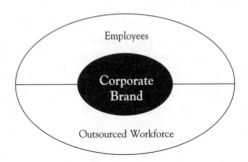

Fig. 3.1: Internal Audiences and Pride of Association

Corporate communication strategies become simple, focussed and potent, with the above approach in mind. Internal communications are strategic initiatives for the 'inner circle' that increase the involvement and motivation of the corporate's immediate audiences. Further, they reach out to a corporate's constituents to promote the company's mission and culture. External communications, on the other hand, have the singular objective of establishing and maintaining a proper reputation in support of the 'corporate' policy. This could include information about its commercial, financial and community policies. In this light, your audience for internal communications become the employees and the larger workforce, while external communications are targeted at stakeholders, customers, investors, media, opinion-makers, financial markets and special interest groups. It is time now to take a closer look at the nature of internal and external audiences that the 21st century Corporate communicates with—

Employees

As a visitor to New York, you soon realize that it is among other things, a city of restaurants—a celebrated world capital of fine dining. So, to sample its best, you need to begin with the Bible of the New York fine dining experience—Zagat's. In the 2003 edition of *Zagat's*, five restaurants took the spotlight. Gramercy Tavern and the Union Square Café took the top positions, while three others—Eleven Madison Park, Blue Smoke and Tabla (an Indian Restaurant) hold strong positions in the Top 20 favourites. They are all owned by a restaurateur who is a living legend—Danny Meyer. For his part, Meyer attributes his success to 'an atmosphere of genuine, unfailing hospitality'. But the true secret of his success is that his customer's do not come first (they come second!), his employees come first. In fact, Danny Meyer gives importance to his stakeholders in the following order of priority—employees, customers, community, suppliers, and investors. At Meyer's restaurants, employees are a high-paid team who view their work as a mission. They are known for their uncommon dedication to their calling—delighting guests. This focus has translated into profits, and uncommon brand recognition for Danny Meyer's restaurants that are among New York's best-loved restaurants.

Wally Ollins would agree with Danny Meyers. As one of the world's leading brand gurus, Ollins would have you know that your employee is your most important audience. According to him, the employee is your organization's most vital brand ambassador. At i-flex, the global IT leader, employee brand-building or internal branding forms a core focus of the company's communication initiatives. Considering that i-flex's 2300 strong workforce is spread across 93 countries, including four centres in India, this initiative adds impetus to employee understanding of the brand, which then translates into customer-results. According to Peter Yorke, Senior Manager, Corporate Communications at the i-flex facility in Bangalore: 'Every i-flexian needs to have a certain amount of inculcation of brand value of the product because the association with the customer happens all the time. So, it is important that each employee knows the direction the company is headed...Moreover, in the IT sector, especially, internal branding assumes greater significance because we are particularly into the product business and there, need to have brand reinforcement. Also, IT tools are technology driven, making communication much easier.' (Yorke, quoted in Jones, 2003, *Hindu Business Line*, p. 1).

At I-flex, internal brand building ranges from open forums and employee awards right down to annual picnics and even, peppy company songs. In today's Business Process Outsourcing (BPO) realm, the internal audience of a corporate has taken on a new dimension—the outsourced workforce. Today, outsourced professionals working in call centres and offshore hubs represent client-companies. For corporate communicators, these outsourced workforces are the newest internal audiences. In the final count, internal audiences particularly employees are the most important link in the chain of corporate prosperity.

Stakeholders

In the late 1990s, the computer education market in India took on a new dimension. It oversaw the entry of global players who specialized in children's computer education. Over a few months, companies like Future Kids, The Fourth R India and Boston Cyberkids set up franchise networks across cities, towns across India. The franchise networks comprised individuals and educational institutions that opted for the latest in children's computer education. Suddenly, it became possible for anybody—young entrepreneurs, retired civil servants, even senior citizens—to set up a basic computer training centre for children. At schools, entire student populations bypassed outdated curricula to benefit from the latest in age-specific computer education. The result was strongly branded franchise centres that taught learner-friendly computer applications to thousands of keen minds. Here, strong multinational, corporate brands acted as a strong guiding force for the franchise holders of the company. In fact, these brands worked to unify different stakeholder groups to build on a 'value-of-association' link. What it also accomplished was to create a whole new class of tech-savvy entrepreneurs who established a symbiotic relationship with the parent company. These franchise holders were a typical example of the new stakeholder groups that had joined the ranks of corporate audiences in India.

The term stakeholder is a broad reference to any person or group affected by the performance and reputation of a company. Stakeholders form the innermost circle of external audiences. In an age of strategic alliances, business partnerships and worldwide networks, constituents of a corporate form vital links in the larger worldwide networks that work towards market success. Stakeholders are a wide and diversified audience. While at one end, these might be individuals who are intimately associated with a company as employees, dealers, distributors and franchisees, at the other end, they also constitute of much larger organizations that represent corporate interests such as country partners, master licensees, and regional representatives. Because of factors like time and distance, corporate communications plays a key role in creating 'value of association' with stakeholder communities who are often spread across the globe.

Fig. 3.2: External Audiences and Value of Association

Customers

Customer-nirvana is the way of the future. Ask any first time 'Upper Class' passenger on the Virgin Atlantic's Airways. The journey from customer delight to 'customer-nirvana' is a memorable one. On long interminable international flights, the Virgin Upper Class passenger has access to private bedrooms, showers, exercise rooms and bars. Not to mention, other little perks like manicures and massages. According to John S. Fareed:

Box 3.1
Audience—Entity with Vested Interest

Christine Kapoor is a project co-ordinator at the Ministry of Culture and Heritage in the Provincial Government of Manitoba, Canada. Her work involves participative interaction across a spectrum of audiences—ranging from corporate organizations to ethnic groups. A quintessential 'people's person', she brings her own multicultural experience to bear, in her work with the government. Beyond this, she pursues a lifelong passion for reading and 'learnings'. Here is her unique perspective of audiences for a new era organization:

Vision is where it all begins—in organizations around the world. Be it a corporate brand or an organizational mission, blueprints, strategies and plans-of-action bring professionals and teams together to work towards common objectives. The fulfillment of these goals requires the communications of strategic messages to audiences in every setting. In my own work, as a project co-ordinator with the provincial government of Manitoba, my work involves communication with a spectrum of audiences ranging from Canada's now diverse ethnic groups to corporate organizations. Typically though, our main audiences are communities, interest groups and corporate organizations.

Here, I would define the term 'audience' as any person or group that has a 'vested interest' in a particular issue or initiative. In project management, we address a series of horizontal and vertical communication relationships. I also find in my work, when it comes to communicating with audiences, two often underestimated factors come to the fore. The first is cultural differences, a real time issue in our globalized age, where diverse ethnic communities need to understand each other fully in terms of their differences, ethics and value systems. Why, even the concepts of 'telling the truth' and 'saving face' have its own variants in cultures as diverse as Asia, Europe and North America!

In the new era, what I find, is that organizations of every kind—corporate and non-corporate—are moving from hierarchical power structures to a more egalitarian, 'flattened' form of organization. While this is in itself a welcome change and a sign

(contd.)

Box 3.1 (contd.)

of the times, it presents a new challenge to those of us in project management, who deal with different audiences. For instance, the new era organization calls for transparency, which should also be balanced with 'confidentiality of information'. Vijay Vikram in his book, *Managing the Project Team*, effectively profiles this challenge with the following equation:

$$C = n(n - 1)/2$$

Where C stands for Communication Channels, N stands for the number of people or the audience. So, for three audiences, in terms of the formula, you have 3 channels of communication. But add just one more audience and you are faced with 6 channels of communication! Finally, the organizations of the future, I believe, will be 'equal-pay, equal-work' places, where people and audiences interact with no communication protocol.

'Richard Branson, owner of the British airline company, took advantage of that industry's commoditisation—the same planes with the same seats and peanuts—and turned it into a lifestyle experience and Virgin into a top brand.' (Fareed, 5 May 2003, *Express Hotelier and Caterer*, p.9) The customer lies at the core of a corporate's existence. He or she is the reason that it exists—and thrives. The fission of market success occurs around the core reactor of customer loyalty. For corporate communicators, IMC (Integrated Marketing Communications) is the key tool for building the brand loyalty of the customer. Every corporate communications strategy, worth its reflected success on a balance sheet, must address the customer.

In the new era, we understand the customer in terms of a 'consistent customer relationship' that it delivers. As Kitchen and Schultz point out, 'consistency is delivered via all touchpoints. However, whenever and in whatever form, every time the customer touches the firm or the firm touches the customer, the brand is either built or destroyed. All touchpoints must not only be understood but also managed'. The term 'customer' is a generic one. Anybody could be a customer. Typically, that includes a buyer in a superstore, a client in a stock brokerage, a guest in a beach resort, a visitor to an amusement park, a patron in an art gallery right up to a patient seeking rejuvenation in an Ayurvedic clinic. Think of it in terms of your own choices. Your most fervent brand loyalties will lie with products that have carved a niche in your life. Decades before IMC and CRM (Customer Relationship Management) became buzzwords, Mohandas Karamchand Gandhi pronounced these words on the importance of the customer: 'A customer is the most important visitor on our premises. He is not dependent on us. We are dependent on him. He is not an interruption in our work, he is the purpose of it. He is not an outsider in our business, he is a part of it. We are not doing him a favour by serving, he is doing us a favour by giving us an opportunity to do so'. (Gandhi, quoted in Khanna, 2000, p.59).

Investors

Investor relations in India are best exemplified by the relationship that the Reliance Group struck with its investors when they heralded the equity cult in the late 1970s. That bond has endured till today, when thousands of Reliance investors have seen the group through its turbulent climb to market leadership. The Annual General Meetings of the Reliance Group are an exemplar of investor relations at their strategic best. At company meetings every year, investors come out, all charged-up with enthusiasm and loyalty for a company whose growth they feel personally responsible for. In a market characterized by fickle investor loyalties, this kind of commitment is practically unheard of. The Reliance Group is known for its meteoric rise to the firmament of Indian industry. Its go-getter attitude backed by its market-dynamic leadership is reflected in the way that it researches and executes its corporate communications initiative. With diversified interests from Textiles, Telecom to Oil Refineries, the Reliance Group deftly manages its corporate image, in a business environment that is as ruthless, as it is unpredictable.

In their insight-filled white paper, 'What You Need to Know to Measure Investor Relations', presented by the Commission on Measurement and Evaluation Institute for Public Relations, David Michaelson and John Pinfeather emphasize that all investor relations programmes are aimed at both individual and institutional investors. In today's diverse capital markets, they are a vital audience whose confidence and concerns need to be addressed constantly. In a global business climate driven by change, investor relations have become an integral part of every corporate communications strategy, especially when a corporate is listed on the capital markets. Individual and institutional investors are influenced by what the corporate brand (and hence the company) stands for. The brand image stands supreme in their estimation of the company. For this reason, Annual Reports today are considered excellent vehicles to build the corporate brand. The investor is the financial lifeline of every corporate in today's money market. The same commitment reflects itself in thousands of other corporates and groups around the world. In the final analysis, investor relations are the newest way of addressing the oldest business relationships.

The Media

One of the strangest stories in recorded music history that highlighted the importance of the media, took place in the 1970s. In 1977, the cult jazz rock band Steely Dan fronted by its composer-duo, Donald Fagen and Walter Becker released a song, 'FM' on their album 'Aja'. The song is also remembered because it featured the 70s supergroup—The Eagles on the backing vocals. When the song hit the charts, the band realized to their dismay, that while FM radio stations lapped it up, rival AM band radio stations refused to play it—because of the 'FM' title. Within days, Steely Dan hit upon a stroke of musical genius. They re-edited the song FM for the AM stations.

They picked the harmonically compatible word 'A' off their title track 'Aja' and spliced it to 'FM'. This removed all traces of the word 'FM' in the song, that was now called 'AM'! The now satisfied AM stations gave the song plenty of airtime. Before long, this Steely Dan classic was merrily making its way up the charts—with the much needed airtime from AM stations!

Box 3.2
Successful Brands Understand their Core Audiences

Ashwin Rajagopalan heads Pratika—an integrated communications outfit with the goal of providing its partners with a suite of marketing solutions to enhance their brand image. His firm was founded on a simple premise: 'All brands are not equal, at least not in the minds of the consumer'. Pratika, which means 'image' in Sanskrit has come to be associated with creative, timely and cost-effective marketing solutions to help marketing plans turn into reality. (Visit Pratika at www.pratikaindia.com). Ashwin has a management degree and is passionate about brands. He has worked at both ends of the media spectrum with a four-year sales and marketing stint on one hand and over three years in the media on the other. Here is his take on the world of corporate audiences:

Amongst all other challenges that today's corporate (particularly in the Indian context) has to grapple with, is defining its audience and continuously devicing effective means to communicate with it. Put simply every corporate audience can be segregated into an external and internal audience. Most companies fail to recognise the power of the internal audience (the company's employees) and the impact this group has on the brand(s). I believe that a corporate needs to address both these audiences with a similar approach. There is a core audience and a non-core audience. The core audience is usually the same for all brands/companies— potential customers/users as well as investors while the non-core audience is a much wider spectrum and differs slightly depending on the nature of business. The non-core audience comprises of 'influencers' who are almost as important as the core audience. Influencers are synonymous with word-of-mouth which has become a critical marketing communication element.

Successful brands usually understand their core-audience well, know how to address the key influencers but most importantly know the value of communicating with their internal audience. Just imagine a company that spends millions on communicating with the external world but fails to connect with its staff. My favourite example is a five star hotel, which claims that they are

(contd.)

Box 3.2 (contd.)

the finest in that city and spends time and money on press relations and advertising to drive home that point. But on the other hand they fail to make an impression with their 600-member team. Then you have a situation where this team is not convinced that they work for the finest hotel and negate the external communication effort.

Nike is one brand that has addressed its internal audience—Philip Knight their founder believed that every group had one key influencer, one person an entire group wanted to emulate—the Coolest guy in your class. This resulted in Nike using major sports heroes like Michael Jordan in their external communications. Nike's brand strategists believe they do not just sell sneakers but that they actually sell 'heroes'. The best part is if you ask any of the employees in Nike's corporate office in Oregon, USA you will hear the word heroes before sneakers!

Communication firms like ours have a complex task in today's environment—The number of marketing messages has increased dramatically while the audience's time to absorb these messages continues to shrink at an alarming pace. We believe the key is creating messages that are relevant for the specified audience and messages that can be beneficial and actionable. We help each one of the brands break the clutter within the category they operate in. This has become vital to make an impression in the audience's minds. My favourite case study is a new for old exchange offer for a premium watch brand. We needed to give a tried and tested concept a tweak to enhance response—All used watches that were brought in would be restored and sent to the NGO for resale. An aggressive press strategy ensured that target customers got the message—Bring in your watches for a cause.

The results were terrific—over 500 used watches were exchanged for new ones in the space of a fortnight. (Nearly all of them represented incremental sales!)

In their insight-filled book, *News for a Change: An Advocate's Guide to Working with the Media,* the authors quote the legendary American journalist Walter Lippman, describing the media as a beacon that moves from one newsworthy story to another. That is a reassuring truth that corporate communicators of today live with. As they look to to harnessing the power of the media through its three techno-avatars—the print media, the audio-visual media and the digital media. As builders of corporate brands, they are acutely aware of the media and its power to create images that matter—for market success. In our age, the media plays catalyst to the process of image-building and vital decision-making across all audience groups. And, the difference is immediately apparent. Some corporates revel in the limelight, while others stagnate and disappear into obscurity. In Chapter 5, we will look at the importance of media management in building the image of an organization. It is in the manner of things to end with a word of necessary caution when speaking of the media. Like other natural processes, image-building through the media is a strategically planned and delicate process. When push comes to shove, every corporate communicator knows the truth of the ancient Tao saying: 'When faced with a problem, look in the mirror. In it, you will find the problem and its solution'.

Financial Markets

In the early 1990s, Saatchi and Saatchi in London was the place to be—especially if you wanted to be a part of the world's most successful advertising business. The company was set up by the Saatchi brothers—Charles and Maurice. One was a creative genius, the other, a financial wizard. For the next twenty years, Saatchi and Saatchi blazed a trail in the advertising firmament. Their ad campaigns became signposts of frontiers for a host of global brands. Bold overtures in the British financial markets led Saatchi and Saatchi to bid for Midland Bank, Britain's fourth largest bank with $77 billion in assets. For a while, it seemed like Saatchi and Saatchi could do no wrong. Then, in the mid 1990s, the Saatchi Brothers were kicked out of their own company, in a celebrated boardroom coup that made world headlines for weeks on end. The company never quite recovered from the blow. Neither did its reputation in the financial markets. In a few years, the company split into two entities—Saatchi and Saatchi agency (which ironically, did not employ the Saatchi brothers!) and Cordiant Communications Group Plc, which retained a shaky market standing as UK's second biggest advertising agency. By May 2003, Cordiant was a shadow of its former self—valued at $ 98.3 million. And so it was, that the unfolding saga of Saatchi and Saatchi and Cordiant became a grim reminder of two market realities—the fragile nature of investor confidence and the uncertain flow of financial markets.

In today's financial markets, corporates invest in hardselling advertising campaigns before a public issue of shares. The aim—to positively influence investor confidence. This is why for the corporate communicator, financial markets are an extension of the investor relations areas. In an era when the watchword of any business is to 'think global', communication within financial markets has to be addressed in ways that are conducive to the future growth of the corporate. In a business environment racked by turbulent financial conditions, financial markets are a point of reference through which the international financial community judges a company's financial standing. The right information at the right time can often prove to be a corporate's saving grace. And, it always pays to remember that financial markets are the home of your future investors.

Regulatory Bodies

In August 2003, the Indian Parliament banned the sale of colas on its premises. This followed a environmental study conducted by the New Delhi-based Centre for Science and Environment, that revealed the presence of the pesticide Lindane in leading cola brands. The government ban of colas on the Parliament premises sparked off similar boycotts in schools and institutions across the country. Overnight, the sale of leading brands like Coca Cola and Pepsi plummeted, despite assurances by the company's managements. Earlier in February 2002, the same companies had been under fire, when their brands of mineral and packaged drinking water were found to have traces of residual pesticides. In each case, inordinate efforts were put into talks with the government to resolve the issues related to the pesticide controversy. One attendant result of this issue was the importance that companies began to place on their communication initiatives with the government and its regulatory bodies. Corporate brands play an important role in influencing social pressure groups, policymakers or public opinion at large. For example, companies that are seen to operate in categories that are environment-unfriendly (like oil exploration, mining), try to cultivate an image of being environment-friendly. The international environmental campaign by the Shell Corporation is one such example.

Equal emphasis is placed on positively influencing consumer and government perceptions about individual brands in respective categories. This has the added benefit of positively influencing any policymaking in this regard through public opinion. In today's corporate world, every corporate organization is accountable to the law of the land. And, in every business scenario, the Government and its allied agencies form the most powerful regulatory influence. The Government goes about its role of watchdog, through the appointment of several industry bodies to oversee the conduct of business in the various sectors. While interaction with a single government itself can prove to be a multi-faceted task, the issue only magnifies for multinationals based in different countries. Either which way, a corporate must plan on a strategy to establish a two-way communication process with every category of government organization that it will come in contact with, in the course of its day-to-day business. Today, corporate communicators take on the delicate challenge of addressing the Government and its regulatory bodies in a targeted and specific way.

Fig. 3.3: Core Corporate Audiences

Opinion Makers

Burson-Marstellar is the largest PR agency in the world. And, there is compelling reason to understand communications from their world-view. Since its inception in the early 1950s, the agency has created a stand-alone reputation for communication excellence in various parts of the world. Here are excerpts from the Burson-Marstellar website on the role of opinion-makers in today's networked world: 'Today we are surrounded by a growing number of television programmes, newspapers, magazines, Web sites and chat rooms. These outlets are where consumer advocates, health care professionals, financial experts, political advisors, media commentators and other opinion makers hold center stage. We are a population inundated with opinions, facts and rumors, and they have a tremendous influence on how we communicate, work and live…It (the PR agency) accomplishes this (the opinion-making initiative) by having messages about the individual, company or company product or service communicated through a credible third party such as a trusted journalist, physician, television or radio commentator, entertainer or influential Internet figure. In essence, a public relation agency optimizes the power of endorsement by successfully influencing those who influence a targeted audience.' (sourced from www.bm.com)

Opinions make reputations. Word-of-mouth continues to be one of the most powerful tools of information-dissemination in our networked world. The role of opinion-makers in society has been a long recognized one. Reputations, more often than not, begin with opinion-makers. Today, corporate communication pays due attention to that societal reality, when it specifically chooses to addresses specific segments of society, with a view to influencing its overall opinion. While it is true that practically everyone is an opinion-maker, what counts is how powerful those opinions are in a particular society or community. Corporate communications strategies today place an onus on seeking out relevant opinion-makers and informing them about relevant issues. In terms of building a corporate's brand, this category usually comprises leading citizens, senior economists, markct observers, financial journalists, and business barons. Their insights mould and shape the views of the communities that they live in. It is a cornerstone of practice around which every corporate communicator builds his professional expertise.

Potential Employees

In the year 2001, Infosys, the beacon corporation of India's software realm, received over 6,00,000 applications for jobs. To anyone who was looking, it was very apparent that the Infosys message of being 'Created by Values, Powered by Intellect' had taken on a whole new meaning for an entire generation of young Indians. Here, a company that had worked on its 'value-of-association' had built an enviable reputation in the job market as the preferred employer. Let's take this observation a significant step further. Pick any corporate website at random. And, visit its 'jobs/careers' section. You will find here, that there is a strong emphasis on the work culture of the company. In it, you will find characteristics, personality-types and qualities listed for the available job designations. Whether they are detailed or whacky, job descriptions are the first step towards communicating with a key external audience: potential employees. All communications in the direction of this target audience seek to communicate the brand, its core values, the work culture and the reasons to make a career decision with the company.

When Wally Ollins observed that a company's most important audience is its employee, he set the stage for the recognition of potential employees among a corporate's external audiences. Corporate communicators today treat potential employees as one of their key audiences. Working with the companys' HR departments, they help to instill a sense of pride in potential employees, while attracting and retaining the best talent. A company that presents its true image will attract the right kind of employees. So, when a corporate communications initiative addresses potential employees, it is fulfilling a core responsibility. Typically, it could range from an appointment ad to a corporate film presenting a career in a company. And, the results show. A company that is consistently portrayed as an innovative front-runner will consistently attract the best talent. At best, it is the simple application of the 'birds-of-a-feather' concept, where like-minded people in the pursuit of a core vision synergize to achieve it.

Special Interest Groups

'It was a Sunday in 1984
The Lord was resting, the Devil did a show
In a town called Bhopal, people had slept
Many did not wake up, the rest, they wept
Time is running out....'

—The Banned (2001)

In February 2001, Greenpeace India and a determined group of rock musicians called 'The Banned' made a concerted stand for two Indian eco-causes: Bhopal and the Narmada River. It involved the release of a 12 track album 'No More Bhopals', followed by an eight day campus-tour in Chennai city, that reached out to an estimated captive audience of 25,000. There were no 'tickets' for the concert. In fact, the only criteria for admission was a carefully collected bag of junk deposited in a community trash can. The lyrics featured above are from the title track—No More Bhopals. Each time over, the raucously successful concert tour ended with a signature campaign demanding justice for Bhopal's victims. In just eight days, over 26,000 signatures were collected. The 'No More Bhopals' effort marked one more memorable initiative by a high profile 'pressure group' or 'special interest group' to highlight an issue in the public light. Across the planet, thousands of such causes are being fought out everyday in the public limelight.

Dag Hammarskjold, the legendary UN Secretary-General once observed that the United Nations was not intended to lead countries to an earthly paradise, but to prevent them from descending into a war-torn hell. It is a fact of corporate history that companies have been ranged against special interest groups over issues relating to society and the environment. In the recent years, corporate India too has woken up to the reality of pressure groups. Looked at objectively, pressure groups are an important part of any democratic tradition. The right to dissent is as sacred as the right to do business. Whether as individuals or as a group, everyone has the right to express their stand and views in society. As much as the concept of corporate citizenship is entrenched in the fabric of our society, the special interest group too is an important indicator of its democratic health. Corporate communicators today look to working with—not against,—special interest groups to ensure harmony between the corporate and its community. Communicators work to ensure that the communication process is imbued with interaction and transparency. Again, cola companies have to deal with environment groups, beauty pageants with culture police, tobacco companies with anti-tobacco lobbies and atomic plants with anti-nuclear protestors. The list goes on. It is the evident responsibility of today's corporate to deal with issues brought up by special interest groups. Like we said, the emphasis here is on working with pressure groups to resolve an issue—as opposed to working against them.

In the final analysis, an in-depth, dynamic knowledge of the market environment and target communities leads to effective corporate communications. Once there, the use of the right communication techniques at the right opportunities adds to the impetus of the corporate's growth. Taking into consideration the market's dynamic nature, it is important to ensure that the corporate's image remains consistent with every piece of communication, while strategically projecting the vision and mission of the corporate. An intensely successful corporate comprises empowered leaders and high performance teams that are motivated to achieve common goals.

The Future is Wild

In June 2003, Discovery Channel, arguably the world's number one infotainment channel, premiered a documentary series titled 'The Future is Wild'. The documentary had a fascinating premise:

what would the inhabitants of Earth look like, in 200 million years time? The documentary —an awesome blend of paleontology, biology, geology and animation technology—threw up some fascinating answers. In parts, it viewed like a science fiction film. One watched in it, the merging of the three continents Australia, Asia and North America. 'The Future is Wild' predicted the emergence of the Babookari—a monkey-like creature that lives in the grasslands; Carakiller—an eight-foot tall bird and the Falconfly—a gigantic insect; all dramatic, yet natural evolutions of life as we know it on earth today.

On the corporate planet, you will find change sweeping the domains of influence. Audiences in the corporate realm are evolving too—though in a less dramatic way. Corporate communicators in these diverse, global settings are now acutely sensitive to the communicative processes that build brands powerfully. For this reason, communicative processes today create and nurture a brand voice for the organization, while ensuring its efficacy in a business world driven by radical change.

In its broadest sense, the three core audiences of corporate branding are consumers (customers), shareholders (investors) and stakeholders (Employees and other similar groups). The corporate branding initiative exercises act on these three classes of audience in three different ways. Shunu Sen, the late management guru, proposed this model for understanding the corporate brand: 'The vision of the company (aimed at the shareholders), its mission (aimed at the employees) and its corporate position (aimed at the consumers). From Sen's perspective, a company's vision, mission and positioning are the key components of the overall corporate branding.' The challenge ahead of today's corporate communicator is to communicate the corporate brand and its core messages to a diverse, growing spectrum of audiences. Beyond producing profits, cutting costs and reducing risks, the new era Corporate makes an extraordinary effort to reach out to its internal and external audiences. And there is just one reminder to those who discount its power to create corporate success. Remember, it helped a petrol pump attendant from Aden to create India's greatest equity cult.

Signposts

Internal audience is a collective term that refers to the inner circle of audiences that every corporate organization addresses. It shares a symbiotic relationship with its corporate and is intrinsically linked with the future and growth of the corporate. Internal audiences build on their 'pride of association' with the organization.

External Audiences are a broad reference to the diverse, scattered entities that a corporate organization addresses, as part of its effort to build its brand. Typically, customers, investors, the government and its regulatory bodies, the media, pressure groups and opinion-makers are some of the prominent external audience groups.

Employees, for the corporate communicator, are the most important target audience. The creation of an internal work culture through employee brand-building or internal branding is crucial. Employees are the most important link in the chain of corporate prosperity.

Stakeholders refer to any group that is affected by the performance and reputation of a company. Stakeholders form the innermost circle of external audiences. In an age of strategic alliances, business partnerships and worldwide networks, stakeholders form a wide and diversified audience that have specific communication needs.

The customer is the 'most important person' on the premises. He or she is the core of the corporate's existence. IMC is the key tool available to corporate communicators for building brand loyalty for the customer.

Audience-Initiative

This initiative, you will find, goes much deeper than it appears to. Think of the corporate or institution that you are most familiar with. If you are still a student, it makes the most sense, to apply this initiative to your institution. The principles of corporate communication apply to non-profit organizations as much as they do to profit organizations. In this exercise, you are invited to identify and list audiences for the corporate/institution that you choose. And, having done that, you build a communication model that will be used to communicate to the institution's diverse audiences. As you will find, there is a three-step process involved here.

The first step involves understanding the corporate/institution—in terms of its brand or institutional vision. Here are some of the questions that prove useful for this first crucial step. What does the organization stand for? How is it viewed in its local community? Has its brand/image been effectively communicated, since its inception? Does the organization stand by itself or is it represented by an individual or a group? What are the pros and cons of its image-building initiative so far?

Having zeroed in on the core facts of its communication, you must then move to the second phase, which is to identify the audiences to which the brand needs to be communicated. You could begin by listing out distinct audience groups. Do they constitute internal or external audiences? How are those audiences listed in the order of importance, when it comes to communications? Are there different approaches for internal and external audiences? As a corporate communicator, how do you consistently and effectively communicate with them? Also, ask yourself whether any audiences groups would require a unique communication approach.

Finally, as a third step, develop a communication model— an approach, diagram, model—that you would use to explain the communication model that you propose for the corporate/institution. In our experience, this initiative has an astounding effect and real learning value when the actual communicator for the chosen organization is present and evaluates the various approaches presented and then presents the existing approach for the institution.

Sources

Publications

Collins, J.C. and Porras, J.I. (2000). *Built to Last.* Random House Business Books, London.

Croteau, D. and Hoynes, W. (2001). *The Business of Media: Corporate Media and the Public Interest.* Pine Forge Press, Thousand Oaks.

Khanna, Satish. (2000). *The Future Manager: A Value Builder for Tomorrow's Organisation,* Tata McGraw-Hill Publishing Company Limited, New Delhi.

Kitchen, Philip J. and Schultz, Don E. (2001). *Raising the Corporate Umbrella: Corporate Communications in the 21st Century.* Palgrave, New York.

Mahendra, Mohan. (1990). *Advertising Management: Concepts and Cases.* Tata McGraw-Hill, New Delhi.

Wallack, L., Woodruff K., Dorfman L. and Diaz I. (1999). *News for a Change: An Advocate's Guide to Working with the Media.* Sage Publications, Thousand Oaks.

Audiography

Banned, The. No More Bhopals (2001). Bodhi Records Pvt. Ltd. Chennai.

Periodicals

Fared, J.S. (5th May 2003). 'Bed and Bored: Creativity Helps Differentiate Your Property', *Express Hotelier and Caterer,* Mumbai.

Fernandez, Joseph. (June 2000). 'Corporate Communications', Business Mandate (MMA).

Jones, N. (23rd June 2003). 'Making an Impact', *The Hindu Business Line—Life,* Chennai.

Sen, S. (May–June 2003). 'The Danny Myers Story', *FHRAI,* New Delhi.

Sen, S. (May 2002). 'Two Sides of the Same Coin—Sense and Nonsense', *The Hindu Business Line.*
Rangarajan, T. S. (September 2002). 'Impressions', *Frozen Thoughts*, p. 18.

Websites

www.instituteforpr.com *
*(What You Need to Know to Measure Investor Relations Commission on Measurement and Evaluation, Institute for Public Relations, David Michaelson, President, David Michaelson & Company, LLC John Gilfeather, Vice Chairman, RoperASW)
www.medianonline.com
www.communicationsmgmt.org
www.bm.com

Interviews

Ashwin Rajagopalan
Founder, Pratika,
Chennai

Arup Kavan,
Managing Partner
Ogilvy PR Worldwide, South India

Christine Kapoor
Project Co-ordinator
Provincial Government of Manitoba, Canada

David Appasamy,
Chief Communications Officer
Sify Corporation, Chennai

4 Advertising: Beyond the Brand

If it doesn't sell, it isn't creative.

—David Ogilvy, on advertising

WHEN Sachin Tendulkar's MRF logo-ed bat thwacks the ball at the Centurion grounds in Johannesburg, South Africa, you hear it resound across the world. A whopping six, it reverberates in living rooms across South Africa, Dubai, India, Singapore, Hong Kong, all the way around the world to the Silicon Valley—where homesick software engineers yell in jubilation as India's Little Master notches another six in his career. As the applause dies down, it is time to take a closer look at your screen. Notice anything? Look long enough and you will find another phenomenon—a much bigger one—unfolding on the screen, at the moment that you are immersed in the split-second action governing that match. And no, it isn't the partnership that Tendulkar and Sehwag are building their records on. Nor is it South Africa's legendary fielding order. It is not even the roaring crowds of both countries, cheering their heroes on. So, here's a clue. It has to do with the sport mania that sweeps the imagination of millions across the world. It lives the sweat-streaked, ecstatic spirit of sport. And, it has to do with those four unobtrusive letters on the right hand corner of your TV screen. And, it reads: ESPN.

Sport bursts into action in your life, as you watch Sachin's six soar at Johannesburg, share a moment of doubles glory with Leander Paes and Mahesh Bhupathi at Wimbledon, savour a split-second victory of Michael Schumacher at Monte Carlo, and relive Brazil's glorious victory at the Football World Cup 2002. ESPN is one of our sport-crazy planet's most popular channels. Even more fascinating is the story of its ESPN's brand avatars. The channel's whopping success has spawned a family of sport-related brands, each of which compete with their parent brand in dynamism and foresight.

So, what does the ESPN brand family really offer you? On a lazy evening, when you have nothing to do, you could click on to catch global sporting action on ESPN. More action? well, try the offerings of ESPN's sister channels, ESPN-2, ESPN News or ESPN Classic. That done, you could still potter around the house, with ESPN playing on the radio. Or, visit ESPN online at its website—**www.espn.com**. And if all that sporting action stirred the sportsperson in you, step around the corner, if you are in the right city, and pick up the latest sporting gear from the ESPN Store—their retail outlet. Worked up an appetite? It's time to catch up with your calorie count at the sports-themed restaurant—The ESPN Zone. Time to head back home. And the last thing you remember before falling asleep, is reading the glitzy ESPN Magazine.

If that is an avalanche of brand information, try this: ESPN is owned by one of the world's most iconic brands—Disney. To the corporate planet, Disney is a media icon that has learned the value of branding. The Disney empire has a global presence stretching from the Americas, to Europe to Japan. And, its brand essence revolves around wholesome family entertainment. It is best known for its children's movies, and it has theme parks, Internet sites, books, toys, a cable channel and a cruise line for family vacations. As ESPN's illustrious parent company, Disney is at best, a silent presence behind the former's adrenalin-pumping existence. And, ESPN is just one example of the many brands that compete for our attention and loyalty in everyday life.

Our lives and perceptions in this new era are shaped by a 'brand reality'. Every moment of our waking hours seems prompted by a brand choice. Everything from the toothpaste we use, the clothes we wear, the vehicles we commute in, the PCs we work on, right up to the mattresses we curl up on at the end of a stressful day.

They are all prompted by persuasive brand messages that have found their way to our homes and inner lives. These choices have worked, because the strategies to communicate their appeal and usefulness have worked.

The brand concept, as we have it today, traces its origins back to the cold, windswept highlands of Scotland. This is the gritty, hard land brought to life by films like Braveheart and Rob Roy. Here, brewers manufacturing scotch whisky 'branded' their barrels to distinguish them from the produce of other brewers. In time, as legends of Scotland embraced the tradition, Scottish distillers and their amber offerings. And, today, Scotch whisky occupies a unique niche among connoisseurs of fine liquor. Scotland is also home to another legend, which is a brand in its own right. An otherwise sleepy Scottish village, the Loch Ness, is a virtual pilgrimage spot for millions of tourists, who know it as the home of the legendary Loch Ness monster. Nessie, as she is affectionately known, has yet to oblige her visitors though. A lucrative memorabilia industry has sprung-up around her legend. And, the Scottish Tourism Board is not complaining!

In the world of brands, advertising remains the most powerful and persuasive tool of brand building. Fittingly, advertising as we know it today, began as a little known function of traditional journalism. In the 1950s, if you wished to place an advertisement, you would make your way to your city's newspaper office. Here, you would present your information at the design department. This information would then be converted to an essential black and white advertisement, which would find its way into the next edition, based on an advertising tariff. Economies and environments then became more corporatized and technology-driven. In time, the corporate world saw the evolution of advertising and public relations which emerged as specializations in their own right. With the corporate brand at its core, every advertising strategy becomes a powerful tool of market growth.

In the new era, advertising has clearly changed, taking on a truly brand-centric avatar. In the world of brands, advertising remains the most powerful and persuasive tool of brand building. In its early days, advertising was seen as the preserve of the marketing department, while public relations was seen as a management prerogative. Not any more. Corporate communications today embraces them both to form a larger strategy that is implemented at every level of the organization. Today, corporate communications leads the phalanx of strategic communication tools for corporate growth. This chapter dedicates itself to an understanding of brands, in the context of a modern corporate. And, through advertising, we look at compelling strategies to communicate a brand to a corporate's diverse and challenging spread of audiences.

The Rise of Global Advertising

In the 1950s, after the smouldering lessons of World War II, global markets began to rise, in the United States and Europe. Overnight, products were beginning to find international buyers. The stage was set for the emergence of the global marketplace. In the din and clamour of the trading places around the globe, it became rapidly clear that companies with their products and services needed to speak with distinctive voices. In India too, advertising was a post independence phenomenon, though it traced its origins to a clutch of international agencies that were set up in the 1920s and 1930s.

By the 1950s, advertising in the country had taken on a flavour of its own. For years, Calcutta was the advertising capital of the country, with memorable campaigns created by luminaries like Satyajit Ray, Subash Goshal and Subrata Sen Gupta. Then in the early 1960s, Bombay became India's advertising capital. And, so it has been, though other advertising fraternities continue to produce memorable work. Advertising's early years were an era unto themselves. And, the marketplace was quickly littered with costly mistakes—badly planned product launches and poorly conceived market strategies. But marketplaces also lead to quick learning, based on experience. The writing on the wall was amply clear. The answer was the brand. And, so it came to pass. Companies became brands. Products became brands. Services became brands.

Advertising and branding are distinct from each other. Though they are often mistaken for each other. Advertising is best known by the definition suggested by the Definitions Committee of the American Marketing Association, which is 'any paid form of non-personal presentation of idea, goods or service by an identified sponsor'. Ironically enough, the most relevant advertising definition in our context first showed up in the issue of the *Advertising Age* dated 28th July 1932. Here, advertising is defined as 'the dissemination of information concerning an idea, service or product to compel action in accordance with the intent of the advertiser'. (*Advertising Age*, quoted in Mohan, 1990, p. 2). More than 70 years later, *Raising the Corporate Umbrella*, took up from where the *Advertising Age* had left off. In the 21st century, 'action in accordance with the intent of the advertiser' leads to 'consistent consumer experiences'. In this light, corporate advertising represents the pinnacle of building corporate brands through the media.

MRF   Buena Vista Beach Resort   Kinley Water

Fig. 4.1: Corporate Advertising at Work in Diverse Market Environments

The Emergence of Brand Presence

Branding on the other hand, is the big picture. Kitchen and Schultz offered us this insight in Chapter 2: 'A brand, very simply, is a collection of perceptions in the minds of the consumer...A brand is built with consistent consumer experiences delivered by the organization, not just promises in marketing communication or the advertising'. In the final analysis, Kitchen and Schultz point out the three-step process to building a brand in the new era:

♦ Consistency builds trust.
♦ Trust builds loyalty.
♦ Customer loyalty builds a brand.

—(Kitchen and Schultz, 2001, p. 123)

Sheik Abdul Taher of Radical, the brand consultancy has this take in *Advertising Beyond the Brand*: 'In today's chaotic globally accessible/identifiable-locally flavoured marketplace, where buying is based on need and the consumer is not an "idiot", but your wife and she demands quality at a price that she wants to pay; and where the USP of the bygone era is bygone-advertising that works will be advertising that intrigues, persuades and ultimately, sells. It must justify a brand's worth to the consumers, provide value and satisfy a real need in everyday life. And it must do this when dozen other competing brands are jostling along with your brand for shelfspace, mindspace and heartspace. Your advertising better get it right the first time. Because, in today's bazaar, there's no second coming'. (Taher, 2000, p. 13)

In other words, brands are powerfully communicated by advertising. But advertising is only one tool in the armoury of brand strategy. From the vantage point of brand knowledge, the corporate communicator is afforded a unique view of the global marketplace. And, the way ahead is drawn by clarity of vision. The corporate brand represents the core vision of the company. This vision then influences customer perceptions of the company's individual brands, products or services. Corporate brands do influence decision-makers. Consider the Taj Group in India and the exclusive hospitality experience that it offers. Looming large against its formidable backdrop is the unmistakable corporate presence of its parent group—The Tata Group.

As the second chapter revealed, corporate communication concerns itself with the promotion of the corporate brand. In this regard, cost-effective corporate communication requires a structured and disciplined approach. The corporate brand's core messages need to be crafted, to be successfully communicated to audiences. To achieve this end, corporate communications media are usually integrated. This is the singular reason that corporates today are able to communicate in so many directions at once to internal and external audiences. Corporates in the 21st century will use advertising to create an identity, build their brands and manage their reputations.

Branding the Corporate

In the spotlight of corporate branding, the Centre for Competence for Corporate Communications at the University of St. Gallen in Switzerland, has a branding-specific view of corporate communications: 'Corporate branding creates "positively loaded knowledge" in the minds of all relevant target communities in order to build trust in the company, its products, services and actions. In the minds of the customer, this knowledge then differentiates it from its competitors'. They suggest that the corporate brand is made of factual and emotional elements. These two factors play in the building of a corporate brand. Taking this model an important step further, the Centre presents a three component model of the corporate branding process:

Fig. 4.2: Corporate Branding and its Synergy

(a) Target Communities

The term 'target communities' is a favourite in the lexicon of corporate communicators. It refers to all target groups relevant for the corporate to achieve its goals. Typically, these communities include customers, shareholders and employees as well as public and political domains. Here, 'mediated interaction' with financial analysts, journalists and political lobbyists is seen as being pivotal to this process. Further, this approach also looks at segments like business partners and competitors.

(b) Content

Everything that a corporate says and does to create knowledge about itself in the outside world is termed 'content'. Corporate communications strategy must then reflect the true identity of the company. Any contradiction in a corporate's content will create a dissonance in the eyes of its target communities. Again, the strategy needs to be adapted to the interests and needs of the particular target communities while attaining the goals the company wants to attain with them.

(c) Methods

'Methods' under the corporate branding refer to the various communication initiatives used to interact with a corporate's target communities. These might include employer communications with the employees, consumer relations with the consumers, media relations with journalists, investor relations with the financial community and government relations with the political domain. (Sourced and developed from www.communications-mgmt.org)

Exploring the Brandscape

Advertising in the new era, we have discovered, is reflective of that approach. In mid 2002, Hutchison Essar announced their unified brand for cellular services, Hutch for three territories in India— Andhra Pradesh, Karnataka, Tamil Nadu and Delhi. As the brand hit the cellular markets, it began a powerfully persuasive campaign in print, outdoors and memorable promotions. The Hutch campaign took proprietary control of the word: 'Hi'. Day after day, the consumer stepped out to a cheery face greeting her. A year later, we were introduced to a enchanting TV commercial that featured a little boy and his dog taking a walk in a tropical setting— somewhere along India's west coast. Its multi-lingual tagline read: 'wherever you go, our network follows'. Asim Ghosh, Director, Hutchison Essar quoted as saying 'Hi' was an expression of Hutchison's 'open and fun' approach to the world.

Keith Kirby, Director of Global Branding, Hutchison, (who also created Orange, the global brand) spelt out Hutch's future role: 'Hutch was chosen as the brand name because "people call us that, it's simple and easy to say, it's real and its three tri-star logo was designed to symbolise its dynamism and creativity", (Challapalli, 2002, p.1) Kirby added that Hutch, which was 'part of the big story' would evolve and change over time. Hutchison Essar saw that Hutch's services would be "feature-rich" and ensured that the brand build-up concentrated on the "totality of the consumer experience". In a worthy postscript, OgilvyOne, the outdoor division of the Ogilvy Group won the Golden Lion at Cannes for the Hutch campaign. Not ones to shy away from a well-earned moment in the spotlight, Ogilvy took out tongue-in-cheek hoardings that read: "This year we brought home the lion. The pride will soon follow."

Honours apart, the Ogilvy presence in the Hutch campaign marked an important milestone. This was the artful application of Ogilvy's 360 Degree brand communication—arguably the best known, and most potent approach towards building brands on the corporate planet. This approach is the subject of the superbly crafted book, *The 360 Degree Brand in Asia: Creating More Effective Marketing Communications*. Authored by Ogilvy supremos, Mark Blair, Richard Armstrong, and Mike Murphy, the book is about a revolutionary rethink in brand building—and advertising. A must-read for corporate communicators, the *360 Degree Brand in Asia*, studies eight

Asian brands including Milo, San Miguel Light Beer, Brand's, Left Bank Café, IBM e-Society, and Kelvinator (India).

Among these, the one that stands out on its own is the Singapore campaign for 'God'. The 'Love Singapore Movement'—a group of 150 Christian churches—wanted to increase the awareness of God among Singaporeans. The awesome story of the 'God' campaign's success is told here with relish. So, what is 360 Degree Brand communication? 360 Degree Brand communication, according to the authors, is an approach to marketing that sees no limits on the number of contact points possible with a target customer—media will be found, and activities created, to maximize involvement with the brand, whenever and wherever they are needed most...To reiterate, a 360 Degree communications approach starts with the problem—or the Brand challenge—and then 'finds the media and messages that best answer that problem.' (Blair, Armstrong and Murphy, 2003, p.15). The Ogilvy 360 Degree Brand Communication is one of the key brand building approaches in the global marketplace. And, they all merit our attention. Perhaps the last word on the topic goes to Arup Kavan of Ogilvy PR Worldwide. In a candid moment, at the end of an exhaustive interview conducted for this book's research, Arup observed: 'The name or the approach that you use to build a brand does not really matter. All that matters...is that it works !!!'

Box 4.1
Advertising is the Great Corporate Hope

Professor Francis Jose heads the Research Wing of the Department of Commerce, Loyola College, Chennai. Over a two decade career in academe, he has taught subjects as varied as business communication and consumer orientation. His doctoral thesis, Effectiveness and Consumer Orientation of Medical Systems (with specific reference to selected physicians) has taken an unique look at consumer effectiveness of 5 diverse medical systems. He can be contacted at josefrancis_99@hotmail.com. With interests from homeopathy to holistic consumer experiences, Professor Jose brings his unique understanding to modern corporate advertising:

(contd.)

Box 4.1 (contd.)

In the new era—an age of profit orientation and globalisation—corporates worldwide are seeking to re-invent themselves through advertising and other tools of brand-building. There is sound business reason for this premise. In our informed age, the truth about everything, companies and their products, will be known in the least possible time. People will share the truth. Which is why short term market strategies might perhaps yield fast money. Long term, customer-focused market strategies, on the other hand, will build lasting, immortal brands!

An immortal corporate brand is about synergy. A brand experience is built around an augmented customer experience of a core product or service. Advertising is a key brand building tool—in some cases it's most powerful market ally. In its essence, advertising is the artistic expression of the advancement of science. Here, advertising promotes a brand to build market presence and produce profits.

In the long term, a strong brand extends an angel arm towards its community through corporate citizenship. In that endeavour, corporate advertising profiles the caring face of the new era company. Not everything about profits and market leadership needs to be mercenary. Consider this. Pfizer's legendary success with Viagra gives it the added R&D impetus to produce cheaper, more effective medical solutions that will change the lives of millions around the world. The Wellcome Boroughs foundation for The History of Medicine renders yeoman service in the ongoing study of modern medicine's progress.

Beyond advertising powerful persuasiveness and great creative ideas, its maverick fraternity needs to realise that many customer-groups today trust a brand like a patient trusts a doctor. So, a commonly evolved code of ethics that recognises the grey choices is a growing need in our new era marketplaces. In the final analysis, Advertising is to me, the great corporate hope to say the truth to the most impressionable audience with a view to building a brand and creating profits. With it comes the realised customer-promise of good products, cost effectiveness and easy availability.

Building Brand Passion

Here is one compelling question that you have undoubtedly considered, in all of this: Does branding really work? Do all brands need advertising? Those answers clearly lie in the real world. Here are three compelling reasons drawn from real life that illustrate the ability of brands to change our lives—and the world we live in.

In early 2002, a young dentist based in Pennsylvania, USA returned home to India for a short holiday. It was a journey filled with memories, as he was coming back for the first time in five years. Apart from his professional calling, the dentist was a connoisseur of the writing experience. Writing with fountain-pens, that is. It gave his writing, a flow he simply missed in micro points, ball points and felt pens of the new era. During his sojourn in the US, he invested in a premium Watermark pen that delivered on its legendary quality. Something, however, was still missing. The answer became apparent, when he re-visited India. He sorely missed the writing experience offered to him by the China-made Hero Pens of his childhood. And, so it was, that our dentist headed back to the land of eminently available, much advertised Sheaffers, Parkers and Waterman pens, armed with a set of trusty Hero pens that for him, delivered the 'real writing experience'!

In the Indian context, Hero Pens are a memorable piece of exotica. But for thousands of students growing in a pre-liberalized, regulated economy, they marked the peak of the writing experience. Hero Pens filled an important writing need for all occasions. Important exams, prize-winning essays, even that hesitant letter to your first love—all got written by the trusty and exclusive Hero Pen. It wrote different. And, it felt different. But it was not advertised differently. In fact, it was hardly advertised. Stationery retailers sometimes mentioned it in their advertisements. But the pens were aggressively retailed. They were displayed prominently with stationery retailers, who still swear by their efficiency. For brand builders, the Hero Pen will continue to stand out as a brand that occupies a unique niche—thanks to a very offbeat brand loyalty.

It was translucent. It was spectacular. And, it was ready to take on the Internet. The launch of Apple Computer's iMac in the late 1990s is already a classic case in brand strategy. The revolutionary iMac, backed by an enviable brand strategy, rode into the US markets with guns blazing. The strategy worked. With Chiat/Day, the legendary ad agency and Edelman Public Relations Worldwide working the global advertising and public relations initiatives, iMac's launch created an overnight sensation. It reflected the jubilant mood of a decade earlier, when Apple had first launched the Macintosh in 1984. Its triumphant entry into the consumer market was reminiscent of the 'first-day-first-show' hysteria in India's cinemas. Across America, queues built up outside computer stores waiting for the first iMacs to hit the market. Elsewhere in the globe, similar situations acted themselves out. The iMac brand took Apple Computer out of its loss spiral and put it on the trajectory to market growth. An already classic example of a product brand that did its corporate brand proud. For the next step in the unfolding iMac saga, visit **www.apple.com**.

Steve Jobs, Apple's legendary co-founder captured the spirit of his brand when he once observed that 'it was better to be a pirate than join the navy'. Since its heady days of taking on IBM, Apple took its cult status to new heights, when it described itself as 'the computer for the rest of us'. In the HBO film 'Pirates of the Silicon Valley', the story of Apple and Microsoft are told with unusual insight. In particular, you are struck by the contrast between Steve Jobs' maverick management style and Bill Gates' softspoken, but potent business leadership. And, in many ways, the resounding success of the iMac took up from where the film left off. Once market rivals, the Apple and Microsoft brands have partnered today to impact technologies that would 'create a dent in the universe'. Look no further than the corporate advertising campaigns of Apple and Microsoft to understand the truth of that observation.

In August 2003, Harley-Davidson—a whole wind-streaked way of life—turned 100 years old at Milwaukee, USA. You could almost hear the roar of motorized approval from around the world. The Harley-Davidson Company kick-started a global fourteen month event to celebrate its 100th anniversary. It typified a whole way of life, where Harleys thundered across America's windy stretches, typifying the spirit of freedom. The event sponsored by the Harley-Davidson Company, attracted participants from all over the world. The legendary bike with its many variants, has inspired a fanatic following. In fact, amongst the Harley enthusiast ranks, are those who swear by specific models. The Sturgis remains a blazing favourite. Now, past its hundredth year, the Harley-Davidson Company continues to draw on its worldwide following, USA, Europe, Australia and in the Asia-Pacific.

When Dennis Hopper and Henry Fonda revved up their custom-built Harleys in the 1960s cult classic 'Easy Rider', they advertised a whole new way of life that grabbed a generation's imagination. In the decades to come, the Harley built on its cult status to become an exclusive ride experience. Strangely enough, the Harley cult has an international following, drawn from every stream of life. From Hollywood stars, millionaire stockbrokers, hippy bikers, fervent believers to enthused senior citizens. The Harley-Davidson success is about brand passion. A communal belief in the horse-powered legend's ability to evoke a way of life. Sample that fervour at **www.harley-davidson.com**. Or better still, visit the shrine of the Harley enthusiasts—the Daytona Week—to watch the power of a brand to change its world.

It takes an intelligent, uncompromising corporate communicator to successfully deploy a successful brand strategy in a competitive market area. In this dynamic arena packed with aggressive competitors, *Built to Last* provides a beacon for market leadership: 'preserve the core and stimulate progress'. For the brand to succeed, brand communication must evolve, while retaining the brand essence. Look at the market leaders that matter. And, watch their advertising change in wondrous ways, while the soul of their brand remains the same.

The Fabric of Brand Success

For the market observer, the fabric of brand success is an intricate delight. Interwoven with it are numerous multi-hued strands of customer-loyalty, each of which contribute to the overall tapestry of the brand-experience. Across product and service categories, the same pattern unfolds. Customers prefer certain brands. They ignore others. For the chosen few, there's the loyalty of a lifetime. And, none of these decisions is a happy accident. They are always the result of brand building initiative that has borne fruit. Well-crafted, a brand experience is one of the finest and most persuasive forms of artistry that we will experience in our collective lifetime. The brand experience has several touchpoints that lead to customer retention—and loyalty.

Across India, especially in the vibrant south, the Basics brand occupies a unique niche in the mind of the clothes-conscious customer. The 'smart casuals' brand's origins are humble enough. They are rooted in a two-man tailoring outfit that specialized in shirts and trousers for the export market and multi-brand outlets (MBOs). Today, Chennai based Hasbro is an on-the-go enterprise run by its entrepreneur brothers, Hanif and Suhail Sattar. The company has a pre-eminent brand presence in South India with its formal wear division, Genesis and its smart casuals brand, Basics. It has innovatively chosen to reach out to the lesser known towns and cities of the South. Here, a significant customer segment for formal wear and smart casuals has virtually created itself. Of these, Basics has the most visible brand presence, driven by a radical advertising strategy.

In their own words, the Sattar brothers build their products around a core brand experience: 'latest fashion, pocket-friendly, great ambience, fantastic service and great variety, topping it all was great value-for-money.' Hasbro aimed to offer this experience through Genesis and Basics. While Genesis was set up in 1992, the Basics brand hit the shelves in 1995. This scenario allowed Hasbro to target its existing formal wear customer segment for its Basics smart casuals choice.

The company opened stand-alone outlets that offered both the brands, with a unique shopping experience. For the rest of the country, the Basics brand formed part of the multi-brand outlets such as Ebony, Globus, Lifestyle, Pantaloons and others. As Hanif Sattar points out, the company's stand-alone dual-brand outlets served to reinforce the Genesis/Basics brand identity by creating and maintaining its image. Multi-brand outlets, on the other hand, maintained the reach of these people. Typically a Genesis/Basics

1995–1996   1998–1999   2003–2004

Fig. 4.3: The Evolution of Brand Genesis

shopping experience would include: a contemporary clothes choice, backed by a common ambience, friendly staff and optimal prices. Each outlet would centre around a core team of three shop floor personnel. They would oversee the outlet's team and ensure that the customer stepped out, delighted. Word-of-mouth was to become their biggest brand building asset.

Playing catalyst to this brand experience was Radical Advertising and Consultancy Pvt Ltd—a young, maverick team of brand specialists, with attitude. And, their brief was clear: create compelling advertising that would evoke a response from a target audience of young male customers, in their early twenties. The first year they targeted the young male college student. Shortly after that, the Basics brand went out to what Abdul of Radical terms the 'first job guys'—the segment of the population that had just started earning, and had aspirations to the yuppie lifestyle of the 1990s. There were obstacles, hurdles and constraints. But as Radical was to prove, the limited budget only served to increase the creativity that went with it!

In 1996, Chennai played host to three spectacular hoardings, strategically placed near the Genesis/Basics outlets. Each hoarding featured a compelling picture, juxtaposed with a relevant Basics fabric. The approach was the same. An apparently unrelated visual backed by a vignette of the Basics product accompanied by a witty comment and very little else in terms of copy. And, you could always trust the copy to address the target group, who were reading it.

Box 4.2
The Customer is not an Idiot

Sheik Abdul Taher, Prakash Jha and Raj Jacob run Radical Advertising and Consultancy Pvt Ltd. They take their brand passion into the Indian marketplace with a stand-alone evangelical zeal. Known best for their work on the Genesis Basics campaign, Radical has since created memorable work for several other brands. In this insight, Abdul brings the Radical perspective into new era advertising—and brands:

I no longer wear a shoe, I wear Hush Puppies. I no longer use a toothpaste, I use Colgate. I no longer drink coffee, I drink Nescafe.... I no longer.... Well you get the picture well by now, I guess.

Married to the brand
Brands give us comfort, offer guarantees of quality and security, much like what a wife would look for in a husband. Brands own a set of values that makes us buy them, paying more than mere products or lesser-known brands that may offer us the same core benefits.

A brand doesn't sell itself...it makes people buy it.
The other day I walked in to a lifestyle store, had a couple of brands in mind—searched out the counters and picked-up what I wanted. Well like me everybody else there was doing the same. Now the question is where did the process of 'selling to me' go? We come to 'brand' again. What we see now in lifestyle stores or supermarkets across the world is the result of branding. Branding 'pre-sells' the product or service. Brands are bought...products are sold. See the ultimate of 'brand-centric' buying that is happening over the net... People are buying without even seeing the products in reality...based on what? 'Brand' of course.

If you can brand it ...you can make people buy it.
To borrow Al and Laura Ries' phrase... 'a branding programme should be designed to differentiate your cow from all other cattle on the ranch. Even if all the cattle in the ranch look pretty much alike.'

(contd.)

Box 4.2 (contd.)

Successful brands stand for something particular to someone...
not everything to everyone. 'The real thing', 'Just do it', 'Yeh dil
mange more', 'United Colors of Benneton', 'Hamara Bajaj', 'Heinz
means beans'......

Gone are the days when I used to go to my *Nadar Kadai* (a
typical *kirana*/general store in Chennai) and ask for 2 kg atta and
1 kg oil. Today it's 2 kg Annapurna atta and 1 kg Nature Fresh
oil. Ever wondered about water being sold as brands? Please be
frank with yourself. What about oxygen? Well it has not yet caught
on here in India but it is on its way. As of now, there are only a
few oxygen bars in India.

A brand is radical or it isn't
Let me clarify before you brand me. This has nothing to do with
being extremist. The only kind of extremism marketers around
the world love is that of single mindedly making moolah. And
thanks to the successful brands that are doing it. But for every
successful brand, there are umpteen in its category that didn't
make it or that lost their way and died. The difference between
survival and death can be a radical factor.

RADICAL, if you haven't already guessed is an acronym.
RADICAL stands for Relevant, Attacking, Dedicated, Insightful,
Creative and Loving. Let me take you through a brand that I
have been involved in building for the last seven years—BASICS.

Be relevant or else...
Picture the emerging market scenario. Proliferating brands,
shrinking shelf space, cut throat competition, media clutter,
skyrocketing media costs, shifting attitudes, sceptical attitudes. In
today's tougher marketplace, where buying is based on need and
consumers demand quality at a price they want to pay, brands
must offer consumers value and satisfy a real need in everyday life
and be relevant in the consumer's evolving life. Basics, for instance,
became relevant as a brand simply by offering a product with the
best 'price–value' equation.

Attack, or else...
Single mindedness and a killer instinct can make the difference
between life and death. Brands don't happen in isolation. In a

(contd.)

Box 4.2 (contd.)

situation where consumers are having one-night stands with brands
more than ever, brands have to singularly position themselves.
Sometimes taking an attack approach can give you that singular
position. In a time where every possible brand was promising a
lifestyle with 'a belong to this group' kind of attitude, Basics did
just the opposite. It said 'don't belong...just be...in effect **"just be
yourself"**.

Be dedicated, or else...
Today consumers are more impatient than ever before.....and if
they fail to connect with a brand...they don't say 'hey-look, you
are not the same guy I know'...they simply go away. Brands that
suffer identity crises do not stand a chance. So it's imperative that
brands evolve clear sustainable personalities and then invest time
and money to keep it that way.

The Basics communication since its conception has been
consistent. Its advertising though product lead has always been a
product demo wrapped in a creative story telling format...to
communicate its unique identity of 'jus be yourself', one with
which its buyers identify.

Be insightful, or else...
Today's ideas arise out of serious problems. Problems with jobs.
Problems with budgets. Problems with simply feeling insecure in
an uncertain world. Because of these problems, people question
their own motives. Do I need this brand? What does it mean to
my life? Why do I want it? A brand that's insightful is one that
ties imagination to truth, that's real, that can connect with its
products....It's an ability to see the future and tell what its product
basket must have that the consumer will want tomorrow and not
what 'the consumer should want tomorrow'. And Basics with its
successful product portfolio did just that.

Be creative, or else...
Being creative is nothing but a unique message, a message that
competition cannot copy in content or form. To be creative it
takes insight inspired by a profound understanding of reality. It
also takes creative work that locks on to the problems and issues

(contd.)

Box 4.2 (contd.)

that give brands meanings. Real creativity begins in reality—in everyday behaviour and the belief of everyday people…. Creativity is an evolving animal that suits this time and this place. Basics has been guided by this creative mantra in its communication. When other brands chose to show sleek wannabe models wearing khakis in 1997, Basics ads feature a Khaki kept open with the punch line…'Jump in' and consumers still continue to jump onto the Basics brand wagon.

Be loving, or else…
To borrow John Hegarty's (UK's creative guru) expression… 'information goes in through the heart'. When people feel good about a brand's advertising, they feel good about the brand. If the advertising makes them smile, if it offers an escape or captures a spirit that simply feels good, people feel a kinship with the feeling— and through it with the brand. They begin to want it…just because they like it. This is advertising as goodwill ambassador. It opens the door to a relationship by engaging the consumer's attention and extending an inviting hand.

OK. SO WHAT'S A 'BRAND'?
Simply put, it's a name with a set of values, promises, characteristics or anything that can make a consumer buy it. Simply put, a brand is RADICAL or it isn't.

And, Basics ads always ended with the injunction: 'jus' be yourself'. The other significant feature of the Basics campaign is that it scrupulously avoids one very human pitfall of brand advertising. Companies often get tired of their advertising before their customers see or understand it. The Basics brand campaign steers clear of this pitfall. Each campaign is meticulously planned for customer response, with enough lead-time allowed for market results.

Since 2002, Ogilvy PR has taken on the PR account of the Genesis and Basics brands. Planned media coverage is one contribution that Ogilvy PR has worked into their brand building process. It could be anything from a brand profile in a business

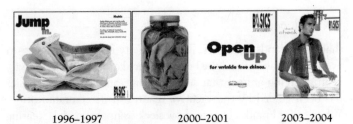

1996–1997   2000–2001   2003–2004

Fig. 4.4: The Basics Brand in Retrospect

periodical to a celebrity opening a Genesis/Basics brand store. That apart, this Ogilvy affiliate has zeroed in on innovative brand building ideas like events at exclusive pubs and hangouts for potential Basics customers. All in all, the Genesis/Basics brand campaign has key insights that can be applied to brands in diverse business settings.

And, now for the verdict. In its sixth year now, the Basics campaign is a thriving example of pioneer brand strategy. It has, in the process, acquired a hopeful band of fashion label imitators, who do their best to imitate. Beginning from its two-man tailoring outfit in Chennai's commercial district, the Hasbro Group today oversees 13 exclusive stores across India with a brand presence in over 30 multi-brand outlets. Internationally, they have a brand presence at 50 multi-brand outlets in the UAE as well as two stores in Sri Lanka. Its advertising strategy now spans publications like the *Economic Times, Cosmopolitan and Outlook*. On home turf in Chennai, at least 25 hoardings that are constantly updated, continue to capture the attention of actual and potential customers.

Of all the figures that make the Basics success story, this one tops them all: When the Basics brand campaign began in 1996, it notched up a turnover of Rs 60 lakhs. Six eventful years later, in 2003, the turnover of the Hasbro Group had quadrupled to become Rs 20 crores. In the final analysis, the success of the Hasbro Group attributes itself to its founding team's understanding of their customers' needs, creating a brand experience that typified it and initiating an advertising–PR campaign that delivered real-time results.

Advertising and the Spirit of our Times

Someone once defined advertising as 'the cave art of the 20th century'. This wild comparison cloaks a core truth of this art, craft and science—all rolled in one. Still, it is possible to believe that the hunter in the Stone Age and the corporate in the Information age, both have a common need—to publicize their core mission and achievements. And, advertising remains the most powerful and persuasive tool of brand building. Countries and states are brands. Let's take the case of Asia. In West Asia, Qatar promotes itself with a exotic flavour of Arab culture with the tagline: 'Once seen, never forgotten'. The brand strategy here looks to create curiosity and evoke a visitor response to a previously unknown destinations-with a first time visit. Moving to South Asia, there is India's own bit of tropical paradise—Kerala, the brand essence of which is driven in with the phrase 'God's own country'. Kerala has assiduously cultivated its brand image to put itself on the global traveller's market. God's own country has a brand strategy that has worked wonders. In South East Asia, Malaysia celebrates its diversity for the tourist with the 'Truly Asia' campaign. Three countries. Three brands. One touristy aim.

Advertising continues to grip the popular spirit of our times. It is, if you like, a symbol of our aspirations. Coke became the number one beverage company in the world, with its promise of refreshment. Nike inspired a generation of sport with the theme, 'Just do it'. IBM invited its users to 'THINK'. On the other hand, Apple Computer's dedicated tribe of maverick users have always known that it pays to 'think different'! More recently, an Italian ice-cream company made the bold decision to provocatively name their ice-cream range after the seven deadly sins of human nature—gluttony, lust, wrath, envy, greed, fear and sloth.

Beyond eye-catching advertisements, campaigns and billboards, brands have been popularized through airplanes, balloons, cloud formations, oceanfronts, rock faces. The Cow Placard Company in Switzerland now offers to advertise corporate logos on cows in the Swiss countryside. It is seen as an innovative way 'to boost the rural economy'. With the corporate brand at its core, every advertising strategy becomes a powerful tool of market growth. You watch it when you watch a James Bond film ride on market associations that range from Reid and Taylor for suits, and BMW for cars. You sense it, every time MRF rolls out a new and improved tyre. You feel it every time Basics Clothing grabs your attention with its compelling billboard. You know it, when you watch ESPN play the brand game. And, play it so well.

Signposts

A brand is a collection of perceptions in the mind of the consumer. Brand strategies revolve around distinguishing a product or service from others, maintaining its brand image and building that image consistently through channels of communication.

Advertising, is in an accepted sense, 'the dissemination of information concerning an idea, service or product to compel action in accordance with the intent of the advertiser'. In the 21st century, it translates to 'action in accordance with the intent of the advertiser' leads to 'consistent consumer experiences'.

Brands are built through a three-way process that communicates a corporate's 'content' through communication 'methods' to predetermined target communities. Corporate brands evolve through a 'preserve the core and stimulate progress' approach.

Advertising remains the single most powerful and persuasive way for a corporate brand to build its presence through the media in the new era. As the 360 Degree Brand approach points out, 'if it moves, it's the media'.

Brand-Initiative

One quick step into the brand future. A biotechnology company approaches you to create their brand image. Their aim is to popularize a slew of tightly researched biotech products for the Asian markets. Their Unique Selling Proposition (USP) is a base of biotech products for daily use—ranging from health to cosmetic products, drawn from modern research in Asia's traditional medicine systems. Indian and Chinese systems form the core of their research capability. Beginning with a year-long brand campaign in the home market, they aim to target a diverse spectrum of audiences, the main among these being the newly aware, upwardly mobile target segment. They are typically within the 25–35 years age group segment, and are health-conscious enough to invest in a premium biotech product that points to a healthier, more natural lifestyle.

How would you build this brand? And, how would you address the key audience described here? Your brand campaign would need a company name, a logo, a mission statement, an umbrella brand that oversees two separate categories of health and cosmetics. Apart from a corporate identity programme, you could look at a nationwide corporate brand campaign that builds on the theme of modern research built on traditional medicinal systems. A good way to evaluate such an initiative would be to call in an advertising professional—creative or client-servicing, to present his or her take on the campaign. Such an evaluation might seem hard or demanding at the first look but you would gain a wealth of insight on the true value of the brand campaign's effectiveness.

Sources

Publications

Blair, M., Armstrong, R. and Murphy, M. (2003). *The 360 Degree Brand in Asia: Creating More Effective Marketing Communications.* John Wiley and Sons (Asia) Ltd, Singapore.

Croteau, D. and Hoynes, W. (2001). *The Business of Media: Corporate Media and the Public Interest.* Pine Forge Press, Thousand Oaks.

Kitchen, Philip J. and Schultz, Don E. (2001). *Raising the Corporate Umbrella: Corporate Communications in the 21st Century.* Palgrave, New York.

Mohan, Manendra. (1990). *Advertising Management: Concepts and Cases.* Tata McGraw-Hill Publishing Company Limited, New Delhi.

Periodicals

Bhimani, Rita. (18th April 2001). 'Is Your Corporate Communication Working?' *Catalyst, The Hindu Business Line.*

Bhushan, Ratna. (5th August 1999). 'Advertising is not about winning battles, it is war...' *Catalyst, The Hindu Business Line.*

Challapalli, Sravanthi. (6th June 2002). 'Hutch says Hi', *Catalyst, The Hindu Business Line*, Chennai.

Fernandez, Joseph. (June 2000). 'The Advertising Industry: Reinventing the Future', *Business Mandate*, Chennai.

_____ (June 2000). 'Corporate Communications', *Business Mandate*, Chennai.

Radhakrishnan Sankar. (21st February 2002). 'Genesis of a dream', *Catalyst, The Hindu Business Line*, Chennai.

Sen, Shunu. (12th September 2002). 'Consumer insights count', *Catalyst, The Hindu Business Line*, Chennai.

_____ (18th April 2002). 'Advertising is one element of the marketing mix', *Catalyst, The Hindu Business Line*, Chennai.

Subramaniam, Harsha. (18th April 2002). 'When media brands advertise', *Catalyst, The Hindu Business Line*, Chennai.

Taher, Abdul. (June 2000). 'Managing Chaos...Oops...Advertising!' *Business Mandate*, Chennai.

Further Reading

Choudhury, Pran K. (2001). *Successful Branding.* Universities Press, New Delhi.

Morrison M., Haley E., Sheehan K.M. and Taylor R.E. (2002). *Using Qualitative Research in Advertising: Strategies, Techniques and Applications.* Sage Publications, Thousand Oaks.

Valladares, June. (2000). *The Craft of Copywriting.* Response Books, New Delhi.

Websites

www.apple.com
www.genesisbasics.com
www.harley-davidson.com
www.online-pr.com
www.corpcomm.co.uk

Interviews

Arup Kavan
Managing Partner
Ogilvy PR Worldwide, South India

Professor Francis Jose
Department of Commerce
Loyola College, Chennai

Sheikh Abdul Taher
Creative Director,
Radical Brand Consultancy and Advertising, Chennai

Hanif Mohammed,
Managing Partner
Hasbro Clothing, Chennai

5 Public Relations: Into the Strategy Realm

Here's to the success of our impossible task!

—The Soviet dissidents' toast in the 1970s

JEFFERY Vardon is taking his place in the sun. Twenty feet below him, the Bay of Bengal's white-crested waves are crashing onto the moss green wave-breaker, on which his lithe figure stands poised. A rainbow-like mist is settling on this desolate part of the North Madras coast. As the young man clad in ethnic Indian attire transforms himself into the epitome of flowing artistry. Before you can say, 'The Hot Shoe Dance Company...', he assumes an Icarus-like pose—the ultimate aspiration of man in flight. And, then for a few unreal seconds, it happens: 'Take!'

Jeffery Vardon is airborne—his lithe figure, silhouetted against the tropical afternoon sun. Rapid-fire clicks and the whirr of camera shutters follow, in quick unison. And then, with an almost feline grace, he is back on his feet. The sound of light applause from the camera crew, leads him to a moment of theatrical impulse. For the nth time in his two-decade career, Jeffery Vardon takes a practised and graceful theatrical bow. So, what is one of India's leading choreographers doing on a wave-breaker in a windswept corner of the North Chennai coast? The answer lies in a passion-turned-profession that Jeffery has pursued for nearly two and a half decades—Dance.

A quintessential performer, Jeffery Vardon is one of India's few qualified dance instructors. His artistry enables him to flit effortlessly between styles and forms, thanks to his classical training in Russian ballet, backed with diplomas from the Melbourne-based Victorian Dance Company. Over the years, he has participated in over 78 productions that have taken him across India—and around the world. His merit as a dance professional has led to recognition by the top names in the entertainment and media industry.

Across the worlds of advertising, films, theatre and modern dance, Jeffery Vardon has established himself as a consummate interpreter of movement. His distinctive style and form has found expression on every platform of the media. You'll remember him for the Nirma detergent ad in the 1980s, featuring Sangeeta Bijlani. More recently, his work was featured in Kamal Hassan's grim tale of two brothers 'Abhay'(Alavandan, in its Tamil original). Dance has lead Jeffery on a cultural journey that has spanned the continents of the world. From Moscow's disciplined dance studios to London's stadium stages. From North America's neon-lit venues to Southeast Asia's glittering stages. And, then in 1997, Jeffery quit a lucrative career as a travel professional in Chennai to make dance a passion-turned-profession. And, he called it 'the Hot Shoe Dance Company'.

In addition, a core team of dancers who come under the aegis of the Hot Shoe Dance Company perform for corporate events and entertainment programmes, giving the enterprise a high-profile visibility. Like its founder, the company is the confluence of cross-cultural influences. On a good day, you'll find Jeffery drawing from elements as diverse as Bharatanatyam, Classical Ballet, Latino Dancing, Tai Chi and Kalaripayattu—Kerala's time-honoured martial art form. (You'll even find Jeffery's musical innovation: New Vogue—a musical form that incorporates Latin American music with the beats of the South Indian percussion instrument—the mridangam!) Beyond its reputation for consummate artistry, the Hot Shoe Dance Company's ascent to market prominence was turbo-charged with a powerful PR (Public Relations) strategy. And, that remarkable story is told in the second half of this chapter. Read on...

Public relations in India, like the rest of the globe, has come into focus for its pure potential in terms of a communication strategy.

Indeed, what public relations is to the corporate world translates into propaganda for the political realm. In the mid 1990s, British Prime Minister Tony Blair stormed to power, with his 'New Labour' party that swept the imagination of an entire generation in the United Kingdom. Driving his campaign was an assiduous propaganda strategy, by a team of communication specialists, who came to be known as the 'spin doctors'. As the 1990s wore off, the term 'to put a spin' came to signify the art of manipulating information. Closer home in India, the meteoric rise of India's film-star politicians have already proved to be classic propaganda strategies. The Congress Party's 'My Heart beats for India' and the BJP's 'India Shining' campaigns, though, are now viewed as examples of how-not-to-plan-propaganda!

And, then there's public relations—PR as we popularly know it. The public relations industry has shot into prominence with the recognized need for professional communications strategy that work in the short, medium and long term. In an age of proactive strategic management, public relations initiatives are widely seen as 'a barometer of public opinion, sensitizing management through research, measurement and evaluation, to the concerns and expectations of the organization's publics' (Navin, 2003, p. 1). India's public relations industry has an estimated annual turnover of Rs 12 billion. The industry itself has an annual growth rate of 40 to 50 percent.

When it comes to 'PR', everyone is doing it. Apart from the usual slew of celebrities, industrialists and film producers, the government seems to have joined in the fray. Leading the roster, is the Andhra Pradesh government, when it hired a PR agency for about Rs 20 million to handle the National Games' public relations programme—the first initiative of its kind. The Himachal Government signed up with the frontline PR agency Perfect Relations to inform the public about its development initiatives. More famously, in 2002, Narendra Modi's government issued a CD Rom in the *India Today*, as an image-building initiative. As Sunil Sethi, the anchor of the celebrity programme, Limelight on Star News puts it: 'It is wall to wall PR. There is no public life without PR.' (Navin, 2003, p.1). Practically every organization within the public domain today strategizes with public relations initiative. Governments, industry, healthcare, education, even non-profit organizations—they are all there. Public relations offers a three-pronged approach, in terms of long term strategy, image-building and crisis management, all of which lead us to believe that this is the definitive age of public relations.

The Critical Mass

In the path-breaking book, *News for a Change: An Advocate's Guide to Working with the Media*, you will find this insight launch the book on its trajectory of academic excellence: 'It's not about reaching everybody. It's about targeting the few who make a difference. It's about starting a chain reaction. It's about getting to critical mass' (Gunther, quoted in Wallack, Woodruff, Dorfman and Diaz, 1999, p. 52). An insight applicable to every communications initiative—and, indeed, public relations strategy. Taking up from the insights offered by *Raising the Corporate Umbrella*, this chapter bases itself on the premise that corporate communications is the traditional turf of public relations practitioners. It is, in that respect, an evolved response to the communication needs of the 21st century Corporate.

To begin with, our first step into the strategic realm of public relations begins with an understanding of its nature: 'Public Relations is the practice of creating, promoting, or maintaining goodwill and a favourable image among the public towards an institution or public body. It could also mean the condition of the relationship between the organization and its public. To elaborate, Public Relations is the planned and sustained effort to establish and maintain goodwill and mutual understanding between an organization and its publics. Going by the traditional approach, an "organization" can be a government body, a business, a profession, a public service or a body concerned with health, culture, education—indeed any corporate or voluntary body large or small. "Publics" are audiences that are important to the organization'. (Navin, 2003, p. 1).

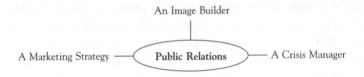

Fig. 5.1: Public Relations in its New Era Roles

In the previous chapter, 'Advertising: Beyond the Brand' we looked at the brand as being the core reactor of the modern corporate. This chapter focusses on understanding how the modern corporate uses PR as a brand builder: first, by starting a chain reaction of image building and then attaining 'a critical mass' of brand reputation. In that light, we will look at public relations in its three avatars, namely—a market strategy, an image builder and a crisis manager. Over to the real-time application of public relations strategy in today's businesscape.

A Market Strategy

Like everything else that we live with, public relations has undergone a world of change in the way that it is perceived—and practiced. 'PR' has gone beyond mere 'press relations' to become a full-fledged strategic area for the modern corporate. In the more assured days of the 20th century, public relations and marketing had different agendas. Public relations looked at corporate relationships and the build-up of universal goodwill. Marketing looked at consumers, demands, and importantly, profits. Public relations was the qualitative, feel-good factor, whereas marketing rolled up its sleeves and got down to the business of making money. Of course, it all mattered because good public relations created an opportunity-rich environment for the marketing strategy to do its job. As the 21st century braced itself for the invigorating atmosphere of a new competitive era, all that changed—forever.

In their book *Raising the Corporate Umbrella*, Kitchen and Schultz shed light on the turbulent interaction between the fields of public relations and marketing. And the birth and synergy of the new corporate strategy area known as Marketing Public Relations (MPR):

'Marketing Public Relations (MPR) is the use of public relations strategies and techniques to achieve marketing objectives. The purpose of MPR is to gain awareness, stimulate sales, facilitate consumption, and build relationships between consumers and companies and brands...' (Harris, quoted in Kitchen and Schultz, 2003, p. 177). MPR is the effort to tie the corporate brand and the various product brands together more closely. Taking the conceptual steps into this realm, they throw up the corporate and product brand model proposed by Thomas Mosser of Burson-Marsteller, the world's largest public relations firm. In brief, every institution has two key assets: its 'Brand' (by which is meant the institution's image, reputation, financial assets, performance and people), and its 'brand' which are the products and services it offers. The corporate 'Brand' and product brand have a symbiotic link—i.e., they are intrinsically dependant on each other.

That is the theory. So, is there a real-time application of this brand model at work? More importantly, does Marketing Public Relations work in a corporate environment? The answer to that question is an emphatic yes. The application of MPR is a reality in India and abroad. We found this PR approach applied and adapted in the country offices of India's pioneer overseas education group: Campus-Abroad.

Creating a Student Market

In 1978, more than a decade before India opened up to globalization, a young entrepreneur in Chennai, fresh from an educational stint abroad, realized a nascent need in India's burgeoning student population. His own experience as an overseas student led him to the realization that aspiring students in India had no avenues of consultation when it came to pursing their dreams of overseas education. At that point, overseas education was a privilege with a few thousand students leaving every year for universities in the West. A one-stop advisory that would guide students through the applications, admissions and immigration processes was the need of the hour.

That vision of Dr Paul Chellakumar was realized in the setting up of Campus-Abroad, India's pioneer overseas education and counselling organization. In pre-liberalized India, overseas education was not a priority. From day one, Campus-Abroad and its founding team knew that this was one niche that was to be created. 'Our earliest experience indicated that word-of-mouth was our strongest asset in the student community', recalls Dr Chellakumar with candour, 'Our natural recourse at that point was a public relations programme that would get across to this key audience of Campus-Abroad'.

A good decade of market effort backed by PR initiative saw Campus-Abroad set its base up across India's four southern states. In time, this was to prove a good administration decision. As Campus-Abroad charted its moves through India's nascent student markets, it realized that its audiences were growing. Beyond growing student enrollments, there was also a growing network of schools, polytechnics, universities and institutions to be addressed around the world.

And then in 1991, it happened. India's year of liberalization opened the floodgates of Globalization, re-inventing the aspirations of a whole new generation of Indian students. Suddenly, overseas education was an achievable dream. And, the surge in India's student markets' had the market leader riding the crest of its growth. It quickly became apparent that Campus-Abroad would have to take a first step in addressing the new niches that were cropping up in overseas education and its allied areas.

Campus-Abroad's market strategy revolved around teams of student counselors who interacted with students. In their other role, they acted as representatives of Campus-Abroad at academic events, international education fairs, and embassy events, pertaining to overseas education. Wherever you see a Campus-Abroad team, the approach is the same—an assertive, friendly approach backed by professionalism and integrity. Campus-Abroad centred its student market effort around the assiduous 'use of public relations strategies and techniques to achieve marketing objectives'. This quantum growth in the market meant that Campus-Abroad had to address diverse audience spectrums at the same time. As it crossed its second decade of existence, the Campus-Abroad Group became a 'Brand' with affiliate organizations that offered smaller 'brands' of specialized services. In chronological order, they are:

Courses-Abroad

A group affiliate which played country representative to specific courses offered by international universities for students from India.

America-Abroad

A Los Angeles-heaquartered affiliate that represented American universities primarily in India, Europe and the Asia-Pacific region.

Chances-Abroad

A Chennai-based immigration and employment consultancy that oversaw process formalities for aspiring immigrants and professionals wishing to work abroad.

Campus-Abroad Mauritius

Once again, a pioneering overseas education firm set up for the first time in the verdant island nation of Mauritius.

Campus International

An overseas educational service with a unique approach: it focusses purely on student academic requirements without any university affiliations.

Let us take a moment now to understand the audiences that the Campus-Abroad Group now addresses. During its early days, there were precisely two target audiences: students and universities. Today, the Campus-Abroad Group addresses the following audiences: current students, potential students, students' parents, schools and colleges in India, scholarship foundations, foreign schools, polytechnics, institutions, universities, foreign embassies, foreign alumni, visiting academics and franchise offices across India.

In early 2003, when Campus-Abroad celebrated its silver jubilee, it initiated a year-long advertising and public relations campaign centred around the theme: 25 years of excellence in overseas education. The statistics were impressive. In two and a half decades, Campus-Abroad had a growing alumni strength of 6000 students. Every academic year, its offices meet over 5000 students. Over the years, at least 65,000 students had been counselled on overseas education. Globally, the Campus-Abroad Group has a network of 83 affiliate universities across 20 countries. Not to mention, two country offices in the US and Mauritius. Pioneering a niche in India's student markets, Campus-Abroad discovered that an aggressive market strategy was clearly not the solution. Instead, the group looked to an assertive market initiative, driven primarily by public relations strategy to build on its leadership position in the market. And, it paid off.

The Image Builder

Even Richard Branson swears by it. As the founder of the Virgin Group, he delights in madcap maverick publicity-blazing events that popularize his group. (In his rollicking autobiography, *Losing my Virginity*, he candidly admits that his PR capers bring him more publicity and cost a lot less than million-dollar ad blitzes!). In the first chapter of their admirable book, *News for a Change*, the authors provide one, and indeed the only, rule for public relations as an image builder: 'You can't have a media strategy without an overall strategy' (Wallack, Woodruff, Dorfman and Diaz, 1999, p. 10).

Truer words were never spoken for the unsung tribe of PR professionals. All too often, the 'PR' for public relations is often taken to mean 'press relations'—a case of mistaken identity that most PR professionals manfully try to compete with. As new era companies and organizations come to terms with the corporate realities of competition and change, they find public relations as an image builder is a strategic tool of success—and survival. The image is all, many will have you believe. Or, is it? Image building, through public relations is one guaranteed way of improving business, both, in terms of marketshare and goodwill. As Arup Kavan of Ogilvy

Box 5.1
The Final Connect is the Last Mile

Based in Chennai, Arup Kavan leads several Ogilvy Public Relations Worldwide initiatives in South India. With over a decade in advertising, exposure to disciplines like direct response, and hands-on sales and marketing experience, he has strong views on the powerful role Public Relations can play in brand building:

"A good public relations programme, as far as I'm concerned, ties in strongly with the brand's marketing objectives. It recognizes key audiences—the end user, the buyer, the influencer, the trade channel, current and prospective employees, etc. It develops key messages relevant for each audience. It prioritises between the many audiences. It develops a strategy that focuses on delivering key messages to those audiences that matter, in a memorable and credible manner that is more likely to lead to the desired audience response.

PR programmes demand a holistic understanding of brand communication. It is becoming fashionable for PR outfits to earnestly explain that their version of PR is 'more than just media relations'! Media relations is and will remain a key armament in the PR war cabinet. PR offers the brand owner a breath-taking opportunity to study his brand issues and needs from an audience perspective. And to then deliver targeted communication, relevant to the particular audience. Research is key, and regrettably rarely invested in by a brand owner already under budgetary pressure to test and run the last set of 30 second commercials he agreed to in a weak moment!

PR sets out the brand's messaging. PR can influence perceptions, attitudes and behaviour. PR runs on the Pareto's 80:20 principle, leveraging the fact that 'the few have an extraordinary influence on the many'. PR provides last mile connectivity to each of the targeted audiences – internal and external. The brand owner who does not invest in a professional PR programme is simply out of touch with reality!"

PR Worldwide points out in his view, PR continues to be a highly cost-effective strategic tool to reach a wide audience in the long term (See Box 5.1).

By extension, a powerful PR strategy will give a corporate the image and exposure it needs. This leads to better market performance, resulting in higher profits. In image building, the media plays only a part of the role in overall public relations strategy. As the collective experience of the world's top companies proves, it makes gilt-edged business sense for any company to build its image with a mix of advertising and public relations. According to Ramkumar Singaram of Catalyst Public Relations, a Chennai-based public relations firm, most multinationals allot 70 percent of their annual promotion budget towards advertising, leaving the remaining 30 percent for public relations. Today's markets however, are media-saturated, and corporates need to increase their visibility through a well planned, effectively handled image-building PR strategy.

Let us take a look now at media relations, as it is now known. Why should a corporate initiate contact with the media at all? The answer to that question lies in the dynamic, changing businesscape that you see around you. Behind the scenes, intense lobbying and networking are the order of the day. Sooner or later, every corporate and organization is confronted with the need to get its point of view across to the largest possible audience. Such a scenario calls for a proactive image-building strategy—and therefore, a rapport with the media.

Here is an example. Let us assume you represent the apex organization of the auto ancillary industry in your state. This year's budget has unfairly taxed your sector, spelling financial doom for many of its small industries. The most potent way to express your grievance is to take your case to the government, publicizing it through the media. The end result is that you gather all possible support for your cause. In the PR strategic armoury, media relations is definitely the most powerful image-building tool. Of course, the reason that press relations is now known as media relations is because it addresses news organizations in the print, audio-visual and digital media. And its success depends on its 'newsworthiness'. The team at Catalyst Public Relations that specializes in business-related news shared their insight with us. These are key examples of newsworthy events that are highlighted by the media:

- Product/service/concept/company launches
- News of awards/commendations/affiliations/prestigious recognition
- Inaugural Functions/expansions/diversifications/financial results
- Foreign tie-ups/high value orders/joint ventures/ collaborations
- New management/board level appointments/key business opportunities
- Philanthropic activity/corporate citizenship initiative/welfare schemes
- Exhibitions/workshops/contests/trade fairs/buyer-seller meets/ expositions
- Apex association/industry federation/corporate organization meets
- Crisis Management/damage control exercises/trade and industry problems

— Courtesy: Catalyst Public Relations, 2003

Fig 5.2: PR's Definitive Corporate Newsmakers

Into the Spotlight

When Jeffery Vardon visited Median in December 1999, he brought with him one of the strangest and most challenging initiatives that we have had to work on. In two months, a little over 60 days, he was about to embark on the artistic dream of a lifetime. One of Chennai's leading and most accomplished choreographers, Jeffery's two year old venture, the Hot Shoe Dance Company was planning to stage its first major production in Chennai. And, Jeffery was there, because the company 'needed the media' to spotlight its effort. With limited resources, the Hot Shoe Dance Company were planning a mega production. The cast of 70 dancers were already in gruelling rehearsals, while a skilled production team was working on the sets, props and costumes. Adding to the challenge was the fact that it all centred around a single production to be held in late February 2000 at Chennai's preferred indoor venue—The Music

Academy. To complete the dream, the Hot Shoe Dance Company needed a strategy that create, maintain and nurture an image for its home audience.

When the team at Median rolled up its sleeves, it zeroed in on a PR-centric strategy. The critical first step was creating a long term strategy that would communicate with audiences. To do this, we stepped into help shape 'the overall strategy'. Soon enough, the Median team was pitching into the script of the production as well. The presentation itself was a riot of song, dance and stage forms that were being introduced to Chennai for the first time. The show was driven by a soundtrack comprising popular Latino music. It also showcased artistic moments expressed through elements of Indian classical dance and modern dance. And, through the swirl of its movement, it told the poignant story of a love lost and regained. The name of the production, we decided, would be 'Dance!—A Celebration of the Millennium Spirit'. Not only did the title establish a brand link with the Hot Shoe Dance Company, but it captured the spirit of the time.

Fig 5.3: The Hot Shoe Dance Company takes Flight

By the middle of December 1999, the overall strategy of the Hot Shoe Dance Company was in place. One initiative of this period was a photo shoot conducted in a little-known corner of the coast in North Chennai, where foam-crested waves crash on concrete wave breakers. (This chapter starts by attempting to recapture that moment, in that day in late 1999, when we completed a memorable photo shoot there). It was time then for the media strategy. Based on our experience in media, we now knew that the Hot Shoe Dance Company was an imminently newsworthy story.

Our first target audience was the media. Our aim was to ensure we got as much pre-press publicity as possible in order to sell tickets. (There was no budget for an ad campaign or for that matter, even an advertisement!) Our first step was to draw up a list of 33 media organizations across the print, audio-visual and digital media. These included the top news sources of the region—*The Hindu*, *The Indian Express*, NDTV, Sun TV, and news sites like Chennai Online and Satyam Infoway. And, they addressed the English and Tamil news organizations in the city. The next step was a compelling media release—the kind that caught the attention of a harried news editor sifting through piles of press releases. The nifty media release spotlighted the production of the Hot Shoe Dance Company, giving details about its finer aspects, in terms of its production, script and characters.

Along every step of this challenging assignment, we were guided by the insights provided by *News for a Change* (Wallack, Woodruff, Dorfman and Diaz, 1999, pp. 80–81). In particular, we found the Media Event Planning Time Line presented by the book extremely useful in strategizing for media coverage. Briefly, the checklist guides you through a primer of how to interact with the media before, during and after a press conference. Here, the guidelines lead you through a timeline that starts a month in advance, a fortnight in advance, a week in advance, at the conference and after it. In our personal experience, we found that its application in our setting worked like a dream. A week before the actual show, the media was invited for a show preview that included a spotlight with the company—its cast. The show also featured video footage from rehearsals, followed by an actual performance from the show itself. Soon after, it was showtime.

The curtains rose on 21 February 2000, to an ecstatic audience response. The 70 strong cast put their soul into their performance, giving their home audience a treat of artistic styles celebrated through music. In terms of media strategy, the pre-event publicity had worked, with at least 16 news organizations giving the company some kind of coverage. The media attended the event in full strength. Star News covered the event on its weekly bulletin. At the venue, we co-ordinated personalized interviews with the cast, and ensured that the media got its story. There was ample post-event publicity that caught the city's attention. Two weeks later, as we reviewed the success of our initiative, we found that at least 25 of the 33 news organizations that we had interacted with, had responded with coverage for the Hot Shoe Dance Company. The company rode the wave of publicity to become Chennai's lead dance school.

Box 5.2
Public Relations—The Way Ahead for Market Growth

Ramkumar Singaram, drives the CATALYST Public Relations practice in Chennai. One of South India's most prolific and successful agencies, Catalyst PR occupies a unique niche in its chosen field. For its 130 annual clients, most of them, Small & Medium Enterprises (SMEs), Catalyst PR has ushered in the age of market-friendly, client-focussed public relations practice. Here is Ramkumar's view of the Indian PR scenario in the century to come:

Public Relations in India is all set to reinvent itself in the 21st century to suit the unique needs of its corporate organizations. In this dynamic scenario, we at Catalyst PR see our clients in three categories of business organizations: Corporates, Small & Medium Enterprises, and Small Players. Corporates have traditionally adopted PR practice for market growth. Whereas Small and Medium Players have recently understood its potential. Small Players, on the other hand, have yet to fully comprehend the relevance of PR in the day-to-day conduct of their business. But, even that is changing.

At Catalyst PR, our expertise reaches out to all categories, Small & Medium Enterprises are our chief focus. And, the reason

(contd.)

Box 5.2 (contd.)

is evident. In the last decade, these enterprises—the mainstay of our economy—have felt the pressure of liberalization and globalization on their traditional market turf. They have watched their home markets get eroded by multinationals and corporates, who are using aggressive culture-specific market strategies to gain other traditional customer bases. One classic example comes to mind. A multinational toothpaste suddenly made inroads where a traditional tooth powder once reigned supreme. The unsettled nature of our markets strikes even the most established players. For these traditional businesses, often family-owned, a public relations strategy is a cost-effective, goodwill-building approach that yields desired market results.

The approaches of the different organizations could not be more different. In our experience, we find that corporates approach us with a market results-oriented strategy asking us to work out media costings based on it. A SME or a Small Player, on the other hand, comes to us with a seasonal budget, and asks us to work out the most powerful strategy, which is invariably a mix of long-term PR and cost-effective advertising. Across all our client organizations, there is widespread strategizing for the vernacular language media. Ironically, the markets of deep South have not yet been impacted by the Internet. And so, Public Relations takes recourse to the most traditional platforms of information spread. By this, I mean, traditional village fairs, weekly markets, religious events and the like. Public Relations, marketers find, is a potent tool for the emerging field of rural marketing.

As for the future, in the decade to come, I see the SMEs looking to PR strategies that were the sole preserve of the corporates. And, by extension, Small Players—the small, almost unnoticed businesses of our day-to-day lives—will reach out into existing PR practices followed by SMEs to boost their business growth. Add to this, emerging media platforms such as full time business channels in local languages, and you find an entire new dimension to the awareness of PR among these organizations. All these organizations have a single market agenda: survival in an increasingly competitive marketplace followed by success in terms of market growth and customer loyalty. Towards this end, Public Relations remains their most potent tool of market growth.

The Crisis Manager

Dag Hammarskjold, the second UN Secretary-General once remarked that the UN was not created to take nations to paradise, but merely to save humanity from hell (Hammarskjold quoted in Tharoor, 2003, p. 3). Apply that thought to PR in its role as a crisis manager, and you will have an idea of how PR works in a crisis situation. PR, in essence, recognizes that the process of building a corporate image is a double-edged proposition. The same truth confronts corporates, communities and organizations across the world. In its avatar as a crisis manager, public relations plays the peace-keeping role of reducing conflict, while trying to maintain goodwill.

Crisis management is the corporate world's worst-case scenario. And, the global businesscape is littered with wrecks of corporates that took the wrong turn. Corporate crises have time and again proved to be only the tip of the iceberg upon which titanic corporations have hit and sunk themselves. And, the wrecks are legion. Enron, Union Carbide, Worldcom are some global examples. Closer home, the collapse of Home Trade, a decade after the stock scam of the early 1990s was a grim reminder that corporate India is inherently vulnerable to corporate crisis.

In our experience, we have discovered that public relations in its avatar as a crisis manager plays a role very similar to that played by the humble unseen UPS (Uninterrupted Power Supply) units in our work environments. A good UPS unit deals with the minor spikes and surges in power that would otherwise damage your personal computer.

In case of a power shutdown, it provides your PC with valuable back-up time, and prevents any damage to its memory or hard drive. Crisis management is the uninterrupted power supply of corporate existence. It deals with the minor issues that crop up in the day-to-day functioning of a corporate. And, in case of a sudden crisis, it swings into action to keep the lifeline of communication going between a corporate and its publics.

Raising the Corporate Umbrella presents a compelling definition of a corporate crisis: 'Crisis is defined as a people-stopping, show-stopping, reputationally defining event, which creates victim and/ or explosive visibility'. (Lukasweski quoted in Kitchen and Schultz, 2001, p. 203). It goes on to describe the three kinds of crises that affect an organization:

• Operating Situations
(Crises arising out of the day-to-day operations of an organization— accidents, disasters, onsite or offsite)

• Non-operating Problems
(Situations arising outside the scope of activity—e.g. crime, harassment, sabotage)

• Combination operations/non-operation scenarios
(These include take-overs, acquisitions, stock price changes and disgruntled employees)

Tomes and volumes have been dedicated to the study of crisis management and ways to control them. And, they would agree that every crisis calls for a corporate crisis response that is timely, transparent and responsive. Importantly, a crisis response should proactively control any further damage to the lives or reputations of those concerned. In the often dreaded event of addressing the media and other publics, *News for a Change* offers us four guidelines:

1. Try to stay calm and be courteous...
2. Never exaggerate, evade or lie...
3. Never say 'No Comment'....
4. Plan for a crisis in advance
            (Wallack, Woodruff, Dorfman and Diaz, 1999, p. 100).

How often do you hear of companies that arrive in a blaze of publicity? In series of lavish events and conventions, they promise to change their customers' lives forever—through stocks, franchises, products and networks. They possess the makings of a corporate success—swank offices, glitzy business plans, hi-profile teams and aggressive campaigns. Companies that become the cynosure of the media—and put their spin on definitions of success. Of course, you need to look really hard, for beyond the buzz of hyped achievement, the clamour of apparent success, often exists a void—devoid of any business vision. And, then for the nth time in business history, it happens—a minor event kicks off a series of events that leads to the ultimate collapse of the organization—much like collapsing dominoes. The organization crumbles. Reputations crash. And, communities suffer. The shutdown of the company leads to a breakdown of communication—and pandemonium among its stakeholders. Here, you will find that the lack of a crisis response worsens matters. And, in the carefully chosen words of the Queen rock anthem, another one bites the dust! In such a scenario, an effectively handled crisis management initiative could make a vital difference.

On a lighter note, even crisis management has its humorous moments. During the SARS epidemic that paralyzed Hong Kong in March 2003, a clever public health official in Hong Kong found an innovative way to evade uncomfortable questions. He stood a safe distance from the waiting media crew, and announced that he would not answer questions. The official reason was that he was not sure whether the microphones were sterilized!

Prowess for the Corporate World

In March, 2004, the Hot Shoe Dance Company took the centre-stage in Chennai for their fifth annual production. In the established tradition of the company, it was a glitzy production that spotlighted a 70 strong cast with an even larger production team. The production played to a packed house and rave reviews. The Hot Shoe Dance Company has time and again re-invented itself in its annual production to give loyal home audiences something to rave about. As this book went to print, there was an avalanche of artistic ideas already in place for future home productions. And, that is only the beginning.

In five hectic years since its inception, the company has built an unmatched reputation for its unique artistic culture. In the real world, the Hot Shoe Dance Company today operates from three swank venues. It has gained immensely from its association with O-2 a health studio run by the Savera Group—one of India's leading hospitality chains. Aerobics, Ballroom, Jazz. Latino and Modern Dancing are some of the styles showcased by the company. As of now, the school has a total strength of 300 students from tiny tots to aspiring models, fitness freaks and expatriates, to senior citizens even. The company's overheads are kept low, with a core dance team and hired-out venues. When not under the spotlight of musicals or theatric productions, the company's core team of dancers perform for corporate launches and events, as a means of extra revenue. More importantly, the Hot Shoe Dance Company is a corporate entity, with an amazing brand recall. Their media coverage is the envy (and puzzle) of every other artistic group in the region.

The Hot Shoe Dance Company got it just right. 'PR', to them, is first a corporate growth strategy, then an image builder and finally a potent crisis manager. The Campus-Abroad Group did not do badly either. In 2003, the group celebrated its 25th year of market leadership with a slew of PR initiatives, driven by a steady presence in the media. Its target audiences clearly defined, the organization grew from strength to strength in an intensely competitive environment, to create new markets for itself by targeting lesser known towns and cities in south India as potential student markets. Two organizations. Two diverse audiences. A similar approach. As these organizations discovered, the application of PR formed a crucial part of their corporate communications initiative.

Corporate communicators today are on familiar turf, when they look to public relations in its three modern avatars: as a market strategy, as an image builder, and as a crisis manager. After all, corporate communications is an evolved response of the traditional practice of public relations. Still, corporate communications is a field in nascence, and is expected by many of its seers and practitioners to find exalted prominence in the key agendas of the 21st century corporate. As this book went to print, we contacted the two organizations highlighted in this book to get an update on their growth. The results speak for themselves. The winning moves in the corporate arena are made by those who understand the intricacies of strategy. In the light of this chapter—the aspects of public relations strategy that it has highlighted—the true potential of public relations still stands to test. But, remember, it took a determined choreographer and his young dance company to their place in the sun.

Signposts

- Public relations is the practice of creating, promoting or maintaining goodwill and a favourable image among the public towards an institution or public body.
- A market strategy, in PR terms, is the long-term initiative by a corporate to use public relations strategies and techniques to achieve marketing objectives.
- Image building is the core thrust of a PR strategy. It refers to the specific efforts made by the organization to create, maintain and nurture an image specific to its diverse spread of audiences.
- Crisis management is the contingency plan of corporate existence. It is the emergency plan that will determine how a corporate will react to any contingency that confronts it. Deployed in time, it is the ultimate tool of damage control.

PR-Initiative

Here is a challenging one. Consider your place of study or work—make it your PR client. And, create a public relations strategy that will see it through the 12 challenging months to follow. To do this, you might want to place the organization in the light of its current market position, its available resources, its spread of audiences. You could strategize on the basis of a reviewed quarterly result. Remember that the entire public relations initiative, will be seen in the following terms:

- A market strategy.
- An image builder.
- A crisis manager.

Think this one out, and you will find that you can apply these three aspects of PR initiative to virtually any organization. Rely on a radically different approach to build on successes of the past and reduce the failures of the future. Begin with the conceptualization, the strategy itself, its three elements and finally a quarterly forecast of how you will work towards its success, with clearly researched and evaluated results.

Sources

Publications

Wallack, L., Woodruff K., Dorfman L. and Diaz I. (1999). *News for a Change: An Advocate's Guide to Working with the Media.* Sage Publications, Thousand Oaks.

Periodicals

Bhimani, Rita. (18th April 2001). 'Is Your Corporate Communication Working'? *Catalyst, The Hindu Business Line.*

Challapalli, Sravanthi. (18th April 2001). 'PR People are Listening Posts', *Catalyst, The Hindu Business Line.*

Kitchen, Philip J. and Schultz, Don E. (2001). *Raising the Corporate Umbrella: Corporate Communications in the 21st Century.* Palgrave, New York.

Navin, Puja. (20th January 2003). 'Public Relations: Winning Solutions', *Catalyst, The Hindu Business Line.*

Radhakrishnan, Sankar. (18th April 2001). 'PR is More Holistic and Universal than Media Relations', *Catalyst, The Hindu Business Line.*

Subramaniam, Lata. (12th September 2002). 'Making PR Integral', *Catalyst, The Hindu Business Line.*

Tharoor, S. (16th March 2003). 'Indispensible, not Irrelevant?' (The Shashi Tharoor Column), *The Hindu Magazine*. Chennai.

Websites
(further research reading)

www.melcrum.com
www.pr-people.com
www.pr-online.com
www.ogilvy-pr.com
www.campus-abroad.com
www.corpcomm.co.uk

Interviews

Arup Kavan,
Managing Partner
Ogilvy PR Worldwide, Chennai

Dr. Paul Chellakumar
Chairman
The Campus-Abroad Group, Chennai

Jeffery Vardon
Director
The Hot Shoe Dance Company, Chennai

Ramkumar Singaram,
Chief Executive
Catalyst Public Relations, Chennai

6 The Traditional Media: Between the Lines

And the end of all our exploring
Will be to arrive where we started
And know the place for the first time...

—T. S. Elliot, Four Quartets

SHE is a vibrant subcontinent, a cultural cauldron and a political miracle. Across her land area of 3,287,263 square kilometres, she celebrates a world of diversity. From north to south, she stretches across 3,214 kilometres. From east to west, she measures 2,933 kilometres. She has a land frontier of 15,200 square kilometres—much of which is guarded zealously by the Himalayas. The Arabian Sea, Indian Ocean and Bay of Bengal lap up to her splendid coastline stretching 7,516 kilometres. Visit her northern reaches in Himachal Pradesh, and you will brace yourself for the icy climes of the Himalayas that rival the Alps of Europe. Head to her northwestern frontier near Rajasthan to experience the sullen heat of the Thar Desert. Her humid eastern border introduces you to the song of the cicada in the mangrove-fringed coastline of Bengal. And, let us not forget her slices of tropical paradise—the Andaman and Nicobar islands, at the extreme end of the Bay of Bengal. Or for that matter, the Lakshwadeep islands, nestled in the sparkling Arabian Sea. Head for her vibrant south, and you will experience the extremes of the tropical experience. She is India.

India's culture revolves around its spirituality. For 5,000 years, six world religions have made India their home. Hinduism is her largest faith. Hindus constitute about 82 percent of the population. Islam comes second, with about 12 percent of the population subscribing to it. The other religions have small, but significant presences. They include Christianity (2.4 percent), Sikhism (2 percent), Buddhism (0.7 percent), Jainism (0.4 percent) and others like Zoroastrianism, which constitute about 0.4 percent of India's population. India knows how to celebrate her contrasts. Software cities next to villages, international class highways through pristine countryside, glitzy amusement parks next to heritage villages. Nothing really, is a surprise in India.

India is a political miracle. The seventh largest country on the globe, she spans 28 states, six union territories, six major ethnic groups and an unevenly distributed population of over one billion people. Though she covers only 2.4 percent of the world's landmass, she is home to about 16 percent of the world's population. And, then there is the way that she communicates. Her constitution recognizes the use of one official language (Hindi), one principal language of commerce (English) and 17 other officially recognized languages. They include Assamese, Bengali, Gujarati, Kannada, Kashmiri, Konkani, Malayalam, Manipuri, Marathi, Nepali, Oriya, Punjabi, Sanskrit, Sindhi, Tamil, Telugu and Urdu. And, here is the unbelievable part: India uses only 1652 spoken languages to communicate!

Despite this veritable babel of languages, India has done an admirable job of connecting its diverse populations with communication technologies and networks. Every strata of society has tapped into this resource. From the Punjabi farmer, using his village's only phone, placing his next order with the fertilizer retailer in the next town, to a Country Sales Manager sending his latest market report online to regional managers across the country, to a Central Union Minister using the video conferencing facility to interact with his western counterpart to assess a flood situation in the Brahmaputra. India is a wondrous example of a country with new era communications at work.

For centuries, India had a thriving oral tradition, backed by a limited written tradition. The introduction of the printing presses by its resident European powers was to change all that. In 1780,

James Augustus Hicky's *Bengal Gazette* or the *Calcutta General Advertiser* became India's first hub of journalism. Coincidentally, at the same time, English became the 'primary language of commerce'. Between the years 1818 and 1947, the Indian Press came into its own—with a diverse spread of English and vernacular papers. By 1924, the British ushered in the age of radio-broadcasting. Ironically, the very systems set up by India's colonial rulers to serve as a means of communication and control, became propaganda weapons of its freedom movement. Mahatma Gandhi and Jawaharlal Nehru, both icons of India's freedom movement, understood the power of the media. India today remembers her years dependence through sepia-toned newspaper reports, static radio broadcasts, not to mention grainy, black and white film footage that never tires of telling its story!

After 1947, the Indian mediascape altered drastically. Besides its press, there was the emergence of radio, film and television. The emergence of AIR (1936) and the birth of Doordarshan (1959) were important milestones of this period. Decades later, the 1975 Emergency was seen as a watershed period for the Indian press. For 19 long months, the Indian press underwent a trial by fire, after which it emerged stronger and more vibrant in more ways than one. According to *The Handbook of the Media in Asia*: 'After the Emergency, the press evolved into a highly professional, market oriented business. It introduced new technologies, designs, and magazines, and a new style of journalism. For example, newspapers and magazines, and a technology in printing and production. They use computerized typesetting equipment and print facsimile editions'. (Vishwanath and Karan, quoted in Gunaratne, 2000, p.90). The traditional media continues to play catalyst to the emergence of modern India. The course of her history has been significantly impacted by the catalytic power of her media systems.

The Handbook of the Media in Asia offers us a staggering avalanche of facts on the media in India: As of 1996 (the last available official data), there were 39,000 publications, covering the daily, fortnightly, weekly and monthly categories. Of the 4,453 newspapers that informed India, 320 were in English and 2,004 in Hindi. In terms of radio, India had about 116 million radio receivers serviced by over 200 radio stations by 1997. As far as television, public and private audience are concerned, studies indicate that India has about 60 million 'TV households' (and 18 million cable-TV subscribers). This translates into one of the largest captive television audiences in the world, ranging from 296 million to 448 million. Here is one more staggering fact. The total population of the United Kingdom's population, where the English language originates, is about 60 million. The total population of the United States is 250 million people. India, however, is the world's largest English speaking nation with over 250 million speakers, who use it on a daily basis!

The ABC of Communication

Every corporate communicator knows it, as you should too. There are two truths to the communications process that you play catalyst to, as a corporate communicator. The first mirrors itself in the words of the Microsoft Corporation's founder, Bill Gates: 'The first rule of any technology used in a business is that automation applied to an efficient operation will magnify the efficiency. The second is that automation applied to an inefficient operation will magnify the inefficiency.' (Gates, quoted in *Frozen Thoughts*, November 2002, p.9).

The second truth comes to life in that universally accepted communicator's insight: 'It is not what you send, it is what they receive'. The target audience is always the end-point of every communications initiative. This brings us to the famous poser that the communications guru, Harold Laswell popularized in the 1940s: 'Who says what to whom via what channel with what effect?'. The message that your audience receives is the only message that will matter. *The Manager's Handbook* by Arthur Young tells this hilarious story concerning J. Edgar Hoover, the legendary FBI director in the 1950s. Concerned with 'sent and received' messages, it is aptly titled 'Crossed Lines', this story observes that ambiguous communications can cost a business money and waste time. It can also lead to faulty decisions as the following, perhaps apocryphal story illustrates:

'A young man was put in charge of the FBI's stores and stationery. Eager to make an impact, he decided to save on costs by reducing the size of the memo paper. One of the new sheets landed on the desk of J. Edgar Hoover (the legendary FBI director in the 1950s) himself. He disliked it on sight— the margins on both sides were too narrow for him. Across the top he wrote, in some irritation, 'watch the borders'. His purpose was misinterpreted. For the next six weeks, it became extremely difficult to enter the USA by road from either Canada or Mexico!'

(Young, 1987, p. 132).

In our experience, we have discovered the three cornerstones of corporate communications. In the order of importance, they are:

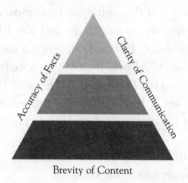

Fig. 6.1: Three Cornerstones of Corporate Communications

• Accuracy of Facts
The corporate, as a living entity, communicates its brand to its internal and external audiences. Core messages are drawn from this centre, to be disseminated to the various corporate audiences. These evolving core messages need to be faithful to the brand vision. Across the platforms of the print, audio-visual and digital media, these messages will differ. An example. Think of your favourite car model. Now, imagine that its price is slashed by a whopping 10 percent. As its corporate communicator, you now need to address two audiences—the potential customer and the investor community. Here is one way to strategize for an accurate 'core message' on this

one. Drawing on your company's brand vision, you inform the customer, through an advertising campaign, of the new incentive to buy. In tandem, you inform the investor community through its monthly online newsletter about higher sales figures that are likely to be realized through the price cut. One message, two audiences. The golden rule here is: build accurate, brief, clear messages around the brand.

• Brevity of Content

The word 'brevity' simply means 'keep it short'. Any communicator will tell you that it is always 'easier' to churn out reams of content. Evolving a short, crisp and yet apt piece of advertising copy is the real challenge, which is why a sound knowledge of three media formats should see you through most situations: advertising copy, the journalistic feature writing style and the PR media release format. Having said that, Robert Gunning is a respected American writer, who has consulted with over 100 newspapers including the *Wall Street Journal* and the *United Press International*. His 'ten principles of clear writing' are a highlight of the immensely popular book '*News Writing and Reporting for Today's Media*'. They are:

1. Keep sentences short, on the average.
2. Prefer the simple to the complex.
3. Prefer the familiar word.
4. Avoid unnecessary words.
5. Put action into your words
6. Write the way you talk.
7. Use terms your reader can picture.
8. Tie in with your reader's experience.
9. Make full use of variety.
10. Write to express, not to impress.

(Gunning, quoted in Itule and Anderson, 1994, p. 168)

In other words, keep it short.

Clarity of Communication

Corporate communications—always a 'concept-to-completion' process—requires clarity of communication. To accomplish this, corporate communicators often echo the poser of communication guru, Harold Laswell: 'Who says what to whom via what channel with what effect?'. Clarity of communication is about understanding the message, its sender, receiver, channel and desired result. This real-time example illustrates the point. When Kinley Water—a product of the Coke Company—wanted to reach out to its existing customers, it chose to use a newsletter. Let us look at their strategy in terms of Laswell's approach. Kinley Water wished to build greater product awareness among its current customers through a circulated newsletter with the objective of building greater customer loyalty—and a larger market share. In early 2002, the company used its network to directly distribute the newsletter with every Kinley 'bubble-top' reaching at least 10,000 homes and offices in Chennai.

Putting Print to Paper

Some things have not really changed, since 1445. A good time to remember that is the next time you see the humble rubber stamp. In principle, the rubber stamp resembles its ancestor—the movable type, invented by the German printer Johann Gutenberg in the mid 15th century. One key premise of this book is that corporate communications draws centrally from traditional media, namely print and audio-visual media. Here, the print media becomes a key tool of corporate branding.

Take the business or visiting card. A business card is the smallest branding tool. It identifies the employee against the background of his or her organization. It goes on to provide vital information about the person, job profile, the organization and its overall brand image. And, then there is corporate literature. Brochures, booklets, flyers, folders, inserts, newsletters, pamphlets and user manuals are all established potent means to communicate

Box 6.1
The Craft of the Print Medium Remains the Same.

S. Muthiah is an Information Consultant, who is best known for his pioneering work for the Heritage cause in Chennai. His prolific career is marked by a long innings with the TTK Group. A Journalist and Writer, he has written for *Madras Musing*, *The Hindu* and a host of other publications. Over the years, he has specialized in corporate and institutional biographies. His book *Madras Rediscovered* is one of the India's best known heritage celebrations. An ardent believer in the power of the print medium, S. Muthiah shares his passion for the printed word:

The cardinal rule of any publicity used to build or promote a company's image is that it should have a clear message, aimed at a target audience. Every communicator should realise that he or she must operate on the lowest common denominator to effectively communicate to a mass audience or in a 'language' understood by the largest number in a target audience. (Like many other essential truths in day-to-day life, we find that not too many communicators, are clear about this!). Any communication, to my mind, should be built with the bricks of simplicity, clarity and brevity. It also needs to be said that creativity in any communication should help it to work, not obscure its main intent.

Here are two memorable instances illustrating this. In the early 1980s, a young advertising agency approached an established pressure cooker manufacturer, whose market appeared to have stagnated. Their pitch intrigued the management. The agency suggested that the problem did not centre on the product—but on its advertising. In a country populated by a 300 million middle class segment that mainly spoke in the vernaculars (at that time), the pressure cooker was being advertised mainly in upmarket English publications, the agency pointed out. Change the focus, and new markets would emerge, the manufacturer was told. In a refreshing surge of entrepreneurial spirit, the manufacturer switched to a powerful vernacular advertising campaign that spoke the language of India's new market. Overnight, the sales skyrocketed, taking the manufacturer into a league of his own.

(contd.)

Box 6.1 (contd.)

In the second instance, three decades ago, four advertising agencies pitched for a transport manufacturer's account. In what was a memorable case of what-not-to-do, one agency built its campaign around a very slick Western theme. One of the advertisements had the headline 'Riding the Rails'. Placed in an American market where the phrase was once celebrated, the idea **MAY** have gathered a momentum all its own. But in an Indian market, where many local languages are spoken, the campaign would have absolutely fizzled out, with the line, an outdated bit of American slang, being meaningless, whatever the translation. Fortunately for the manufacturer, who knew better, the campaign did not see the light of day.

Coming to the print medium, we have today many new technologies: high-speed web, multi-colour offset, digital transfer of images etc. The influx of digital technology has seen execution of copy and design improve in ways that few had foreseen. But specially created copy and visual effects are not in themselves communication—only supplements to it. To my mind, nothing has changed basically. In the new era, the craft of the print medium remains the same. Modern technology enables larger numbers to be more quickly produced with better **average quality**. Believe it or not, for the best result, a few CRAFTSMEN still resort to the age-old letterpress, where the hand-crafted block and the richness of ink supply guarantees the finest reproduction. Strange, but true! And Madras has at least one of them, exporting to Western markets!

In the final analysis, the print medium does still score over the other media, providing detail, impact, mobility and timelessness. For example, an electronics store could choose to reach out to 5,00,000 potential customers through a black and white newspaper ad and then follow it up with a snazzy product catalogue for its 10,000 monthly visitors, followed by 1000 after-sales service booklets for its actual sales. In the final analysis, putting print to paper gives every company a credibility, provided through detailing, unmatched by other media. It is for these reasons the print medium will continue to play a major role in communication.

your corporate's brand to internal and external audiences. Here, a knowledge of print technology is always an asset. To begin with, here is an essential insight into print technologies used in today's corporate environments:

Screen Printing

This is a printing method by which an image is transferred to paper by means of ink squeezed through a stencilled fabric or a metal wire stretched over a frame. Screen printing is a popular manual process that is used for corporate stationery—particularly business cards, letter pads and business covers. Its advantages are that it can be used for smaller or 'limited-run' print jobs and that it can be easily corrected. Screen printing is particularly popular, because it allows for the heavy application of paint and fluorescent colours on practically any material. In corporate settings, you will find it used for posters, T-shirts and point-of-purchase displays. On the flipside, it takes longer to complete and involves a greater margin for human error.

Offset Printing

Offset printing is a mechanized print method by which an image is accurately transferred onto paper based on the photography principle of positive and negative areas. The ink is transferred from the plate onto a rubber blanket and then onto the paper. Based on the design need, offset printing may be single colour, two colour, three colour or four colour jobs. Offset printing bases itself on the CMYK colour principle, where C stands for Cyan(Process Blue), M for Magenta (Process Red), Y for Yellow and interestingly, K for Black. Practically, all colour printing revolves around this four-colour process. In rare cases, special colours like gold are created for specific print jobs. Colour matches are the greatest area of challenge particularly for offset printing. So, a knowledge of the print process and established standards like the Pantone codes always help.

Digital Printing

Digital technology is rapidly transforming the traditional media. And, digital printing represents the latest step on the technology frontier. We use the same technology to take colour printouts for everyday use. Digital printing is centred around the RGB (Red Green Blue) format, where all printed colours are a combination of these three colours. However, the CMYK or RGB platforms can be used for specific print jobs. Today, digital printing is used in everything from business cards to brochures and posters right up to the large glitzy hoardings that dominate our cities' skylines.

Trust in Every Drop

In early 2002, Kinley Water entered the bottled water segment in Chennai city with its bubble-tops. Over a period of 12 months, at least 10,000 homes and offices were targeted as potential customers. Behind this brand entry was the monolithic Coke presence. S.R. Water Company, Chennai's sole Kinley manufacturer and bottler approached the Median team to contribute to its year-long 'integrated marketing communications' (IMC) initiative. In Chennai, as in other Indian cities, Kinley water brought in the assurance of safe drinking water against a backdrop of chronic water shortages and sometimes tainted water sources. The communication impetus was clear: build on Kinley's brand position—'trust in every drop'. This core message that was successfully conveyed through emotional TV commercial campaigns in Hindi ('Boondh Boondh Mein Vishwas') and other languages. The *Kinley4U* initiative is best explained in the three stages that follow:

Fig. 6.2: *Kinley4U*—Building on 'Trust in Every Drop'

• The Conception

The immediate requirement was a one-off newsletter that would communicate the Kinley brand premise to the existing customer network. Our decision was based on the following parameters of communication, economy and potential reach. The newsletter had to present Kinley water in its bubble-top avatar, present it as a hub of 'Trust in every drop' and reach an outer target audience of about 50,000 readers. Economy of production too was cited as an important criteria. While at this, we found the print checklist in Andre Jute's definitive work *Grids: The Structure of Graphic Design*, applicable to this print job:

Brief Checklist

Project
Description
Marketing objective
Background
Product
Name
Usage(when/how)
Product presentation
Sizes/prices
Consumer benefits
Product support
Position within market
Marketing plans
Competition

Reader/consumer
Social group
Age/sex
Occupation
Area/location

Strategy
Type of promotion
Length of promotion
Launch date

Facts to be taken into account
Quantity
Total budget
Size/pages
Number of colours
Existing logo/name style
Product slogan
Illustration/photo style
Deadline
Delivery/distribution

—(Jute, 1996, p. 48)

• The Creation

The imaginatively titled 'Kinley4U'—in technical terms—was an eight page, four colour newsletter, printed on A4 size foreign art paper. It used a concise journalistic style, that presented articles that ranged from 250 to 500 words. The overall content had to be friendly, easy-to-understand and brand-specific. In design terms, we used a contemporary newsletter template emphasizing design-fluidity, bright, interactive colours and the Kinley brand association. In terms of editorial content, the break-up was as follows:

Page 1 comprising of Masthead, two articles—the editorial (Crystal Clear) and one introductory article (Trust in Every Drop).

Page 2 comprising a single technical article on Kinley's water treatment processes titled 'Kinley's Seven Steps to Perfection'.

Page 3 comprising three features—The Coke Story, A Kinley Customer Profile and a piece on the Kinley Call Centre.

Page 4 comprising a trivia/competition section featuring water-facts, a water quiz, a cartoon and a children's competition, as also Kinley contact information.

Once the content and design were integrated, the creative process got underway. At the penultimate stage, the newsletter was thoroughly proof-checked, with its facts double-checked. The softwares used included Microsoft Word (newsletter content), Adobe PhotoShop (Images/Photo scanning) and Adobe PageMaker (for page layout). The content, images and design were then merged into a single creative file.

• The Completion

After the final approval from the client, *Kinley4U* made its way to an offset press in for its print-run. Over two days, a state-of-art offset machine began roll out copies of *Kinley4U*. The first few copies of the newsletter came under the rigorous scrutiny of the 'colour-correction' processes. This ensures that the colours remain faithful to those prescribed by the corporate identity programme. Another important element to be checked is the 'registration' or clarity of the text and pictures. (In all of this, experience will prove to be your greatest teacher, with some hopefully not-so-costly mistakes!). The print-run complete, *Kinley4U* now made its way to the Kinley distributor network. *Kinley4U*, along with other elements of its IMC campaign, went the distance in making the brand the market leader in the bubble-top segment in its target area.

Lights, Camera and Brand-Action!

On 7 July 1896, the traditional media changed forever in India. An advertisement in the *Times of India* invited Mumbai's citizens to witness 'living photographic pictures in life size reproductions by Messrs Lumiere brothers'. On the same day, the Czar of Russia too was introduced to a Lumiere Brothers exhibition of this new technology. This exhibition had toured the cities of the world, introducing awestruck masses to the power of the moving image. In India, Dhundiraj Govind Phalke, a young art printer from a small town near Mumbai, was quick to realize the potential of this new media. Cinema was to become his mission—and obsession. In 1903, he acquired a camera and other essential equipment to produce films based on India's overflowing heritage of mythological stories. He produced the first full-length Indian feature film, Raja Harischandra, in 1912. It was released a year later.

In a career marked by achievements and reverses, Dadasaheb Phalke, as he was later known, became the father of India's film industry. Today, India's highest honour in its film industry is named after Dadasaheb Phalke—the gritty pioneer who gave India's film industry the impetus to become the largest film industry in the world. The *Malayala Manorama Year Book* (1992) notes that India produced 948 films in 1990 to remain the world's number one film-producing country. In the decade that has followed since, the Indian film industry has retained its leadership position. In his book *Broadcasting in India*, P.C. Chatterji observes that India had 12,000 cinemas, of which 4,500 were touring cinemas! In the meantime, the Indian film industry is at the centre of the Corporatization–Digitization–Globalization process, taking on the challenges of the new era. India's new era film production companies today are tightly-run corporates that assiduously cultivate their brands. Some of the best known examples are Amitabh Bachchan's ABCL, Dreamz Unlimited and Aamir Khan Productions.

In a parallel sense, corporate films or videos too form an integral part of this celluloid scenario. Every year, thousands of commercials, infomercials and corporate videos are made to cater to the needs of companies across the country. Largely the preserve of agencies and production houses, corporate films are today a genre in themselves. For corporate communicators, they are recognized as important brand-builders, along with other mediums like radio and television. This section focusses on corporate films and videos, as they represent the most popular medium in the audio-visual media. Likewise, the principles described here can be adapted and applied to the production of radio jingles, television commercials and the like. To start with, here is a professional view on the reasons for potency of corporate videos:

1. Video is capable of conveying large amounts of information to large numbers of people.
2. Video does not require your customers to read; video talks to them and shows them the message you want to deliver.
3. It leads them through a sales presentation as if your sales staff was right there with them. Videos reach out like a hand shake to give a personal touch so your audience becomes familiar with your company, your product, and your people
4. They see real people talking to them instead of typed words and a photo on a web page or print material.
5. It links your services to actual images in their minds.

6. Use it for sales presentations, show it in meetings, conferences, or keep it looping at trade shows.
                          —(www.indievisionfilms.homestead.com)

From Concept to Completion

Corporate films are today known in their three essential avatars:
infomercials, commercials and corporate videos. Typically, in today's
scenario, the production of a 5 to 10 minute corporate film can
take from one month to three months—from its concept to
completion. Larger corporate films can take three to six months.
There are three key stages to their production:

In the pre-production stage, the film's concept and script are
developed. This is a creative process where the corporate communicator acts as a link between the brand inputs of the corporate
and the creative outputs of the film-maker. At this stage, the script,
the schedule and the budget are taken into account. The corporate
needs to be analyzed in terms of its brand, product, services, features
and target audiences. The narrative approach is first decided:
whether to use a presenter, a 'voice-over' or a mix of both. The
script then moves to the 'storyboard' stage. Other details that need
to be looked into at this stage include production budgets, crew
and equipment and shooting schedules.

The production stage comes next. The cameras are now ready
to roll. Here the treatment of the concept and script are all-
important factors. Corporate films have a general flow that
audiences around the world are familiar with. The website
www.indievisionfilms.homestead.com presents this
structure of a corporate film:

Act I, the Opening: Title, graphics, music, host welcome,
general introduction of what this is all about, build interest.

Act II, the Presentation: Profile the product, demonstrate
it, show benefits, sales points, present key company representa-
tive(s) and testimonials.

Act III, the Closing: A review, why they should act, closing
points

End with a personal thank you from the host or senior executive followed by closing graphics, sound, contact information and a credit roll.

—(www.indievisionfilms.homestead.com)

Corporate films were traditionally shot in 16 mm or 35 mm film formats. Today, corporate film-makers take recourse to three digitally driven video technologies. These are the VHS, U-Matic and Betacam systems. Briefly, VHS is the traditional video format. The U-matic with its good output capabilities represents the middle approach. Betacam technology is the high-end choice. It is comparable to the excellent broadcast quality that you see on television. When the shooting is over, the raw footage needs to be viewed for any repetitions and re-shoots.

The post-production stage marks the final step for the corporate film-maker. Here, the entire footage is moved into digital formats on editing workstations. The scenes are then combined sequentially, in tandem with the script. Essential graphics and sound are inserted for a 'rough-cut'. This is then shown to the client for approval. In technical terms, final edits include complete post-production capabilities including analogue and non-linear editing, 3D animation, special effects, digital graphics and voice-over recording. That done, the final edit is completed with colour correction, digital effects and enhanced graphics. This stage includes final narration by a professional voice-over artist, a musical score, sound effects and a final mix of all these elements. After the production is completed, appropriate compression formats like AVMPEG, QuickTime and Real Player are chosen for its viewing. VHS cassettes are an established format for corporate films. They have however been replaced by more recent formats such as CDs and DVD ROMS.

I-Potential Ahead

As the first quarter of 2003 unfolded, the Council of Leather Exports (CLE), the apex body of the Indian leather export fraternity, took its message of 'I-Potential' to its global audience of buyers and

Box 6.2
Corporate Films—Compelling Mediums for Companies

Randor Guy is a Chennai-based writer and film-maker, whose career spans locations as diverse as Hollywood, Colombo and Chennai. A lawyer by training, Randor Guy took his passion for films with forays into the south Indian film industry and a continuing chronicle of work on films in journalism and publishing. Over the years, he has produced corporate films for companies and organizations in India. Here is his take on the art of making corporate films:

If you had the choice of telling a story, which would you prefer—a static print ad, which is easily forgotten among a welter of other ads or a corporate film that grips the attentions of your viewer? This is a choice that confronts every corporate building its brand image today. A corporate film is a vehicle of communication that carries with it, the idea of a company, its history and everything it stands for—as a brand. An assiduous brand building exercise, it aims at creating a niche image for the company, that seeks a footing in the competitive markets of the future. For that reason, corporate films tell compelling stories of their companies. They effectively communicate brand vision, while selling products and services. They also create iconic corporate legends.

Perhaps the earliest example of corporate film making began humbly enough in the 1940s, at the Photography Department of the Detroit-based Ford Motor Company. Here, Michael Omalov the legendary cinematographer, pioneered innovative film making techniques that told compelling stories of the Ford Motor Company and its iconic status. Today those Ford films are a classic in their own right. Back home in India, a remarkable film promoting a public swimming pool called The Royal Bath at Madras. It was an innovative and successful effort for its time!

Like its more glamorous celluloid cousin—the feature film, the corporate film begins with an idea. The idea evolves into countless drafts that become an accepted synopsis. This then evolves into a screenplay, which brings together the elements of film making

(contd.)

Box 6.2 (contd.)

and the film production team. The live shoot, sound recording, animation and graphics follow. This done, the film is brought to digital life on the editing table. Corporate films, I believe, have changed, for the better. No longer do film makers agonize over expensive decisions like 35mm film, black & white or colour options, and colour corrections. The techno-strides of the digital age have ensured that corporate film making has become more interesting and challenging. Your story is only limited by your imagination.

On a sunny day in Los Angeles in 1996, the truth of this realization dawned upon me in a very special way. While at a friend's film laboratory, I happened to chance upon a video conference session where a film director shooting in the Arizona Desert was giving colour correction instructions to his editor in Los Angeles. In a matter of hours, key changes were made, while the director could carry on with the rest of his shoot, thousands of miles away.

Of the corporate films that I have made, there are two that come to mind for their unique approach. The first was a forty minute corporate film for a company called Light Roofings Ltd in the early 1980s. The theme centred around the need for fire resistant roofing material for rural communities. The story revolved around a cynical village community that learns to use fire resistant roofing—the hard way. Here, an entire village burned down, except for one home that, of course, used the roofing material. In yet another film done for the Federation of Indian Export, we worked around a bold theme that has now gathered credence: 'Every Indian has something to export'. In what sounded like a revolutionary idea at that time, we pointed out that everything from yoga to village handicrafts and Indian food had an export value. This extended to the fact that every Indian, wherever he or she was, was in fact a potential exporter. An evocative idea for the liberalizing market in the 1980s. In the final analysis, I believe that a corporate film remains a company's most effective way to tell its story. It is powerful. It is cost effective. And, it tells its compelling story for posterity.

potential buyers. The CLE core message was simple: I-Potential is India's Potential in the global leather market. The tagline to I-Potential read: 'Think Leather, Think India'. This core message was carried in the apex organization's communications—in its glitzy corporate brochure, its website and in its sixteen-minute corporate film titled 'I-Potential'. Created by Ogilvy PR Worldwide at its offices in Chennai, the I-Potential case study will give you an idea of how corporate films are made.

I-Potential was about projecting the new face of the Indian leather industry. In its pre-production stage, it was decided that I-Potential would take a different approach from the run-of-the-mill corporate films. It was to represent a quantum leap from anything the CLE had initiated in the past years. According to Arup Kavan of Ogilvy PR, I-Potential needed to present the three arms of the Indian leather industry—leather footwear, leather garments and leather goods and accessories—in the light of its growing acceptance from global buyers. The 'hook' was the careful use of testimonials from buyers. No narrations. No persuasive voice-overs. Just the on-camera testimonials of global buyers, who made their way to India, year after year. The second highlight was the Indian leather industry's corporate citizenship initiative—on the fronts of workforce welfare and pollution control.

The film opens to a montage of text ('supers') and graphics capturing diverse facets of India's leather industry. The soundtrack incorporates techno-music that serves the purpose of tuning into the viewer experience. In between these shots were clips of the various facets of the leather industry—tanneries at work, assembly line production, leather fashion shows. After 2 minutes and 50 seconds, this visual sequence fades to spotlight an American buyer who states that when it comes to leather products, 'India is on par with any other nation in the world'—an interesting 'hook' for an essentially western audience. The film then launches into an animation sequence that presents a tri-coloured I-Potential namestyle with the tagline: 'Think Leather, Think India'.

In its middle section, I-Potential opens to the footwear component of the Indian leather industry. It records the observations

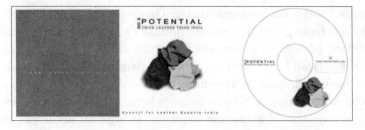

Fig. 6.3: The Unfolding of I-Potential

of American, European and South East Asian buyers, who have bought leather over the last 25 years. Each testimonial mirrors the impression that Indian leather is undergoing a process of gradual, continuous improvement. This section also juxtaposes the new era leather industry against its more traditional predecessor. Shots of glistening leather shoes are juxtaposed with clips of 'Kolhapuri' slippers being manufactured.

Six minutes into the presentation, it is time for the leather garments industry. The 'supers' here indicate that suede leather, used in leather fashion wear, is India's speciality. Shots of design studios creating leather fashion concepts are contrasted with clips of factories specializing in leather garment manufacture. This segment winds up by featuring the top fashion brands that use Indian leather: Pierre Cardin, Liz Clairborne, Tommy Hilfiger and Versace.

Ten minutes into I-Potential and you are introduced to the world of leather goods and accessories. Here, the viewer is introduced to a diverse range of leather goods being retailed. (Everything from hats, bags, lifestyle products—even saddlery for horses!). Emphatic buyer-testimonials follow. The section concludes with the presentation of a collage of global brands that use Indian leather for their products: Harrods, Next, Gens and Yves St. Laurent.

In closing, I-Potential calls the viewer's attention to the Indian leather industry's role as 'a responsible industry'. It begins with the candid admission that the industry reacted to the environmental pollution issue in the early 1990s. An international environmental expert then notes that its 'speed of implementation' in pollution control norms has been remarkable. The corporate citizenship role is then highlighted through the industry's emphasis on worker welfare, healthcare, green belts and occupational safety practices. An American buyer then states that he patronizes Indian leather for his brand, only because he is convinced of its effort to be a responsible industry. Sixteen minutes later, I-Potential concludes to its tri-coloured animation sequence. It urges its audiences to 'recognize opportunity' and to 'seize opportunity' in I-Potential— India's potential in leather. The concluding shot of I-Potential features the CLE URL: **www.leatherindia.org**.

The New Order

When T.S Elliot spoke of 'arriving where we started' and 'knowing the place for the first time', he unknowingly captured the thoughts of those who stand at the frontiers of traditional media, contemplating wondrously its expanding frontiers. Their world has changed forever. The definitive conclusion to this chapter finds itself reflected in the words of Andre Jute in his book, *Grids: The Structure of Graphic Design*: 'The key to efficient communication in print and on screen is logical organization.... The result is comprehension and, where required, persuasion.' (Jute, 1996, p. 122)

Traditional and new media are not competitors. Rather, they are strategic partners that offer a world of brand building opportunity. *Kinley4U* and I-Potential, two diverse initiatives for corporate awareness, reflect that effort. Notably, both initiatives in traditional technology formats relied on digital technology to add impact to their core messages. The traditional media, as always, will continue to change and evolve, charting new territory in the communication of brand realities. They will focus on communicating core messages in a compelling manner to 'distant, individually-unknown, mass audiences'. (Jute, A., 1996, p. 122). But, as we travel from the domain of the traditional media to the realm of the new media, one more thought-provoking encounter awaits us, in the words of a legendary American author who looked out of his beautiful home by the picturesque Mississippi River, in the late 19th century, to scan the vistas of the world's cultural legacies. In an inspired moment, Mark Twain wrote: 'India is the cradle of the human race, the birthplace of human speech, the mother of history, the grandmother of legend, and the great grandmother of tradition. Our most valuable and most instructive materials in the history of man are treasured up in India.' Truer words were never spoken. India has its 'traditional media' to thank for playing catalyst to that immeasurable legacy. Thanks to it, India celebrates her diversity in its mediascape.

Signposts

The three cornerstones of corporate communication practice are: accuracy of facts, brevity of content and clarity of communication. Every brand communication needs to build itself around these cornerstones.

Traditional media is the broad reference to existing and established media technologies in the print and audio-visual realms that play catalyst to the networked era that we live in.

Print media technologies refer to the popular print processes in today's corporate environment. They include screen, offset and digital printing. *Kinley4U* is a typical example of the print media.

Audio-visual technologies refer to the established fields of radio, television and film in which media initiatives—jingles, commercials and corporate films—are used by corporates to build their brand identities.

Media-Initiative

Both of the following are concept-to-completion jobs that are to serve as brand vehicles. The first is to create a compelling corporate or organizational newsletter. Begin by picking a business or organization that you (and your team) know best. Determine the amount of information that you possess and the size of the newsletter. Now, create a single sheet (with at least four articles complete with images) or edit a four-page newsletter—along the lines of *Kinley 4U*. Typically, you could look at an editorial, an opening feature, a guest column, a trivia section. In its essential form, corporate newsletter templates are available on software packages like Microsoft Office, Star Office and AppleWorks. Once it is created, proofcheck it, and print a specified number of copies at your nearest DTP (Desktop Publishing) centre. Consider expanding its communication potential by uploading the newsletter on the easiest available site in the popular 'pdf' format, now popularized by Adobe Acrobat.

The second option is to make a film. This one is admittedly a more ambitious project, that involves the use or hire of cameras, studio time and other resources. In its basic form, a corporate film represents a company/organizations' brand image, while communicating its core messages. Budget for about three weeks of conceptualization, creation and completion. Begin with a compelling script, work in a voice-over or text-driven guide. Complement these with well-chosen graphics or visuals. Keep a tight grip on the shooting and production schedules—cost included. And, then spend the better part of your time, editing it at your nearest digital studio. While you are at this, consider uploading an edited version of the film on a website in a video streaming format. This would be an apt digital touch to expanding the communication reach of your corporate film.

If you believe in testing your limits as a corporate communicator, here's the litmus test. Create your newsletter, print it, upload it on a website. Follow this by creating a corporate film and then complete it in a digital format. Now present these to your group, explaining your corporate/organization's brand vision and your reasons for communicating it in the way that you did. Explain your brand mission, its core message, your strategy. Now, translate them into the content and design aspect of your newsletter and the content and visual aspect of your film. And yes, we would be interested in hearing from you!

Sources

Publications

Chatterji, P.C. (1991). *Broadcasting in India*, Second Edition. Sage Publications, New Delhi.

Craig, James. (1974). *Production for the Graphic Designer*. Watson-Guptill Publications, New York.

Gunaratne, S.A.(Ed.). (2000). *Handbook of the Media in Asia*. Sage Publications, New Delhi.

Itule, B.D. and Anderson, D.A. (1994). *News Writing and Reporting for Today's Media*. McGraw-Hill, New York.

Jute, Andre. (1996). *Grids: The Structure of Graphic Design*. RotoVision SA, Switzerland.

Kitchen, Philip J. and Schultz, Don E. (2001). *Raising the Corporate Umbrella: Corporate Communications in the 21st Century*. Palgrave, New York.

Young, A. (1987). *The Manager's Handbook: The Practical Guide to Successful Management*. Penguin Books Ltd., London.

Periodicals

Frozen Thoughts (November 2002). 'From the Mind of Bill Gates', Vol. 2, Issue 5, Chennai.

Further Reading

Fernandez, J. (1995). South Asian Diaspora Films: A U.K. Case Study (Postgraduate Dissertation), University of Wales, Cardiff.

Mathew, K.M. (Ed.) (2002). *Manorama Year Book 2002*. The Malayala Manorama Company Limited, Kottayam.

———— **(Ed.)** (2001). *Manorama Year Book 2001*. The Malayala Manorama Company Limited, Kottayam.

———— **(Ed.)** (1998). *Manorama Year Book 1998*. The Malayala Manorama Company Limited, Kottayam.

———— **(Ed.)** (1992). *Manorama Year Book 1992*. The Malayala Manorama Company Limited, Kottayam.

Websites

www.smartechindia.com
www.intelliscapefilms.com
www.indievisionfilms.homestead.com

Films

I-Potential (2003), Council for Leather Exports-CLE, Chennai

Interviews

Arup Kavan
Managing Partner
Ogilvy PR Worldwide, South India

CT Ramasamy
Chief Designer
Studio Srishti, Chennai

S. Muthiah
Madras Editorial Services, Chennai

Randor Guy
Writer & Film Maker, Chennai

7 The New Media: Across the Digital Divide

Computers are useless. They can only give you answers.

—Pablo Picasso

IN the wintry month of February 1946, a slumbering monster stirred to life in the quiet American city of Philadelphia. It was 100 feet long, 10 feet high and 3 feet wide, and weighed about 30 tonnes. The citizens of this mid western capital groaned in dismay, for the lights in their homes dimmed and flickered from time-to-time, acknowledging the monster's presence. Its home was a huge room at the Moore School of Engineering at the University of Pennsylvania in Philadelphia. Fortunately, for Philadelphia's gentle citizens, the monster was a benevolent one. It was at its digital best, undertaking near impossible number-crunching tasks. In fact, it was a useful monster. For its master, the US Department of Defense, it was particularly good at calculating the flight path of artillery shells used in military exercises!

They called it ENIAC—the world's first mainframe computer—Electronic Numerical Integrator and Calculator. It contained 18,000 vacuum tubes, 70,000 resistors and 6,000 switches. And, when it was turned on, it used so much power supply, that the lights of Philadelphia dimmed. (Today, the world of computers has come a long, long way from those cold, inconvenient days of giant mainframe computers in Philadelphia.) A decade later, it was India's turn. In 1955, the Indian Statistical Institute (ISI) acquired the country's first computer. Its initial use was in the area of analyzing population statistics and the like. For the next decade and a half, the computer remained the sole preserve of large corporations and mega-businesses.

From the mainframe computers of the mid 1940s to the PC revolution of the mid 1980s, the digital revolution has networked and linked the world like never before. In tandem, telecommunication has progressed from analogue to digital signal communications, leading to its convergence with computers. The result was the Internet. The e-journey of the Internet from its early days as the US defence-related ARPANET (Advanced Research Project Network), and the Telnet has been a long and eventful one. In India, the Internet revolution took seed in the late 1980s, when the ERNET (Educational and Research Network) initiative, with funding support from Department of Electronics (DoE), Government of India and the United Nations Development Programme (UNDP) was launched. The project involved five premier institutions—National Centre for Software Technology (NCST), Bombay; Indian Institute of Science (IISC), Bangalore, the five IITs and the DoE. The second landmark step was the setting up of the National Informatics Centre (NIC). Over the 1990s, NIC initiated a national network that connects most district headquarters in India.

For most of us, the Internet made its official arrival in our lives on 15 August 1995, when VSNL launched its gateway services. Despite an uncertain start, bogged down by low line speeds, the Internet changed our lives in many ways. By 1999, private ISPs (Internet Service Providers) were already on the scene with competitive alternatives. The National Association of Software and Services Companies (NASSCOM) estimates in 2003 indicated that there are about 500,000 Internet connections in India, with about two million users. The convergence of computers and communications for about a decade now is taking India across the digital divide—into the ceaseless buzz of the Information Age. Indeed, there are those like Prof. Bala V. Balachandran of the Kellogg School of Management, North Western University, Chicago, who stress that India must claim its share of the digital revolution—i.e. one half of it. And, this is because, India invented one half of the binary code that drives it!

The new media has very simply, re-invented the way we do business. Not to mention, revolutionize the way in which corporates communicate. By introducing the Internet, the new media became the first gateway of globalization. Through multimedia technologies, it has changed the way corporates around the world conduct business, while managing their images. In this chapter, we look at the new or digital media in terms of its importance to the 21st century Corporate and its communications processes. This chapter begins by addressing the pivotal role that the Internet plays in setting, maintaining and nurturing the corporate image of a company. In doing so, it looks at the role of the corporate communicator in the website creation process. With good reason, this chapter places its focus on the relevance of a website on the Internet as a tool of corporate image building. Web technology represents only one facet of the digital media. Its predominant discussion is due to the fact that it is the key tool of an online corporate communications strategy. This is followed by a broad overview of multimedia technologies and their potential contributions to today's corporate.

Taking a first digital step, the website **www.online-pr.com** offers us an insight on why the digital media is integral to the 21st century Corporate. 'Ideally, corporate communications media are integrated...whether or not online is integrated with other company communications media.'

Ideally, corporate communications media are integrated. In practice, few are. Integration usually occurs around a specific task such as product promotion or announcement of a new mission. Organizations communicate in so many directions at once both internally and externally, they are inherently chaotic. Cost-effective corporate communication requires a structured and disciplined approach to communication that few companies have time or resources to undertake...On-line public relations can be used as a supplementary or principal communications medium to reach targeted audiences.

It is important in both cases, however, to show that using online directly supports a company's survival and success whether or not online is integrated with other company communications media. It is time now to hit the 'Enter' button in the real-time of the new media.

The Digital Planet

It is the single most important agent of change on the planet today. Since its introduction in 1993, it has changed the way we think, work and go about the business of life. The Internet refers to the vast network of linked computers that transfer information and data across the globe. With digital multi-media capabilities, it serves as the largest information resource on the planet. For the networked planet, the Internet brought home the following advantages:

• Cost-effective
The Internet is today the most cost-effective way of communicating with the world. It only involves a one-time cost of installing a computer and setting up Internet lines. Apart from this, accessing information or conducting business through the net is relatively inexpensive. Economy is the Internet's greatest advantage.

• User-friendly
The Internet is an extremely user-friendly medium. With its focus on ease of navigation and user-friendliness, the PC has evolved to become a tool that can be used by virtually anybody. Further, PC evolutions like the Simputer will ensure that the benefits of the digital revolution will positively impact the lives of India's rural masses for time to come.

• Widest Reach
No other technology accesses the world like the Internet does. In terms of reach and resources, the Internet is an overnight technological miracle. A global survey conducted in mid 1998 concluded that there were at least 82 million Internet users worldwide. By 2002, the Internet community was a growing 200 million users using over 20 million computers. As you read this, many more people across the world's 6.1 billion population have connected with the Internet.

• Quick response time
Quite literally, the response time on the Internet is barely a few seconds. Information can be passed on and received from across

the world in an amazingly short span of time. This adds to the first point of being highly cost-effective and a great time saver.

• Largest information resource in the world
Think of the largest library in the world. Well, it is the US Library of Congress at Washington D.C. It is filled with every imaginable category of books and publications. Its bookshelves are known to stretch over an incredible 50 miles. The sheer magnitude and size of this library made it the largest resource for information in the world. That was until the Internet came along. In terms of pure information and data, the Internet is today over 40,000 times bigger than the US library of Congress!

The E-Commerce Factor

In their book, *India's Communication Revolution: From Bullock Carts to Cyber Marts*, authors Arvind Singhal and Everett M. Rogers point out that the Internet is the highway of the global economy. In the light of the business opportunity it has spawned, they point out: 'E-marketing is the use of the Internet to market one's products or services; e-commerce is commercial transactions between two parties on the Internet'. (Singhal, A. and Rogers, E. M., 2001, p. 239) E-Commerce is a logical culmination of the Internet's exponential growth. It is the application of the Internet in conducting commerce of any kind. It includes the online buying and selling of goods, services or information, either between individuals, or between corporations.

E-Commerce has been categorized into three types—Business-to-Business (B2B), Business-to-Consumer (B2C) and Consumer-to-Consumer (C2C). The most visible of these is the B2C segment, with such high fliers as Amazon.com (and several others in India as well), which aim at direct contact with individual customers thereby blurring the conventional dividing line between wholesaling and retailing. It is, however, the B2B segment that will be much larger in size and more stable over a longer period. Here, the Internet is used by a company to deal with its clients and suppliers. Specialized areas in B2B include Customer Relations

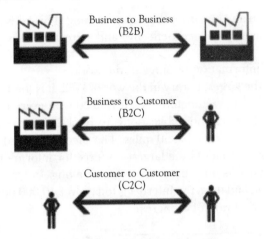

Fig. 7.1: E-Commerce in its three Avatars

Management (CRM) and Supply Chain Management (SCM). These services often rest on a network that connects a company and their immediate clients and suppliers (called an extranet).

The third C2C is a rather small segment, and involves direct client-to-client interaction (e.g. auction sites such as E-bay) or 'gripe-sites' where the users of products or services share their experience and air their grievances. The Internet is a wondrous new world. A strange place, where you can set up a home page—practically free of cost. Or, invest in a state-of-the-art website that incorporates the latest programming and multimedia technologies, in the process, costing you millions of dollars. Of course, for your organization or industry, the answer will lie somewhere in between these two extremes. The choice is yours: a couple of home pages with your Internet address as a 'sub domain' or your own domain where your company's name appears in this format: www.your-company.com or www.your-organization.org.

Bring WWW to Life

A web presence is an important brand decision. Your organization steps onto the Internet with the understanding that it is now open to the global business opportunities of the Information Age. This

Box 7.1
Branding Online—An Offline Function

The most persuasive argument for a website is that it sells. Or, more specifically, content sells. A content development team that has worked on compelling corporate websites, Jonathan and Deepika Davidar are media professionals who provide consulting and solutions for the digital and print media. Their work has a directness giving their clients a unique identity through research, analysis and creativity. They can be contacted at davidar@vsnl.com. Here is their view of the digital media:

A web presence is a statement in itself. It tells the world that you are open to new ideas, technologies, and networking. A website is not an accessory but should be an integral part of your communication strategy. The web can sustain your image, create new business opportunities and give your company tremendous reach. Further, you can publish news about product launches, seminars, training programmes, recruitment drives, competitions, sales, and much more. The fluid, dynamic nature of the web enables you to present information with ease and add/edit/delete any content without much effort.

Remember the power of the web lies in its ability to mirror and keep up with your progress. Unlike traditional media, you can constantly update the web and keep the information current. Also, you can create sections that will appeal to those who are in your line of business. White papers, research articles, tips, solutions, and other such information will attract the right people and, importantly, keep them coming back for more. A corporate brochure, on the other hand, is often a one-time investment that highlights who you are and what you do. It is time-sensitive and has to be recreated with current information on a regular basis.

Branding online has an 'offline' function—to communicate the core values of a brand and reinforce its market growth. In our experience, it has called for a whole new skill set and whole new mindset to creating, nurturing and maintaining a brand. For a start, it brings the much quoted 24/7/365 mode of existence into mind. The key here of course, is to keep the website alive by a well thought out communications initiative that complements the brand strategy.

brings the impetus to produce goods and services with an accent on global quality. If the website represents a particular sector, then it also doubles up as a virtual voice for the sector itself. Your organization steps into this opportunity-filled world, the minute it sets up a website. The first step is to ensure that you have a compelling, comprehensive website whose capabilities are optimal and, more importantly, realistic. Ensure that your website comes powered by the ABC of an online corporate communications strategy: Accuracy of facts, Brevity of content and Clarity of thought. Setting up a website involves three dynamic stages, that were brought to life in a workshop (aptly titled The Webshop!) conducted for the MOP Vaishnav College, Chennai. In the order of time, they are:

> Plan your Website (The Pre-production Stage)
> Create your Website (The Production Stage)
> Host your Website (The Post-production Stage)

Plan your Website—The Pre-production Stage

In planning a website, or conceptualizing it, you need to begin by understanding why it needs to exist. And, thrive. To work out your website strategy, ask yourself these questions:

• What is the purpose of your website?

What is the objective of the information presented in the website? If you are setting up a website to complement your business, then it is necessary to keep this objective in mind and seek to expand its scope. This is the same for organizations and networks. The first step is to clearly set down your website's purpose and its online objectives.

• Who is its target audience?

Having identified the objective of the website, it is necessary to develop it in a manner that would reach out to its target audience. A website for an organization that publishes software guides has a very specific target audience, whereas a weekly magazine's website would have a totally different audience. Let us presume again that the website is being developed for a business. Then the website will have to target the customer base of the business. For instance, a beach resort's website would have the following audiences in mind: tourists, potential guests, corporates, travel agencies and organizations, as well as the casual online visitor. In order to effectively target this segment, the website must offer comprehensive information, exclusive pictures of the resort as well as an online room reservation option.

• How will the website achieve your objective?

This is the clinching factor when it comes to a corporate website. By offering product or service information with online business options, the website does what the office, shop or smartest corporate team can only hope to do, operate round-the-clock to promote your business or organization.

A Website Primer

The website's name is where it all begins. The first step is to check for the ideal domain name and register it. Remember to keep your online strategy in mind, when you choose and register your name. For instance, there are the standard domains (.com, .org, .net.) for corporates, non-profit organizations and Internet-related organizations. Each of these extensions serves a different purpose. The name of your site may be the first thing the browser gets to know about your organization. So select a unique name that reflects at least to some extent what the site and hence, your organization is all about. If you were searching for a certain piece of information on the net, and your search engine lists the sites that contain that information, you make a choice on which site to go to, by assessing the name of the site. Similarly, your site too should have a name that would catch the attention of a browser and encourage him/ her to visit it.

The process involves choosing a name, verifying its availability and booking it through any one of the authorized web-companies linked with Internic—the Internet parent organization. In a tandem move, your webspace is booked on a web server. Based on your requirements, you should choose a server in consultation with your web server company. This choice is based on the programming softwares like Windows-friendly ASP (Active Server Pages), Linux-specific Perl 5.0 and the CGI scripting facility. The space registration and server space comes for a certain fixed fee per annum. This space is booked for a certain period, usually a year, at the end of which you will receive a mail informing you that your domain and registration need to be renewed. At this point, you will contact your service provider who will renew it for you with a local payment. The current set-up fees in India ranges between Rs 1500/- to Rs 2,500/- depending on the server you choose. Your web server furnishes you with details of the server, its FTP (File Transfer Protocol) details, the Operating System, its programming languages, and other relevant details of your web booking.

Create your Website—The Production Stage

It all begins with a site map. A site map is the blueprint of the website. It is a flowchart that shows how your website should look. The site map charts the flow of information in the website and identifies the relevant content, design and programming elements to be incorporated at each stage.

Here the creative team (the writer, designer and programmer) understand the requirements of the client, translate it into web-terms, and express it in the form of a dynamic and vibrant website that lives its online mission. In all of this, you will realize that there are three cornerstones for the development of a compelling website:

Content: The term 'content' refers to all the online data and information contained on a website. It is the soul of your website. And, it is always driven by the accuracy of facts, brevity of content and clarity of thought. With these in place, a visitor would delight in the information coupled with the ease of navigability that it offers. Here are the signposts of web content:

- Always begin with a name, a site map and an overall approach: This is the important first step for any creative web team. Deciding on a name, a site map charting the flow of information for the website and the overall brand approach sets the pace for the work. Whether it is an awesome Flash animation introduction or a traditional homepage, it needs to be compelling and quick.

- Work around the ABCs of online corporate communications: Always be accurate. Remember, the content of your website can be verified by your visitors with any other site on the Internet. If it sounds incredible, it would take him only a few more seconds to countercheck the facts and statistics stated in your content. In terms of content structure, use the time-honoured pyramid format of writing. Briefly, this format states the main piece of information in the first paragraph, and presents relevant information in the paragraphs that follow.

Brevity rules on the web. Always remember that the visitor to your site is reading content off a screen. His attention span is less, because of the glare reflected off the screen. Keep the content concise and its style, crisp. Short, direct sentences (like this one!), which do not exceed 17 words, are the accepted web standard. Vary the lengths of your sentences for easy readability. Keep the sizes of your paragraphs different. And, do not exceed the word count of 506 words per web page.

Whether it is content, design or programming, clarity of thought in each of these areas creates a compelling and successful website. Decide in advance on the mode of presentation of the corporate. The ways in which you will present its image, while complementing it with the choice of graphics and layout. The golden rule here is: Build around the brand.

Softwares to look out for: Microsoft Word, StarOffice 5.1 and AppleWorks

Designing your Website: If content is the soul of a website, then its design is undoubtedly its image—it's outer complementing appeal. Web designers—a select tribe in themselves—weave online magic with graphics, layouts and colours, to create entire online worlds. Readability should be the first priority. Design techniques cannot be allowed to tamper with the Readability. Choose your fonts with care. Here again, Prefer Sans Serif Fonts to Serif Fonts. The other technical guidelines in terms of design, are listed here:

- Stand up for design value. Keep the layout of your website light and use style sheets.
- Understand the web standard for colours—The RGB (Red Green Blue) standard and the 216-colour palette are standards that you will need to work within.
- Design your website with the knowledge that different user resolutions exist. And, ensure that your website is built to common user resolutions (640 × 480 pixels, 800 × 600 pixels, 1024 × 768 pixels).
- Be aware of browser wars. Design your website, being acutely aware of the limits of the most popular browsers, namely, Explorer, Navigator and Opera.
- Quick downloads need quick images. The important image formats are GIF and JPEG. Choose graphic images and design elements that complement the brand and also add to the quality of the website. The right combination of graphics and web layout complete a site.

Softwares to look out for: Microsoft FrontPage, Adobe Photoshop, Macromedia DreamWeaver, Flash, GIF Animator

Programming: The third, lesser-sung aspect of website creation is programming. Beginning with source code HTML (Hypertext Markup Language), that presents a website to the networked world, to higher applications like databases, form registrations, online applications, programming drives the practical side of a corporate website. The success of a website often depends on the efficacy of its programming. Here too, there needs to be an understanding behind the objective of the site, and how it can be accomplished through its programming. The other programming initiatives here may include adding *appropriate* 'meta tags' to your websites HTML code to ensure that important search engines (read Google) register your site.

Programmes to look out for: HTML, DHTML, Java Script

Hosting a Website—The Post Production Stage

The creative process is concluded by the hosting of the website. Once a concept (content+design+programming) is approved, the website comes into its own. The creative process is concluded by the hosting of the website. The approved set of completed Internet files is placed in a folder, and then uploaded onto the server, which is now linked with the domain name. This process is carried placing the web files on the server, using a special uploading web software. Your website is now an online reality.

The package offered by the creative team has site maintenance contract valid for a mutually agreed period of time. This might include, updating your site, editing the existing content, adding or removing pages or graphics, etc. It may even involve redesign of the site, its aesthetics or flow, if the contract is so agreed upon mutually. Once the expiry of the contract, you might be provided the option of an Annual Maintenance Contract (AMC) at the cost of a standardized fee per term.

Softwares to look out for: Cute FTP and WS FTP

Fig. 7.2: A Sampling of Websites from the Studio Srishti Gallery

Other Digital Realms

Beyond the domain of the Internet lie the other less charted realms of the new media. While it is true that multimedia, that awesome mix of animation, audio, video and sound, added to our online experiences, it also comes in handy on platforms beyond the Internet. Used in PC-generated environments, they become tools

Box 7.2
A Website—Digital Extension of the Brand

CT Ramasamy heads Studio Srishti—a corporate design studio. After his graduation from IIT, Delhi, CT worked as a web designer at National Informatics Centre, New Delhi. In 1998, he co-founded Studio Srishti, a graphic design studio that has worked for the who's who of corporate India. Its radical portfolio can be accessed at www.studiosrishti.com. Here is CT's take on the digital media:

The new era, I believe, is a truly special time for the global corporate world. Its nature has been radically altered by the emergence of the New or Digital Media. By the New Media, diverse mediums of communication—animation, graphics, sound, text, even tactile feeling—brought together on a technology-driven, globally networked communications platform. To my mind, the web and multimedia seamlessly blend to form the New Media, as we know it today.

Central to this sweeping change was the advent of the Internet in 1993—a global event that opened our lives to the wondrous possibilities of the World Wide Web. Through it, we have learned of the power of a website. Who could have imagined that a clutch of programmes and 'html' files, driven by acumen and imagination could create corporate history? But as the recent celebrated histories of Amazon, Google or Yahoo remind us, that unknown, intangible tech-driven presence that we know as a website has impacted our lives. And, changed the world, as we know it.

Having said that, a website to me, is a digital extension of the Brand. Done well, it is that distinct unique voice, standing apart, in a global marketplace that is cluttered by cacophonous marketing messages. All at once, it is an archive, a barometer and a chronicle of the corporate and the market in which it operates. Websites—and the web presences they conjure up—do revolve around brands and their core vision. Look at the way IBM, an established juggernaut of the computer industry builds its brand on the Internet. Now, contrast it with the irreverent way in which MTV builds its loyalty with its teen audiences, also using the web. Both the IBM and MTV web experiences are powerful brand-builders for their specific global audiences. One medium. Two approaches.

(contd.)

Box 7.2 (contd.)

A website is the single, most cost-effective way to build a brand presence today. A great unifier, the web is perhaps the only place where a globally known pharmaceutical giant is placed on the same platform as an unknown manufacturer of native medicine. There is a democracy out there at work, as we speak. As a Graphic Designer, beginning my career in the 1990s, I watched the emergence of a new generation of media professionals—animators, content writers, graphic designers and software programmers—all of whom are digitally redefining the way we think and feel about brands. At Studio Srishti, where I work, we have clients coming in for what we call 'integrated media solutions'. Total media packages built around the convergence of communication technologies to build the brands of the new era. Thus, a typical corporate client would like to start from the essentials like the logo, brochure to CD ROM presentations to websites to a corporate film. In getting all his media requirements met under one roof, the client ensures that the brand integrity of his company is intrinsically embedded, and stands distinct. And, that I believe, is the way of the future.

of success in building a corporate's image. In software terms, you could look at anything from the trusty PowerPoint presentation, to more flashy presentations driven by Flash, 3D Max, Macromedia Director and a host of other digital software. Today's corporates enhance their images through communication tools of the future such as CD-ROMs, virtual whiteboards, video conferencing, satellite telephone calls and other emerging tools of connectivity. In the midst of this digital dazzle, it always helps to remember what Marshall McLuhan, who foresaw today's 'Global Village' had to say: 'The Medium is the Message'. And, in the light of the digital revolution, that insight can be translated into the following ways:

The Audience

The new media—the Internet and its digital cousins—have ushered in the era of global audiences for corporates. A website—any website—has a potential audience of over 200 million people. It is the Shangri-La of the marketer, who is making his way to market success. In terms of the power to create, maintain and nurture an image, the new media offers a radically new way for any corporate to chart its future. Again, in the established traditions of online corporate communications, the focus is on audience, publics and targets communities—not just customers or consumers. Corporate communications helps corporates to move confidently into competitive market environments, while persuasively addressing the diverse audiences that surround it.

The Technology

For all its potential and efficacy, the Internet, in its present form is about a decade old. It has rapidly become apparent that the key to the success of an online corporate communications strategy is the use of appropriate technologies. Whether it is the Flash animation on your corporate presentation, or the software for your online customer registration, the use of technologies needs to be based on a sound theoretical approach, tempered by practical experience. An example that comes to mind, is the reluctance of web designers to use heavy Flash animations on websites intended for audiences in India. Their reason was simple enough. With abysmally low line speeds, the download time for the website would increase, in all probability putting potential visitors off for good. It is a different issue today, a good half decade later, that websites in India feature some of the snazziest Flash animations you will ever come across!

Fig. 7.3: A Corporate Flash Animation at Work

The Information Spread

When Marshall McLuhan, the Canadian media prophet peered into the crystal ball of his vision for the future, he foresaw the age of the 'global village'—an era in which a world networked by communications and technologies, would affect sweeping change in every walk of life. In the midst of that vision, he saw the implications for a networked world that lived on an intricate system of communications. As the 21st century unfolds, in the new media, the medium is indeed, the message. Communication gurus always remind us of the golden rule, when it comes to reaching out to an audience, especially a customer-oriented market. It reads: 'It is not what you send, it is what they receive' that really matters. In other words, the audience's perception of your communication is all that will ever matter.

Here is a classic example. If the CEO of your company wishes to inform your loyal base of customers and the general public about a sudden turn of events, let us say a flash strike. To strike an empathy with your audience, it makes perfect sense to address them with a 'Dear Friend,' approach, as opposed to the more stodgy 'Dear Customer', approach. This would ensure at least some empathy and may be a willing ear, where scepticism prevails. Now, let us apply that understanding to the digital media. The success of a digital media initiative does depend on the way it is spread or its mode of dissemination. Understanding how the information will reach the intended audience will help you to plan for its success. It counts to consider whether your initiative will reach the audience online (as in on the Internet) or manually, through a real-time presentation made at a chosen venue. The measure of success is always ensuring that the message you sent is the message that they received.

From Zero to One

Imagine, for a moment, that you have just opened your first digital office. A vibrant operating organization that thrives on the

24/7/365 principle: 24 hours a day, 365 days a year. Its mission: to inform the entire planet about your organization, and the latter's vision and goals. Having done that, it creates and maintains your corporate identity, executes business transactions, networks with your audiences, answers your mails, deals with queries, handles your calls, connects with your global partners and most importantly, networks with your audiences. It takes words and concepts like real-time, digital connectivity, and virtual reality and makes them a living, vibrant way to go about your business.

That is the office of the very near future in which the new media plays a pivotal role. The core reality of today's business organizations. In this scenario, today's corporate has already begun to look at corporate communications as the most strategy with which it can surge into the future. It is fitting at this point to dip into an insight of a man who thinks differently—Steve Jobs of Apple Computer. In the first years of the 21st century, Steve Jobs sees the world embarking on the third era of personal computing. To explain further, the first era was the one in which people used their very basic computers for account, word processing, spreadsheets and creating desktop graphics. The second phase, from 1993 to the present, was all about the Internet. Networking all those computers to helps us communicate. Now, that we're all networked and productive, we're ready for the next great era: people using computers to orchestrate all the new digital gear that has steadily crept into their lives. In Job's own words: 'The next great era is for the personal computer to be the digital hub of all these devices.'

The rise of technology is a never-ending process of evolution. And, emerging technology leaves nothing impossible—virtually nothing, that is. We are approaching such an era in the history of communication where you are never too far from the rest of the world. We are in every sense, denizens of the e-Village called Planet Earth. As the digital new media charts its next course in our lives, it is worth thinking about the long, long journey that the computer has made from 30 tonne giant ENIAC at the Moore School in Pennsylvania, to that beige personal computer on your desktop, right down to that brand new palmtop that is securely tucked away in your pocket.

Signposts

E-Commerce

E-Commerce is the application of the Internet in the area of the buying and selling of goods and services. In Internet terms, we remember them in three categories:

B2B—Business to Business
B2C—Business to Consumer
C2C—Consumer to Consumer

World Wide Web

The World Wide Web is the planet's largest shared resource for information and data.

E-mail

The most popular Internet service is e-mail. Everyday, your e-mail forms part of the six billion e-mails that zip across the globe to their destinations.

Search Engine

The search engine locates any given topic or information on the web. The world's best search engine—www.google.com—searches over one billion web pages to seek out your request.

Web Page

This is the basic unit on the World Wide Web. In it, you find the essentials of the Internet.

Website

A website is an online resource of information that is collected, researched and crafted for the web.

Portal

A 'Portal' is a website that offers extensive information on a topic—and its allied areas. It is a one-stop-shop for curious Internet users. Example: www.msn.com. Similarly, a 'vortal' is a portal website that spotlights specialized information on any single topic. Example: www.automeet.com.

URL

The 'Universal Resource Locator' is the Internet address of any website. The most common domains are '.com', '.org', 'net'. Also in existence are other web-specific URLs.

Digital-Initiative

Having crossed the Digital Divide, the time has come to convert all that projected theory that you have picked up. And, see how it works in time-tested practice. This chapter introduced you to digital media, in particular the basics of setting up a website. Having been through the basics of setting up of a website, it is time now to plan, create and host a website. As in the real-world, this project is best accomplished by a team carrying out various tasks. If you do not have a designer/programmer, then one can be sourced from the nearest multimedia centre. In our experience, a project of this nature does not take more than a day.

Now, to the topic. The closest client at hand is the department or institution at which you are based. And, while you are at it, here are some pointers for the way. Begin with the site map. Chart the flow and navigability of your site. This site can have at least five main links. Look at information pertaining to your institution, its mission, management, faculty, courses, activities, sports, profile, and accommodation. Take it another step further and create hyperlinks for sections that are related to one another. A smaller less imaginative version of this initiative would be to set up a website for your department. In it, you could look at providing information, outlining its profile, curricula, faculty and call for admission in the next academic year. To ensure an assured e-audience, upload this sub-website on your institute's existing website, with a link from the homepage of the main website.

Sources

Publications

Fernandez, J. and Ramasamy, CT. (2001). *The Webshop* (A Course Primer). MOP Vaishnav College, Chennai.

Singhal, A. and Rogers, E. M. (2001). *India's Communication Revolution: From Bullock Carts to Cyber Marts.* Sage Publications, New Delhi.

Periodicals

Fernandez, Joseph. (June 2000). 'Corporate Communications', *Business Mandate*, Chennai.

———— (April 2002). 'The Flow of Excellence', *The Hindu Business Line—Life*, Chennai.

Ramakrishnan, Anupama. (2nd December 2002). 'Looking Up: BT Gets Set to Roll', *Excel-The New Indian Express*.

Navin, Puja. (2nd December 2002). 'Winning Solutions: Public Relations', *Excel—The New Indian Express*.

Websites

www.apple.com
www.online-pr.com
www.studiosrishti.com

Further Reading

Kitchen, Philip J. and Schultz, Don E. (2001). *Raising the Corporate Umbrella: Corporate Communications in the 21st Century.* Palgrave, New York.

Interviews

Jonathan and Deepika Davidar
Media Professionals, Chennai

CT Ramasamy
Studio Srishti, Chennai

8 Businesses and Non-profit Organizations: Communication is Commitment

May the outward and inward man be at one.

—Socrates

THE legend of Candide reflects the learning of our lifetimes. Authored by the iconic French writer Voltaire in 1759, *Candide*, a masterpiece of irony, tells the story of a good-hearted, naive young man called Candide who grows up at a castle in a beautiful country called Westphalia. Life is beautiful for him, as things go, until one day when he is banished from Westphalia for an indiscretion of youth—falling in love with the daughter of the ruler of the land. Banished from the only life he has known, Candide embarks on a remarkable journey across the event-filled old world. In the process, he benefits from real-time lessons in the ways of the world, courtesy the school of hard knocks. His learnings occur through interactions with a series of colourful characters, ranging from con artists to power-hungry rulers. His experiences lead him through the roller-coaster ride of turbulent events, without a shred of certainty. In turns, he becomes a fugitive, a prisoner-of-war, a war hero, a traveller, a heretic, an explorer, a philosopher, and predictably, a connoisseur of life's quiet moments.

At the end of the story, Candide finds himself on an idyllic farm cultivating a garden of exotic fruits and herbs, somewhere between Europe and Asia. With him, are friends with whom he began his event-filled life. One of them is the ever-optimistic philosopher Pangloss. In a memorable moment, Pangloss tells Candide: 'All events are linked up in this best of all possible worlds; for, if you had been expelled from the noble castle, by hard kicks in your backside for love of Mademoiselle Cunegonde, if you had not been clapped into the Inquisition, if you had not wandered about America on foot, if you had not stuck your sword in the Baron, if you had not lost all your sheep from the land of El Dorado, you would not be eating candied citrons and pistachios here.'

Voltaire peppers the entire narrative of Candide with optimistic insights from Pangloss like this one, that justify the mysterious turns of life. But Candide, tutored by experience, knows that life is more than a theory or philosophical discourse. And, his reply brings Voltaire's masterpiece to its fitting finale. 'That's well said,' replied Candide, 'we must cultivate our garden.' Voltaire, through his memorable epic, spoke to an entire generation caught in a turbulent, political era. And, Candide reminded them that the deepest meaning and purpose of life that they could find, was to build and improve upon, that which was around them. In other words, the world was their 'garden'. And, it was for them to build and improve on it.

In the 20th century, Margaret Meade, its most well-known anthropologist, took up from where Voltaire left off. 'Never doubt the potential of a small group of committed citizens to change the world', she wrote, 'Indeed, it is the only thing that ever has'. That insight is at the soul of every non-profit organization that sets about its mission in the new era. It is also embedded in the corporate citizenship role of the modern corporate, as it looks to the greater good of its society. This chapter looks at the use of communication models for the business and non-profit organization. The study of communications today looks at organizations in terms of their objectives. To many researchers, the distinction is clearly demarcated in the phrases: 'profit organizations' and 'non-profit organizations'. In its context, a business here is taken to mean a smaller profit organization that could range from a sole proprietorship, or a family business to a partnership firm. A non-profit organization, on the other hand, is understood to be a non-commercial, non-government entity that is centred around a particular cause or movement. The end, in other words, is the same. The means differ, radically.

In fact, the business offers the first platform for any corporate communication strategy. It builds itself around its unique brand concept. Depending on its size and reach, a business adopts essential corporate communication practice. This way, it builds on its brand and grows. A business represents the microcosm of corporate communications strategy. As it takes the long journey from company-to-corporation, the scope of the corporate communication strategy increases. As audiences increase and domains grow larger, more tools and techniques of strategic communication are deployed to ensure quantum growth and market presence.

The non-profit organization operates on a different turf. The core of the non-profit organization is its mission around which its 'image' is built. To build on this image, it uses social communication, an entire specialization in itself. To keep our focus, this chapter will address the common approaches and points of reference in the areas of social and corporate communication. When it comes to both avatars of the modern organization, we look at new era strategies that create its image, nurture it and disseminate information about goals and objectives. Whether it is social or corporate communication, one thing remains the same— communication, as the title suggests, is commitment.

The Soul of a Corporate

Consider this opportunity. The finest minds in a particular field come together, to form an inner-circle. And, you are invited too. It is awesome, watching the best minds of the age create the future. In the midst of this, you are working furiously to keep up. You have been chosen as the corporate communicator in their realm of corporate excellence. After a year of business preparation, months of market study and weeks of awesome interaction, you are called in to help create the brand, define its parameters and communicate its essence to outer worlds of internal and external audiences. It's different strokes for different folks, you've been told. In the stakeholder universe, for instance, you need to address employees, investors, customers and vendors. No two communications can ever be the same. Yet, they need to convey the same brand essence.

Consider yourself lucky, if you get to be associated with the inception of a corporate. Whether a business, a company or corporation, you are in the right place at the right time, if you are its corporate communicator. You might do this in any of the following corporate avatars: a corporate communications manager, a brand manager, a public affairs executive, a public relations officer, a publicity officer, a community relations manager, a liaison officer or a lobbyist. In all these roles, you get to create the parameters of a brand reality. And in time, when business strategy creates leadership opportunity, you oversee the creation of a market reality.

From Concept to Communication

In our experience, we have found that the corporate communicator essentially oversees three key processes from concept to completion, at the inception of a business. They are:

- The Brand/Mission Statement.
- The Corporate Identity Programme.
- The Corporate Communications Strategy.

The Brand/Mission Statement

A brand statement is the core reactor of a corporate, the hub of business dynamism from which the brand draws energy for its market impact. A brand statement is usually an inspiring statement that is precisely worded. It captures the spirit of the brand. And, it is the soul of the corporate. It is the living, breathing affirmation of a business's presence. What is more is that a brand statement evolves without changing its essence. Like the nucleus of a cell, its premise points to the future growth areas of the corporate organization. It is from the brand statement that the corporate derives its name, logo, slogan and colours. Where brands work, you will find clear, crisp and consistent brand statements. A good way to write a brand statement is to understand the CEO or the founding team. Are they driven and passionate? Or, are they visionary in a quiet way? Are they in the business for the long run? Or are they gunning for immediate market results? Build the business's brand statement based on your understanding of their personality. Remember, that it all reflects the brand's personality. And, do it in a way that is unforgettable....

Here are some 'glocal' examples. Starbucks Coffee wants its brand to 'become a daily ritual in many different cultures'. MRF and its 'Muscleman' set out to create the 'Tyre with Muscle'. The Tatas built on their corporate brand with 'We also make steel'. Infosys, for the world, is 'Powered by Intellect, Driven by Values'. On any day, you know that Wipro would be 'Applying Thought'. A necessary digression here. Apply this thought to some of the best-known non-profit organizations—Green Peace, CRY, World Vision. You will discover an uncanny resemblance between the way that they maintain their image, and the way that corporates manage their brands. In other words, an image is to a non-profit organization, what a brand is to a corporate. More of that later in this chapter.

The Corporate Identity Programme

The second significant step is the corporate identity programme. This is the nuts-and-bolts approach of brand building. Here, the business creates its presence through a corporate identity programme. In its basic form, the corporate identity programme involves a corporate name, logo and slogan. By extension, a corporate identity programme embraces corporate stationery, literature, website and the like. For a business, the corporate identity programme, though small, is a comprehensive one. After taking stock of the business's environment, the corporate identity programme becomes an implemented decision. As mentioned in the second chapter, the best image to be cultivated, especially for a new business, is an assertive presence. This is preferred over a louder, more aggressive image or a silent, passive image.

Typically, a corporate identity programme for a business comprises the following components: Business cards, letter pads, business covers, stamp pads, brochures, flyers, corporate profiles, media releases, corporate website, digital presentation, office memo pads, display boards, neon signs and relevant signage. Remember again that this list covers most of the requirements for a business. As you move to bigger organizations, the list becomes more elaborate and comprehensive. No mention of this programme is complete without a mention of its primer: the corporate identity manual. This admirable work is a professional outline of how a logo and its allied elements are to be used in the various media and across various platforms. In our experience, we have seen manuals that meticulously specify logo sizes for envelopes in America, Europe and Asia. The more detailed manuals run into thousands of pages detailing elements like how logos are to be placed on vehicles and billboards. They specify colours through RGB and CMYK values to ensure global consistency. Among these, environmental identity—the use of a corporate brand name and logo—in various settings is an art, craft and science that charts new ground every day.

The Corporate Communications Strategy

This is the sacred ground upon which brand vision gets translated into actionable strategy. This is also the gladiatorial arena that tests your mettle as a corporate communicator. Every organization with its human element, is inevitably subject to tugs and pulls that draw it in different directions. While the senior management sets the direction, the corporate communicator is called upon to maintain brand integrity—a challenging task in a competitive setting. For this reason, one needs to begin with a strong, persuasive corporate communication initiative that is based on one's business's growth strategy. It should fit the corporate like a cloak that distinguishes it from the other corporates. Here is how the corporate communications strategy works at all levels of the corporate:

- It begins by communicating the brand mission to the internal audiences. It begins with the senior management and works its way to the inner circle of employees and finally to the outsourced workforce. The aid of the Human Resources Department is enlisted in the communication process, for this purpose.

- In tandem, a separate strategy is initiated to address and inform the external audiences in the public domain. This involves potential customers, potential employees, opinion-makers, the media, the government, regulatory agencies, pressure groups and the ubiquitous public domain. The corporate communications strategy here could embrace initiatives in advertising, journalism and public relations, not to forget other platforms like corporate events and sponsorships.

- The third component of a corporate communication strategy is an ongoing and constant research and evaluation initiative. The corporate communicator today has an array of quantitative tools that help him or her to measure the success (or the lack of it) of a given strategy. Impressively, everyone does it. A reputed educational institution that we work with, measured the success of its nationwide campaign by advertising in separate papers— region wise. It then monitored the number of applications from each region, also using its website as a source for application forms. Then, to boost the application drive, it also started a public relations initiative to build its institutional presence. So, in quantifiable terms, the second year's campaign, with its vibrant combination of advertising and PR, resulted in a dramatic increase in the number of applications, over those in the first year.

The Good Life at Chennai

You will find it on the southern outskirts of Chennai, off the picture-perfect east coast road, that leads to Pondicherry. Buena Vista Beach Resort, for three years now, has been offering its clientele a unique hospitality experience. It is fitting (and ironic) that the first strategy case-study picked for this primer revolves around the work that Median has initiated for an affiliate company. Our involvement with this venture afforded us an insider-view of how corporate communication is put to work in a new era organization.

The evolution of the resort as a brand entity itself is a remarkable story. In the early 1990s, the Chennai-based Jos Group was among the first to develop and promote 'Bella Vista' a seaside,

Box 8.1
A Consistent Brand Experience Ensures Business Success

Buena Vista Beach Resort—God's Little Acre—is a celebrated slice of tropical paradise at the southern tip of Chennai. Since its inception in 2000, Buena Vista has created a niche for itself in an intensely competitive market: a beach resort eminently suited for corporate needs. (Visit Buena Vista online at www.buenavistaindia.com). Mark Owen Fernandez, the Executive Director of Buena Vista Beach Resort focussed on the importance of a consistent brand experience:

At Buena Vista, our key brand learnings were born in the school of real life. When Buena Vista Beach Resort opened its doors in April 2000, nothing quite prepared us for the winds of change that would radically alter our marketscape. Fortunately for us, Buena Vista did get its communication strategy right. Months before our inception, we were working at the Buena Vista brand, defining its ambit and re-defining its parameters. Our earliest brand premise was 'The Good Life at Chennai'—an unique hospitality offering of ambience, quality and service for the discerning corporate customer.

Buena Vista's first challenge was the creation of an internal work culture that inspired confidence in our fledgeling ranks. As a start-up enterprise, we realized that our staff were looking for a sense of job security during one of the most unstable phases in the global hospitality industry. At this point, we worked out the nitty-gritty of dynamic communication processes within the organization. One product of those early days was our regular Review Meetings between departments followed by follow-ups on co-ordinated decisions. These built the communications protocol within the organization.

When it came to our guests, a key innovation in the early days was our Rapid Action Management Systems. Beyond our daily working, a guest or group would often have a special request that would have to be fulfilled. And, in practically all cases, we had a solution—or the next best answer. Our market effort was another story altogether. Buena Vista had to make its presence felt in its

(contd.)

Box 8.1 (contd.)

home territory: Chennai. In an increasingly competitive market-place, our sales teams had their task clearly cut out for them: to promote Buena Vista as a resort uniquely suited for corporate conference needs. Here we tuned into conference needs of leading corporates and realized that we could tap into the needs for specialized corporate events: incentive programmes, quarterly reviews, HR training programmes, company events, even board meetings.

Our market teams were fully equipped with sales kits, corporate literature and a pitch to meet every client need. One of our earliest learnings was that our repeat clients responded favourably to innovation. We have had to factor in this 'newness' to keep our client-companies delighted. Each client, in fact, is a learning experience—and a means for us to improve on ambience, service and facilities. With a globally aware client list, the benchmarks were high. In terms of our communication tools, we have used selective corporate advertising, a dynamic web identity, a constant online and direct mailer campaign, backed by the most powerful tool of all: word-of-mouth.

A venture like Buena Vista involves intense interaction with the government, regulatory authorities and special interest groups. Our communication endeavour covers all these fronts. Buena Vista has played a key role in making the nearby beach a cleaner and safer place for the local community as well as the endangered Olive Ridley turtle that nests on the beach annually. As a customer-centric enterprise, we constantly look at new ways to make the Buena Vista experience special for our guests. At Buena Vista, we work at consistent brand experiences that ensure business success. Which is why we find that not a day passes without a new learning!

landscaped enclave. The promoters—a four decade old construc-tion and property development consortium—saw Bella Vista as an opportunity for exclusive residences that would deliver on a commitment of global living standards. The Bella Vista experience centred around elegant villas, cascading fountains and picture-perfect gardens, all of which made it a feast for the senses. And fittingly, its first clients were expatriates—multinational executives and their families, who made Chennai their home with the onset of liberalization. As the nineties unfolded, it became apparent that Bella Vista's potential could be best harnessed, with a full-scale hospitality project that drew an exclusive, corporate audience. The time was ripe for a brand evolution.

In the quest for a logical brand extension to Bella Vista, one choice led the rest. Buena Vista is a Latin phrase that means 'beautiful view'. In April 2000—after a two year hiatus—Buena Vista Beach Resort opened its doors to an enthusiastic public. While retaining the ambience and essence of the parent Bella Vista experience, the resort became a unique hospitality experience on Chennai's east coast. It now centred its appeal around landscaped villas, 30 suites (in the standard, deluxe and luxury segments), three conference halls, banquet venues, a swimming pool and a terrace-top restaurant, not to mention, a spread of Indian, oriental and continental cuisine. The resort's growth was immediately impacted by the emergence of the nearby IT Corridor of Chennai in the city's southern region.

Fig. 8.1: Buena Vista Beach Resort and its Logo

Buena Vista Beach Resort marked the learnings of a decade spent in a dynamic market environment. The primary business audience comprised corporates in the city region, which encompasses a population of 75,00,000 across 172 square kilometres. In particular, the resort chose the nearby IT Corridor of Chennai to fulfill the corporate and leisure needs of the 100 odd companies and corporations in this region. By extension, those who visited the resort, and their families, became potential clients who could be converted into real-time guests. Foreign and domestic tourists continue to be an important, but secondary audience. The resort's corporate communications strategy came under the three heads discussed earlier:

The Brand/Mission Statement

The Buena Vista brand centred itself around three unique guest-experiences: the ambience, the cuisine and the facilities. According to Mark Fernandez, the resort's Executive Director, all of these were captured in the brand premise: The Good Life at Chennai. To begin with the resort's staff were briefed on the implications of this unique hospitality commitment to the guests at Buena Vista. An entire hospitality approach was built around it, an integral part of which was its communications.

The Corporate Identity Programme

The Buena Vista logo features a golden sun, caressed by clouds typifying the beach resort experience. This visual is encircled by an oval unit. An innovative logo touch here was its corporate baseline: 'God's Little Acre'. This was born of an early customer insight that Buena Vista had the makings of a little tropical paradise. Months of brainstorming on that theme led to the pithy phrase—God's Little Acre. Our experience is that this baseline has synergized well with the brand statement—The Good Life at Chennai.

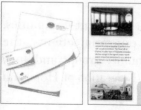

Fig. 8.2: Buena Vista Branding at Work
Corporate Stationery + Brochure + Website

Buena Vista's corporate identity programme comprises the following: corporate stationery (business cards, letter pads, envelopes, stamp pads), corporate brochures, menu cards, signages and billboards. Also included are identity-elements like branded napkins, table coasters, cutlery and table linen. The corporate identity programme along with these branded elements was meticulously designed and planned to ensure brand consistency. Also prominent on the list of brand-building tools is the website (www.buenavistaindia.com), which was built with the guidelines presented in the chapter on new media. Building on customer-experience, it features testimonials and endorsements by guests and corporates who have used the place.

The Corporate Communications Strategy

Buena Vista Beach Resort has consistently adopted best practices in its day-to-day operations namely: rooms, food and beverages and marketing. A select team of hospitality professionals implement top hospitality practices to build on its core commitment of 'The Good Life at Chennai'. Beyond these operational areas, it has involved the use of corporate communications in its everyday operations. In particular, the resort has gone the extra mile in adopting corporate citizenship initiatives in its operations. In terms of its communications model, it has consistently communicated its brand to the following spread of audiences:

- The internal audiences of Buena Vista Beach Resort include its employees, outsourced workforce and globally based board of directors.
- The external audiences include guests, client-companies, investors, suppliers, well-wishers, potential clients, the government, regulatory bodies, community groups and apex industry organizations like the FHRAI (Federation of Hotel and Restaurants Association India).

A key part of Buena Vista's corporate communications initiative has been its role as a corporate citizen. The resort plays a

frontline role in maintaining the three kilometre stretch of the
Neelankarai shoreline that stretches in front of it. It continues to
play a key role in ensuring that the beach is made clean and safe
for the use of the local communities. Over the years, it has
campaigned for cleaner beaches, beach guard patrolling, sponsored
game areas and worked with local citizen groups for greater
environmental awareness. The Neelankarai beach is one of the
nest sites for the endangered Olive Ridley turtle. Every year, wildlife
conservationists base themselves at the beach to protect turtle
hatchlings. This direct link to conservation is backed by citizen
groups of the area, in which the resort plays a key role.

In the three years since Buena Vista commenced operations,
it has evolved into a hub of interaction for achievers in corporate
India. The resort's collective experience indicated that its clientele
were in large part, corporate achievers. And, it has sought to
cultivate that clientele. Every year, it honours corporate 'seagulls'—
men and women, who have stepped beyond their personal success,
to make contributions to the communities they live in. A look at
the guest-list stands testimony to this fact. The Buena Vista Beach
Resort has played host to the likes of Narayana Murthy of Infosys,
Arun Jain of Polaris and C. S. Ramadorai of TCS. To its
many admirers, Buena Vista is home to the Good Life at Chennai.
It is at once a haven of corporate tranquil, nurtured in a tropical
paradise.

Towards the Greater Good

For the non-profit, non-government organization, communication
is truly a living commitment. By virtue of its existence, it has chosen
to make a difference by standing for an ideal, championing a cause
or nurturing an initiative. As the second chapter pointed out, the
twin processes of corporatization and communications have
radically altered the functioning of the non-profit organization. As
Abdul Taher of Radical points out, most non-profit organizations
today are adopting revenue models to sustain their mode of

operations. No longer do these organizations depend on the largesse of donors, but instead, look to aggressive fund-raising initiatives to grow in the future. And, Abdul should know. The team at Radical has been at the forefront of pathbreaking campaign initiatives for the HIV/AIDS cause. Their work for INP+ (Indian Network of Positive People) has introduced a whole new dimension of thinking in the way that non-profit organizations communicate.

In the Radical tradition, Abdul is quick to point out that communications for non-profit organizations use the same principles as brand strategy. The key difference, he asserts, is that a potential audience for a non-profit organization must 'buy a message'. That approach is taken a significant step further in the book *Public Communication Campaigns*. In it, the authors Rice and Atkin define public communications campaigns as 'purposive attempts to inform, persuade or motivate behaviour changes in a relatively well-defined and large audience, generally for non-commercial benefits to the individual and/or society, typically within a given time period, by means of organized communication activities involving mass media and often complemented by interpersonal support'. (Rice and Atkin, 2001, p. 232).

Rice and Atkin go on to qualify this definition with resultant benefits of public communications campaigns that are driven by reform efforts. In this, they acknowledge William J. Paisley's approach towards public communication campaigns. According to Paisely: 'Reform, defined as action that makes society or the lives of individuals better, is a unifying principle of public communication campaigns' (Paisley, quoted in Rice and Atkin 2001, p. 5). When it comes to communicating their cause and image, most non-profit organizations draw from this approach in one form or the other. Non-profit organizations in the new era have necessarily become corporatized in their working. Business recessions and dynamic environments have led most organizations to the revenue model of working.

Appropriate Technology India (ATI), a non-profit organization was established in August 1994 with the goal of introducing cost-effective, environment-friendly, productivity-enhancing technologies for sustainable enterprise development. They help rural producers to better their lives through improved management practices and increased incomes. ATI creates production, processing, and marketing facilities that enable rural producers and farmers to generate more value from their produce and increase their incomes. ATI began with two programmes in Gujarat and the Garhwal Himalayas, both focussed on environmentally sustainable enterprise development.

The first is the Gujarat dairy project, which produced and marketed molasses-urea products (Pashu Poshak), fodder chaff cutters and other livestock technologies. The project concluded in February 2003.

ATI is now entirely focussed on its second programme—a conservation-based enterprise development in the Western Himalayas. ATI presently works in five districts of Uttaranchal—Rudraprayag, Chamoli, Tehri, Pauri and Uttarkashi. From its main office in Ukimath, Rudraprayag district of the Garhwal Himalayas, ATI is conserving biodiversity through creation of community-owned honey and oak tasar silk enterprises. ATI builds partnerships with the public, private and cooperative sectors—and with NGOS and farmer groups to achieve its goals.

Through its effort in Garhwal, Himachal Pradesh, ATI has applied essential brand strategy to two organically produced products—oak tasar silk and Himalayan honey. Both products are locally produced by hill communities in Garhwal. Oak tasar silk is produced, processed and marketed under the brand name Garhwal Silk. The Himalayan honey is harvested, bottled and promoted under the name Devbhumi Madhu. ATI has used its competency areas to provide enhanced processing, organization management and marketing training for the brand promotion of these indigenous products. Both Garhwal Silk and Devbhumi Madhu have stepped into the great Indian marketplace and are creating a distinct niche for themselves. A business initiative that is representative of thousands of other NGOs that are adopting the revenue model globally. To understand how ATI views communication as a commitment, visit www.atindia.org.

Box 8.2
Go Where your Market Is...

A passionate heritage conservationist, Deborah Thiagarajan is an American art historian who has lived in Chennai since 1970. Her keen interest in south Indian heritage led to the setting up of Madras Craft Foundation (MCF) in the mid 1980s. Since its inception in 1996, DakshinaChitra, its heritage village has gone on to become a global exemplar of heritage awareness and conservation. Visit it online at www.dakshinachitra.org. Here, Deborah Thiagarajan shares her thoughts on communicating the DakshinaChitra experience:

DakshinaChitra, for us, is a living museum of the South. And, our efforts to build its image in the eyes of our target communities has always kept us in touch with our founding mission of creating and nurturing an awareness of South Indian heritage. We realized early enough that in order to achieve this goal, DakshinaChitra would have to be a self-sustaining organization. Close on the heels of this knowledge, came the realization that 'Planning is the key'. Whether it was conceptualizing a heritage home, or communicating DakshinaChitra's image.

In the years to follow, our work led us to a unique interface with South Indian crafts communities, the government and corporates. While playing catalyst to this process, we also had to reach out to its real target community: its visitors. Being strategically placed on the East Coast Road, which is now considered Chennai's entertainment highway, we had to make the DakshinaChitra stands out from a swathe of leisure offerings from nearby amusement parks, resorts and entertainment hubs. For this reason, DakshinaChitra became, for its visitors, a totally interactive experience that is based on India's folk arts tradition.

As a visitor to DakshinaChitra today, you get to experience South Indian heritage through exhibitions, special performances, craft workshops and unique programmes. On a good day at DakshinaChitra, you are likely to be engrossed in a throbbing folk dance, stringing your own necklace, weaving a basket, watching a folk puppet show or simply getting your fortune told by our

(contd.)

Box 8.2 (contd.)

resident astrologer and parrot. There are some learnings that only experience can reveal. To our surprise, we found that the 15000 school children, who annually visit DakshinaChitra have turned out to become our most loyal 'brand' ambassadors. They have always returned with their families to relive the DakshinaChitra experience.

In communicating the DakshinaChitra experience to potential visitors, the media has been our most potent tool. In 2001, DakshinaChitra hired Prism Public Relations to build on its public image. We now employ a full time Publicity and Public Relations person. Our initiatives here include media releases, poster campaigns, a bi-monthly newsletter, corporate-sponsored hoardings and craft exhibitions in other cities of India. Here again, DakshinaChitra has built on the synergy between the media's need to have information on arts and culture and our need to have our programmes and initiatives brought out to the public. Our key learning in this area is to 'go where the Market is'.

Bringing DakshinaChitra to life has been a creative challenge to our capabilities. It is certainly one that we have thrived on— as an organization. One of our recent initiatives here is the Friends of DakshinaChitra—a 100 strong group that contributes its time and effort to activities and initiative here at our centre. As it approaches its first decade of existence, DakshinaChitra will cover newer and more innovative territory in becoming a platform of interaction for folk arts and concepts of culture. It is a mission that we look forward to—with a sense of creative challenge.

The Cornerstones of Public Communications

Public communication campaigns have a world of insight to offer us when it comes to communicating a non-profit organization's image and purpose. Public communication campaigns use three basic communication processes to evoke the desired response from their target audiences—awareness, instruction and persuasion. The use of these three processes—or, a combination of them—depends on the nature of the audience being addressed. Here, the resources, strategy and desired response are key factors that shape a non-profit organization's communication initiatives.

Of the three approaches, awareness building is the most commonly used approach. Awareness campaigns work in two ways when it comes to promoting an organization or cause. The first is to create awareness and the second is to increase awareness. Awareness campaigns are generally planned to evoke initiative or responses from vast audiences. They seek to inform and sensitize target audiences about issues and causes, while inviting them to learn more from resources like information desks, websites, publications, counsellors and organizations. During the SARS epidemic in March 2003, governments in south east Asia embarked on public communication campaigns that educated Asian publics about the need to take health precautions and stay calm.

Instruction messages work on the primer principle. They essentially concern health and environment issues. They provide the target audience with a 'how-do-you-do-it' set of guidelines, offering further resources that could help them. Acute water shortages in south India have led state governments to embark on public communication campaigns to conserve water and more importantly, implement rainwater harvesting systems across residential and commercial areas. The third key communication process is persuasion. Here, the emphasis is on persuading a potential audience to either create or change an attitude, by providing a knowledge base that leads to a desired response. In the late 1990s, the Austrian government initiated a successful campaign to inform its citizens about the need to segregate organic and plastic wastes. Beyond a successful public communication initiative, it ensured easy compliance by providing black disposal bags for plastics and green disposal bags for organic and kitchen wastes.

Simply South

Visiting DakshinaChitra is like making a remarkable journey in time. If you too seek it out, you would be enraptured by its experience. One of the most ambitious heritage initiatives in Asia, DakshinaChitra is a world of re-created Indian heritage. It

Fig. 8.3: Public Communication at Work

represents a slice of the celebrated cultures of India's four southern states: Andhra Pradesh, Karnataka, Kerala and Tamil Nadu. As its name suggests, DakshinaChitra is derived from Dakshin—the Sanskrit word for 'South'—and Chitra—an Indian term that refers to a theme, picture or vision. Every step you take into the red brick enclave that embraces it, leads you on a journey through one of the world's oldest cultures—that of south India.

The team at DakshinaChitra has its mission etched out for it. It begins by seeking out 18th, 19th and early 20th-century houses across the four southern states and, in what must be a challenging step, relocates them to the heritage centre. The DakshinaChitra initiative is straightforward enough. The first step is to identify a traditional south Indian home. It could be as imposing as an ancestral merchant home in Tamil Nadu's Chettinad region or an Ikkat weaver's home in the northern reaches of Karnataka. Having purchased it, the team of conservation and heritage experts then meticulously dismantles it. The home is then transported in its various elements to DakshinaChitra, where it is painstakingly recreated, in an area meant for its relevant state. In fact, DakshinaChitra has gone an interactive step further. Beyond homes, it has recreated village streets, workplaces, entire lifestyles that provide authentic insights into traditional south Indian life.

One minute, you are stepping into a magnificent home of Tamil Nadu's merchant community. The next, you are experiencing the austerity of a Sattanur household, reflecting the world of agricultural Tamil Nadu. And from here to the scholastic environs of the Agraharam—the enclave of the Tamil Brahmin community

Fig 8.4: DakshinaChitra and its Logo

bordering a temple. Everywhere around you, life is a rapturous
swirl of south Indian life. The sights, sounds and flavours of
traditional Tamil Nadu come alive—the ubiquitous astrologer and
his parrot with cards that tell your fortune, peacock dancers who
swirl, unmindful of the midday sun and a puppet show that awaits
you in the shade. The south Indian experience continues. You step
into the wooded elegance of Kerala's *tharvadu* (clan) homes, reliving
Arundhati Roy's tradition-veiled world. Minutes from Kerala, you
are ushered into the Karnataka section, where an Ikkat weaver's
home outdoes itself in granite appeal. And, from there, it is onto
the newest section at DakshinaChitra—Andhra Pradesh. Minutes
become lifetimes, as you journey through the compact cultures of
DakshinaChitra.

Conceptualized in the mid 1980s, DakshinaChitra is a
frontline initiative of the Madras Craft Foundation. It was
begun by Deborah Thiagarajan, an American art historian who
has lived in India for over three decades. A non-profit, non-
government initiative, DakshinaChitra began life as a barren sprawl
of coastal land in July 1991. Five years later, in December 1996,
the centre opened to the public. The legendary Laurie Baker
breathed architectural life into it, making its concept a reality.
DakshinaChitra, in its own words, 'is a living, breathing, cross-
cultural museum of architecture, life-styles, crafts, performing arts,
food and music'.

It is first-of-its-kind effort to capture the diverse cultural
flavours of south India. It was around this vision, that one of the

most remarkable heritage initiatives in this part of the world was built. Though a non-profit organization, it is, by necessity, highly corporatized in its operations. The centre's administration is overseen by professional volunteers and paid staff. Adding impetus to its growth was its communications initiative—already a model for initiatives of its kind. Drawing from its experience, DakshinaChitra has found that the public communication processes of awareness, instruction and persuasion, in varying measures, have played a key role in its growth.

To elaborate, DakshinaChitra works at building heritage awareness across the span of its internal and external audiences. Depending on the media and platform, the intensity and duration of these heritage initiatives differ. A visitor to DakshinaChitra, for instance, is first invited to view a 17-minute documentary on south Indian heritage. In the course of the day-to-day operations at its centre, DakshinaChitra runs over 15 activities that require some form of instruction for visitors. These range from traditional arts like pottery, weaving and puppetry to the preparation of traditional south Indian delicacies. Also evident is the use of persuasion to enlist corporate and private sponsorship for DakshinaChitra's myriad initiatives. To achieve this end, potential donors are given detailed insights about the need to protect and nurture the vanishing culture of south India. For these reasons, DakshinaChitra continues to be an emulated example of a worthy mission converted into a communicated reality.

Fig 8.5: DakshinaChitra in Print and its Media Avatars

Its inner circle of audiences comprises diverse spread of groups—employees, volunteers, corporate donors, affiliate organizations, artisan communities and an internal group of friends of DakshinaChitra. Each of these audiences is addressed differently. Employees and volunteers, for instance, are briefed regularly on the need to communicate the DakshinaChitra vision to both internal and external audiences differently. When it comes to corporate donors, Deborah Thiagarajan points out, only nurtured relationships lead to a long-term support and sustenance. In keeping with its objective of promoting folk arts and concepts of culture, the centre is part of an active network of organizations like the Prakriti Foundation, Amethyst, National Folklore Support Centre and the Crafts Council of India. DakshinaChitra is also a creative hub for artisan communities—south Indian potters, soft-stone workers, weavers, fabric printers and other artisans. It showcases their products and performances, while providing technical, organizational and marketing inputs to the craft and folk performance communities of south India. As these lines were being written, DakshinaChitra was launching its own line of branded craft products!

The centre also claims distinction as an example of the synergy between the Government, industry and conservation experts. Its heritage patrons include the Ford Foundation and the Office of the Developmental Commissioner, Handicrafts. And, its Founder-Patrons represent the very best of the Indian corporate realm: American Express, EID Parry India, ICICI, Oberoi Hotels, Sundaram Finance and Sterling Resorts. Though funded by grants and donations, DakshinaChitra assiduously works towards a self-sustenance model. DakshinaChitra venues are a favoured platform for exclusive artistic and corporate events. DakshinaChitra draws over 50,000 visitors annually from India and across the world. These include potential donors, potential visitors, external artisan communities, schools and institutions as well as diverse communities of non-resident Indians. Visit DakshinaChitra online (www.dakshinachitra.org) to understand how a vibrant public communications campaign can drive the vision and initiative of a non-profit, non-government organization—with qualified success.

Evolving to Achieve

If communication is commitment—and, the secret behind an organization's longevity—then these two very 'profit-oriented organizations' certainly take the cake. The world's longest living company is the Stora Company, a Swedish copper mining company that was founded in the 13th century. By pure coincidence, Sumitomo, the well-known Japanese industrial group traces its origins to a copper casting shop that began operations in the year 1590. Two businesses, whose enviable brand reputations span centuries.

These unusual facts come embedded in the rich lore of business insight in Professor S. Ramchander's column 'Value Spiral' in the *Hindu Business Line Catalyst*. In his column subtitled 'The Living Company', Professor Ramachander offers us this insight on a sense of identity and cohesion:

> All successful and enduring systems in the broadest sense are networks and carry a sense of community...Yet, in a long tradition, there has to be a sense of continuity of purpose and character from one generation to the next. Hence, the renewed importance in the literature to culture defined as 'a shared set of beliefs, attitudes and values and sense of acceptable behaviours' as well as a 'way things are done around here' that emanates there from.
>
> (Ramachander, 2002, p. 4)

This chapter sets out to look at the communications approaches of two organizations: a business and a non-profit organization. For a business, corporate communications is where it all begins. In its ascent to market growth, a business adopts a communications initiative that is layered on its market strategy. The initiative itself centres around the three key steps towards a brand reality: the brand/mission statement, the corporate identity programme and the corporate communications strategy. When it comes to the non-profit organization, its avatar of the brand reality is mirrored in its image.

Public communications, we saw, is the way ahead for today's corporatized non-profit organizations that are looking to establish a revenue model for sustenance in today's competitive, market-driven environment. Here, the three key processes used are awareness, instruction and persuasion.

The approaches may differ for both kinds of organizations, but the objective of a communication effort remains the same—to create a brand or image for the organization, to ensure its survival and importantly, its success. In this quest, Candide's message for his generation is a signpost for our organizations: 'Let us cultivate our garden'. More importantly, corporate and social communications strategies set out to achieve an important function for their organizations—to become what they appear to be. So that the organization's image complements its soul. A new era 21st century thought? Think again. Socrates said it first.

Signposts

The brand/mission statement is the soul of the corporate. A brand statement is a precisely worded, inspiring statement that captures the spirit of the brand. It is the unchanging essence of a profit and non-profit organization.

The corporate identity programme is the use of a corporate's brand name, logo and allied elements—in various settings. It is an art, craft and science that charts new ground every day.

Corporate communications, for a business, involves the communication of its brand to internal and external audiences through a strategic initiative towards a common set of objectives, that can be measured and evaluated.

Public communications is the strategic process by which non-profit organizations build their image. It uses three basic communication processes to evoke the desired response from their target audiences: awareness, instruction and persuasion.

Organization-Initiative

Take your pick. And, choose your cause. Play catalyst to the birth of an emerging business or a new non-profit organization. Begin with a brand or mission statement that can be crafted to inspire participation. Then move onto the development of an identity programme that covers the essentials, beginning with a logo that evokes radical response and reflects its mission.

Ideally, this could be followed by a brand or mission statement that is summarized for internal and external audiences with the use of a compact baseline or catch-phrase. Remember to keep your organization's long-term vision in focus as you create the brand or mission statement. Develop the short-, medium- and long-term vision (typically, one, five and ten year projections) of your organization, based on its brand or mission statement.

The next step is corporate stationery. Depending on the size and operations of your proposed organization, this programme could include business cards, letter pads, business covers, brochures, corporate profiles, media releases, a corporate website, a digital presentation and relevant signage. Having said that, the use of a digital presentation to present your organization to your audience will lend credence to its existence. Also establish the different approaches you would take to communicate the brand to its internal and external audiences. This scenario, in the case of a business, can be made more interesting with the assumption of pressure groups and ways to deal with them.

The penultimate step is the creation of a corporate or public communications strategy that delivers on its objectives. In the case of a profit organization, explain how your strategy would work with a focus on the market dynamics and its competitive reality. Establish the means to research and evaluate your results. For a non-profit organization, establish the mission statement in the light of a relevant cause and a realistic means to support it. Beyond donations and grants, you might have to look at a revenue model to sustain your organization. Ensure that your growth strategy is given its impetus by your planned public communications campaign. Either way, conceptualize, create and communicate. And, if your results are spectacular while being imaginative, let us know at **median@vsnl.net!**

Sources

Publications

Kitchen, Philip J. and Schultz, Don E. (2001). *Raising the Corporate Umbrella: Corporate Communications in the 21st Century.* Palgrave, New York.
Rice, R.E. and Atkins, C.K. (eds). (2001). *Public Communication Campaigns.* Sage Publications, Thousand Oaks.
Schramm, Wilbur. (Edited by Steven. H. Chaffee and Everett M. Rogers). (1997). *The Beginnings of Communication Study in America: A Personal Memoir.* Sage Publications, Thousand Oaks.
Voltaire (Edited by Haskell M. Block). (1956). *Candide and Other Writings.* The Modern Library, New York.

Periodicals

Bhimani, Rita. (18th April 2001). 'Is Your Corporate Communication Working?', *Catalyst, The Hindu Business Line.*
Ramachander S. (21st February 2002). 'Value Spiral—The Living Company' *Catalyst, The Hindu Business Line.*

Websites

www.atindia.org
www.buenavistaindia.com
www.dakshinachitra.org

Interviews

Deborah Thiagarajan
Chairperson, Madras Craft Foundation, Chennai

Mark Fernandez
Executive Director, Buena Vista Beach Resort, Chennai

Sharmila Ribeiro
President, Appropriate Technology India, Chennai

Sheik Abdul Taher
Radical Advertising & Consultancy, Chennai

9 Companies and Corporations: Communicating the Corporate

There is no more new frontier, We have got to make it here.

—The Eagles, The Last Resort

•

You know it, when you feel it. The soul of India's biking experience. It lies in the reassuring, deep throb of a gleaming chrome, 350cc beauty. As it surges to life, its harnessed power and exquisite styling mysteriously synergize to bring you power, comfort and ruggedness—with the appeal of a mustang. Settle into the comfort of its saddle seat. Experience its unique throb. Click its unique right-gearset into a cruise mode. Head out into the Great Indian Wide. And, you too experience the India that men and women have known on these magnificent machines. Savour the gentle evening breeze that calms the summer day, as you race down its east coast towards India's land's end—Kanyakumari. Early the next day, the heady spray of a monsoon-kissed morning awaits you, on the palm-fringed coast of Kerala. Head up the west coast through Maharashtra, to India's northwestern frontier near Rajasthan, where the sullen, mirage-like heat of the Thar Desert overpowers you with its intensity. Then, veer into India's hidden slice of paradise. Ride into the magical 'Valley of Butterflies' in Himachal Pradesh, where swarms of colourful butterflies brush past you on your windswept journey. Brace yourself for the icy climes of the Himalayas, while you negotiate the extreme gorges on their endless rock-strewn roads. Pause for a moment, on the humid eastern border. Listen to the song of the cicada on the mangrove-fringed coastline of Bengal. As your journey progresses, you will notice how India celebrates her contrasts. Farmers on tractors, connecting through mobile phones. Busy cyber-cafes in remote villages. And, international class highways that cut through pristine Indian countryside. As you ride back into the home stretch of your journey, you will have discovered the grit, guts and glory, where India's biking experience lies. The Royal Enfield Bullet today holds its own on the variegated nature of Indian roads. Its brand legend, is reinforced by its instinctive bonding with a diverse, but fanatically loyal customer base that varies from India's uniformed forces to a new generation of twenty somethings who use the Bullet to explore India. Thus it is a motley group that celebrates India's diversity and patronizes the Bullet. Right from the army dispatch rider racing out of Sarkhej on Ahmedabad's outskirts towards Rajasthan, who swears by his army green Enfield to the feisty zamindar overseeing his verdant acres on his festooned red Bullet in Tamil Nadu's Gobichettipalayam district to twenty something software professional testing out his gleaming turquoise Thunderbird on the highway outside your city. For each of these bikers, the Royal Enfield implies an experience without parallel. The amazing saga of the company's journey back to market prominence forms the first case study of this chapter. The Royal Enfield case study is, in a sense, a classic one. An established player—a manufacturing company—in a dynamic market environment, re-inventing itself to take on the challenge of the new era markets.

Elsewhere on the information superhighway, India's largest network, Internet and e-Commerce services corporation is fast approaching its next milestone of corporate achievement. Sify Limited, formerly known as Satyam Infoway, is India's pioneer and leader in Internet, network and e-Commerce services. The only integrated end-to-end e-Solutions provider in India, Sify, designs and develops a host of customized e-Commerce and Network Connectivity Solutions that connect critical business systems of client companies across India and the world. At Sify's offices, corporate communications strategy is an integral part of the corporate business strategy that has begun to distinguish new era corporations in India and around the world. Sify is the quintessential new era corporation. Since its inception, it has had to face the market turbulences of a globalized market environment. Its continued growth, longevity and profitability are the latest chapters in its already eventful prosperous existence. At the core of the Sify juggernaut, we found brand vision, uncommon business acumen and market awareness and insight. Its corporate communicators have worked on the organization's networked quality to ensure that it is acutely sensitive to the realities of the global markets in which it operates.

The penultimate step towards an overall understanding of corporate communications is the application of its strategy to companies and their larger organizational cousins, corporations. This chapter picks the real-time examples of two Indian corporate organizations. An established company, and, a new era corporation. To begin with, this chapter establishes the distinction between these two forms of corporate organizations. It then goes on to highlight the broad approaches adopted by them, while strategizing for corporate communications. Both these case-studies prove one point: the new era corporate needs a radically new approach to communicating its brand in a dynamic environment to 'individually-unknown mass audiences'.

The Tao of Brand Building

Corporate communicators of the future will draw their examples from Mother Nature's immutable laws. The analogy of a corporate and product brand with that of a tree and its fruit is one such example. A tree produces fruit, in the way that a corporate brings forth products. Embedded within the tree is the fruit. And, the presence of the tree lies in the fruit—the best way to explain corporate brands and product brands and their symbiotic relationship with each other.

In *Built to Last*, the authors James C. Collins and Jerry I. Porras studied America's corporate icons, to seek out the reasons for their longevity—and continued market success. Along the way, they discovered the quality of being 'a visionary company'. They discovered the Holy Grail of America's corporate legends, which was to 'preserve the core and stimulate progress'. *Built to Last* reveals that these companies lasted, because their vision—a shared ideology—became a legacy that outlived its founders. This explanation holds valid for Disney, IBM, Motorola, 3M, Nordstrom and the like. In all cases, the company's core values remained the same, while its growth strategies provided the company with impetus for market leadership. Central to this process was the creation of an internal culture that would then revolutionize the company's mission. Here, Collins and Porreas speak of 'cult-like cultures' that pervade companies like IBM, Disney and Nordstrom. In all of this, the corporate communicator play catalyst to the key communication processes that build the company's brand in the eyes of its audiences.

Corporate communications builds its efficacy on the subtle, but strategic differentiation between corporate and product brands. There exists a symbiotic relationship between corporate brands and product brands. And, though their objective of each of these is the same, the means by which they are achieved are quite different. So, where does the challenge lie for you as the corporate communicator of a new era company? For one, you must become acutely aware of the mission ahead of you. In principle, you will oversee every aspect of communication that deals with the promotion of the corporate brand. You will be the link between the company and its individually-unknown, mass audiences. The company will go about its core functions of producing profits, cutting costs and reducing risks, while you build its brand, communicate its core messages, and work on strategic communication for its internal and external audiences—a core responsibility that will make you an integral part of the inner and outer circles of the company.

Built to Communicate

Corporate communications, in its broadest application, addresses every aspect of a company's communications with its audiences. It begins by establishing a voice and image, while building on a long-term relationship with its target audiences. The ongoing processes

Box 9.1
A Structured Communication Policy—A Common Language

After his graduation from Cornell University, Rajesh Jambotkar rode the crest of the dotcom wave, with an enviable employment record that spanned frontline organizations in the US and Thailand. He can be contacted at raj@jambotkar.com. As he plotted the trajectory of his career graph, Rajesh paused a moment to share his thoughts on corporate communications:

At the time I joined the company, Ernst & Young was a firm with 80,000 employees and three major divisions. From consulting to audit services, E & Y offered a wide array of products—each with its own positioning and branding characteristics. As company employees and representatives, we were expected to understand our division's products and how they fit into the company's branding scheme. Add to this a rapid product development cycle (necessitated by the economic boom of the late 90s), and you quickly found yourself as an employee inundated with product announcements and updates from internal communications departments. Most importantly, a structured communications policy allowed me to talk with employees from different divisions (or even parts of the world) in the 'same language'.

Roughly 180 degrees west of corporate E & Y's headquarters was a scrawny yet brazen startup named Trapezo. Like other start-ups of its time, the company had a few employees, a bit of seed money, and a box full of dreams about how to expedite the growth of the Internet economy. I joined the company as the eighth full time employee—and quickly appreciated the structure and consistency of the organization I had just left behind. Over the course of two years, the company and its flagship product evolved significantly—we grew to 40 employees and started adding more traditional and conservative customers. These new customers ironically forced us to tone down our rebellious startup image and focus on delivering value and cost savings within a given timetable. With this company maturation, our professional services organization began to change the way we dealt with customers—we developed feedback loops to drive product development and as well as professional looking, paper-based help documentation for the product.

(contd.)

Box 9.1 (contd.)

As the lead customer liaison and product integration specialist—I was actively involved in this transformation. I remember reflecting then how I had previously 'scorned' the rigidity of E&Y's practices, but there I was, trying to instill them in my co-workers. Likewise, as I moved into a management role, I appreciated the change in communication style required on my part. My actions, selection (and omission) of words, and tone were occasionally held under a microscope by the employees I managed. Through trial and error, I quickly refined my communication style to filter out potentially alarming words and actions.

Yet another learning chapter awaited me half way around the world in Thailand. Taking a break from consulting and IT-based ventures, I began exploring opportunities in the education sector. I travelled around southeast and east Asia before returning to Bangkok where I met up with a former American Peace Corps volunteer and his wife. As we discussed our mutual interest in education and community service projects, we realized that we had an opportunity to develop an organization that could benefit travellers and native Thai people. We co-founded Go Without Borders, an organization that offers travel tours and service projects to travellers seeking meaningful cultural exchanges and experiences with Thai people.

Working out of our apartments in crowded downtown Bangkok (very reminiscent of Mumbai!), we developed a logo, product offering, and marketing material that reflected the mission and goals of the company. The process was extremely complex—we were constantly faced with tough decisions regarding our perceived image and choice of wording in our literature. Crucial to our efforts was product differentiation—we weren't offering something completely new, but it was truly unique and we needed to capture the passion we felt about the products in our external communications. That, it did. Go Without Border today has gone on to carve a unique niche for itself in the global traveller lexicon.

Today in my workspace, I am acutely aware of the importance of corporate communications in the networked lives of the organizations that we nurture. Employees' voice mail and email inboxes are to me, a constant reminder of the communication flow around us. In total, my experience has led me to appreciate the complexity and necessity of corporate communications strategy.

of Corporatization, Digitization and Globalization have empowered the corporate communicator's position, while adding to its challenge. The communication of the company's brand and the opening up of audience spectrums have resulted in three key components:

- Corporate communications is a long-term strategic initiative usually created within a company to communicate its brand and core messages. Central to this process is the creation of a corporate voice that is assertive and effective in the interactive and influential modes.
- As a strategy, corporate communications proceeds from the core of the company—its senior management—in a credible and informative way to impact every level of the organization. The internal audiences could include employees, stakeholders, and investors. In the public domain, the audiences typically include customers, regulatory bodies, industry councils, opinion leaders, financial markets, pressure groups and potential employees. As the second chapter pointed out, each audience group is different and calls for specific communicative approaches—with measurable outcomes.
- Finally, corporate communications is an evolved response to the dynamic communications need of the 21st century corporate. As part of its strategic armoury, it deploys the following techniques: advertising, public relations, community relations, corporate literature, corporate hospitality, exhibitions, event management, new media, crisis management, lobbying, investor relations, research, sponsorship management, traditional media and integrated marketing communications.

And, then there are measurable outcomes. This is the ground on which quality meets quantity. Corporate communications ensure that your brand message and communication strategy are consistent with your overall promotional objectives—backed by measurable outcomes. In a rapidly expanding global marketplace, you are communicating your brand and core messages about your products and services to active audiences. Therefore, your strategy must be measurable against predetermined objectives. Every strategy should have measurement capabilities to allow for the tracking of its success. Measurable outcomes play a key role in the working of a 21st century Corporate. Business processes that dominate the working of new era companies are centred around 'the numbers'—quantifiable results that project the measure of success against the predetermined goal.

As a corporate communicator in your company, you will need to evaluate performance on the following quantitative parameters: analysis of media coverage, delivery of key messages, market research and surveys, tracking customer/reader enquiries, tracking media opinion and event attendance. Brand audits merit a special mention. Having fully understood the communication needs of your company, you need to design the most suitable campaign to build its brand. Here, the factors that you will need to take into account are the core message, the target audiences, the available budget, relevant government policy, current public opinion, relevance of the campaign. (Let's not forget competitor activity in the marketplace!). In the two case studies that lie ahead, we will watch the real-time application of corporate communications strategy in the new era marketplace.

The Lone Rider

When the history of brands in India is written, one name will be parked securely in a niche of its own: The Royal Enfield Bullet. Its chrome-and-black presence, instantly recognizable by its distinctive beat is an icon on Indian roads. The company's fanatically loyal customer base across India is a marketer's dream. For close to half a century now, the Bullet has stood for reliability, ruggedness and the gritty Indian quality of sticking it through—no matter what. For decades, Royal Enfield shared its niche with its roadster cousins, the Jawa/Yezdi and Rajdoot. This unlikely trio maintained a cult status on the Indian roads for decades. Royal Enfield first made its entry into India, as a supplier of vehicles for the army in the mid 1950s. Its parent company in Britain set up the plant in Madras (Chennai), India to cope with large production volumes. Strangely enough, the parent company then went into a decline, until it finally closed down in the 1970s. In India, however, the Bullet thrived—thanks to its use among India's armed forces and a formidable group of Bullet aficionados. These were the years of Nehruvian Socialism, where typically a few manufacturers catered to a burgeoning population. The emphasis here was on production—not product development. A still talked-about example of this era was the Ambassador, whose essential design and technology remained unchanged for over 38 years!

ROYAL
ENFIELD

Fig. 9.1: Royal Enfield and the Soul of India's Biking Experience

And, then came the 1980s, when the Indian markets were suddenly swamped by lighter, more fuel-efficient Japanese bikes. Overnight, Yamahas, Hondas and Suzukis began their vice-like domination of the Indian two-wheeler market. The inability of Jawa/Yezdi and Rajdoot brands to effectively and quickly reinvent themselves lead to a fade-out of their brand image. Royal Enfield underwent its own trials at the time. However, following a merger with the Eicher Group in the early 1990s, Royal Enfield managed to reinvent and to regain its market position. (In doing so, the company, in a very corporate way, reinforced what the German philosopher Frederick Nietszche had to say, when he wrote: 'That which does not kill me makes me stronger!') The continuing saga of the Royal Enfield Bullet, its brand resurgence, and presence on the Indian roads forms the first case study of this chapter.

The Eicher Group, one of India's leading automotive groups with diversified interests in the manufacture of automotive ancillaries and garments as well as in exports brought a measure of professionalism into the Royal Enfield operations, at its plants in Chennai and Jaipur. By all accounts, the Enfield resurgence finally fell into place with the appointment of its young biker—CEO, Siddartha Lal, in 2000. Lal and his team have brought about a quality revolution backed by a strategic communications plan that has turned the fortunes of the company around. The new team saw quality in every aspect of the company's growth, as the key factor to market success. The company made considerable investments in modernizing its manufacturing and design technology, that were backed by quality systems. The production line was a typical example. There are, for instance, about 1300 components that go into the manufacture of a single Royal Enfield bike. This entire process now has about 380 quality parameters that need to be adhered to. This means that there is now a bottom-up process where the workman on the assembly line has been made the 'owner of the process'. Simultaneously, the company took the all important step of reinventing its brand.

'It all began with our brand name', says Ashish Joshi, Product Manager, 'In keeping with customer perception, we decided that our company would now be known as Royal Enfield, as opposed to Royal Enfield Motors'. The second step was a simple, yet effective one. Product brands, it was decided, was the way ahead to build the Royal Enfield brand. The company created a new Royal Enfield logo, which is now used on all its bikes. It then classified its standard models under different categories of the Bullet. Broadly classified under the 'roadster' category, the Bullet brands included the following models: Campus, Electra, Machismo, as well as the 350cc and 500cc models. Creating a new niche in the market was its all new cruiser range—the Royal Enfield Thunderbird.

For Royal Enfield, new bikes meant customers. And, before long, Royal Enfield's production, marketing and R&D teams were talking to customers and ascertaining their biking needs. Thus, communication was the key, that aided in the determination of the 'psychological barriers' that prevented potential customers from buying an Enfield bike. The Royal Enfield features its gear on its right, in the tradition of British classic bikes, while most modern bikes have their gears on the left side. That was the first change.

While retaining its traditional Enfield line-up, the gear shift and brakes were switched to fall in line with the other market models. Potential buyers, the company discovered, who typically rode the less-powered bikes, were afraid of the bike's size and of kick-starting it. Better start-up equipment ensured a smoother start for newer versions of the Royal Enfield. Target customer groups were invited to test ride new era Royal Enfields at dealers' places, while company executives gleaned first-hand feedback from them. For existing customers, events like the Royal Customer Meet and the Rider Mania for bikers were organized to build on brand loyalty.

Fig 9.2: The Royal Enfield Bullet and Thunderbird Bikes

Into the Great Indian Wide

Before Royal Enfield took the fast track to building its brand, its team took a significant pause to understand its mission. The result was the Royal Enfield SoCo—which stands for 'Simple Overriding Communication Objective', which is the equivalent of a corporate brand statement:

The Royal Enfield SoCo reads: 'Royal Enfield is the motorcycling icon of India. It delivers a unique motorcycling experience through its power, riding comfort and distinctive beat.'

This statement is the essence of the Royal Enfield corporate brand. In the three years since, the company has created a revolution from within, leading to its resurgence in the Indian two-wheeler markets. At the same time, it has made a concerted effort to reach out to a significant market in the west, particularly in Europe and the United States. How has the company been able to build its brand?

The brand building function at Royal Enfield is overseen by the Product Management Department. Siddhartha Lal, who oversees product quality, is also part of the team. Here, the brand function oversees four thrust areas:

- Advertising, handled by RMG David, the O&M affiliate.
- Brand Management, comprising accessories, clubs, events and special services.
- Public Relations, handled by Genesis PR, the Indian affiliate of Burson-Marsteller.
- Web Management, overseen by D'Zine Garage.

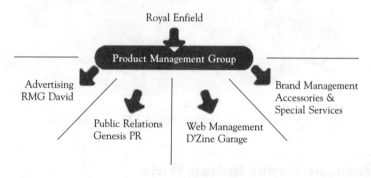

Fig 9.3: The Royal Enfield Brand-builders

To elaborate on the above model, the company builds its brand around the premise of 'a unique motorcycling experience' with its products, accessories, clubs, services and integrated communications campaign. The advertising function is overseen by RMG David in Chennai. The agency handles the print and television commercials for the company. In 2003, there were two key print campaigns running. One was for the more traditional Bullet Electra, with the tagline: 'Everyone makes way for the Bullet'. Here, the emphasis was on the dominance of the road—a standalone reputation that the Bullet can rightfully stake claim to, among India's two-wheelers. The cruiser model Thunderbird, aimed at urban professionals, has a single keyword: 'Escape'. In terms of its brand-stand, the stylistic Thunderbird offered its rider an 'escape' from the grind.

Chaitanya Prakash of Genesis PR called Royal Enfield 'the most loved' of its client-brands. Genesis PR oversees the design and structure of the PR campaign. The SoCo statement of Royal Enfield was developed in conjunction with Genesis PR, which oversees the company's media relations programme. Chaitanya Prakash was quick to emphasize the different PR approaches for Royal Enfield's corporate and product brands. The PR campaign addresses the print, audio-visual and digital media. When it comes to the corporate brand, Royal Enfield is the resurgent, back-on-track market leader, whose performance is its greatest testimony. Product brands, on the other hand, are supported through PR campaigns that spotlight launches and promote the ride experience.

Fig 9.4: The Royal Enfield Brand in its Print and Web Avatars

The Royal Enfield website: www.royalenfield.com focusses on building an online community of Bullet lovers in India and abroad. Vernon Dias of D'Zine Garage points out that the web is the most accountable and credible medium for a brand-building initiative. In September 2003, Vernon observed that 60 percent of the website's traffic were international visitors, while 40 percent were from the Indian subcontinent. He attributed this to higher Internet connectivity in the west. The results of the website initiative have showed. Since Royal Enfield revamped its website, its overall traffic has risen from about 250 visitors a day to 2,600 visitors a day. In this light, Vernon stresses that the Royal Enfield has achieved its web objective:

- To acquire visitors through registrations, e-mailers and offline mailers.
- To retain their interest through content and web-usability.
- To fulfill their needs through online product dealerships.

Interestingly enough, the website played catalyst to the first ever Royal Enfield biker meet held in Goa in 2002, where over 40 bikers congregated for two days. Community-building activities such as biker meets and workshops are another key agenda for Royal Enfield. R. Shankar, General Manager (Sales), points out that Enfield, which started several Bullet clubs a few years ago, plans to revitalize them. These clubs have over 2,500 members and are still growing. The results of these initiatives are obvious. From 20,487 bikes sold in 2000–2001, the Royal Enfield tally crossed the 25,000 mark with 26,610 bikes sold in 2002–2003.

Siddhartha Lal envisions the Royal Enfield future: 'We are firmly committed to being in the power and leisure bikes segment. There's an enormous potential out there and as incomes grow, people want to upgrade to a more charismatic and powerful bike and we are in a good position to exploit this.' As the Royal Enfield juggernaut rides out, an intensely competitive global market is going to size up the efforts of this lone rider. But going by the impetus of the brand in 2003, it is quite clear that Royal Enfield intends to go the long run.

When Icons Shine

The V-formation is an example of nature at her strategic best. Millions of years, migrating birds learned what the new era corporates have also known for a while now: 'Strategy pays'. The V-formation involves a bird at the head that takes the resistance followed by birds on the side. On long intercontinental journeys, this formation has been found to be ideal for birds. Fighter jets, Nascar racers and cyclists take up this formation for wind resistance. And, corporate brands aren't far behind. It is not a rare occurrence for a corporate brand to swoop in on a market target, with the other product brands in tow. This analogy lends itself to a larger interpretation in the context of the new era Corporate.

Corporations and conglomerates today are right on top of corporate communications practices. They swoop in on markets with strategic combinations of product, services and market affiliates. For an example, consider the TATA brand with its affiliate market interests in automobiles, business services, consumer goods, information technology, and software.

Corporate communicators here are challenged to disseminate brand philosophy and core messages across diverse cultures, countries and even continents. Here again, the communicator is confronted by the three strategy options. Kitchen and Schultz outline them in *Raising the Corporate Umbrella*. The first of these is the centralized approach, where the brand and its messages are disseminated in a similar manner across all audience domains. Corporations of the last century with centralized administrations preferred this mode of communication to establish control. The second decentralized approach allows for affiliate companies to make their own communication decisions while remaining faithful to the brand philosophy. This bold new approach is favoured by new era companies and has found many takers in the FMCG (Fast Moving Consumer Goods) sector. Third, the hybrid approach that works on the popular principle of 'think global, act local'— i.e., this approach builds its success on brand vision provided by the parent organization complemented by inputs from the affiliate organizations.

You will find one of the most compelling arguments for corporate communications embedded in the Collins Dictionary definition of a corporation. According to it, a corporation is 'a group of people authorized by law to act as an individual and having its own powers, duties and liabilities'. The creation of a voice, a brand domain, from which core messages emit to a scattered spectrum of audiences forms one of the biggest challenges of corporate communications. As David Appasamy of Sify observes in his insight, there are three crucial steps to corporate communications strategy in the long term: create an identity, build the brand and maintain its reputation.

This approach is simplicity itself. It is a bird's eye view of the deep and intricate process that goes into building a corporate brand. What it implies is that the first step for a corporate—a business, company or corporation—is to create its identity in every relevant form. The second step is to build its brand, within and without the organization, paying particular attention to audiences within the public domain. Finally, having created the identity and built the brand, the conclusive step is to 'manage its reputation'. This last step is a lifeline for established companies and corporations that are building on the impetus of their brand vision and goodwill. It also helps to remember that no two corporates on this planet are similar. Like persons, they differ in every respect. Strategies then, will differ. And, the task of the corporate communicator remains the same. Create the identity, build your brand, and manage your reputation.

Innovating for the Infoway

The Sify office at Chennai's Tidel Park complex is a high-energy zone, spread across a networked space of over 100,000 square feet. The 24/7/365 workstyle is a reality here. Making it real is a committed workforce of over 400 IT professionals, each of whom brings their own competencies to Sify's mission of 'Making the Internet work for you'. Sify provides integrated end-to-end solutions and a range of products and services for both corporates and consumers. In Sify's own words: 'We are the only integrated end-to-end e-Solutions provider in India. We design and develop a host of customized e-Commerce and Network Connectivity Solutions that connect your critical business systems and offer a seamless data network directly with customers, suppliers, vendors and staff'.

Over the last seven years, Sify Limited has assiduously built its brand around these competency areas. Sify's CEO, R. Ramaraj brings his unique understanding of IT to aid the realization of Sify's business vision. In this striving, the corporation has emerged the clear leader in its chosen realm of Internet and networking. In the tradition of the Internet pioneer that it is, Sify rode the crest of the

Fig 9.5: The Sify Corporate Logo

IT boom in the late 1990s. When the markets slumped, Sify quickly proved its mettle as a market leader, in the months that followed. The corporation focussed itself on new and emerging market opportunities, explored new technologies and gained ground in market survival-turned success. So, how does 'Making the Internet work for you' translate into Sify's corporate mission? That answer lies in the core reactor of Sify's online avatar: **www.sifycorp.com**. Enter its online domain and you are introduced to the vision behind its success:

Our Purpose

Our purpose is to make a qualitative difference to the lives of millions of people and organizations by harnessing the power of India and of the Internet. We will do this by empowering them with the potential of the Internet and by leveraging the capabilities of Indian Knowledge Resources.

Our Vision is to be the dominant and profitable India centric Internet company by:

- Building on India's unique advantages.
- Being the leader in terms of market share, quality, revenue, growth and gross margins.
- Adding value to our stakeholders: namely investors, customers, peers and associates.
- Being enablers and catalysts of the Internet for positive change.

—(www.sifycorp.com)

Box 9.2
Corporate Communications—The Company's
Business Strategy Extension

David Appasamy stands on the frontline of corporate communications practice in India. As the Chief Communications Officer of Sify Corporation—formerly known as Satyam Infoway, he takes on the challenge of building its corporate brand, across a challenging spectrum of audiences. He can be reached at davidappasamy@sifycorp.com. A quintessential corporate communicator, he brings his unique people skills and untiring enthusiasm to his mission of corporate brand building:

The need for corporate communications, while gaining acceptance, is often confused with marketing of a corporate brand. The fundamental need for corporate communications goes much deeper than that. For it is to do with the corporate citizenship, and the business strategy of every organization. Much as citizens of a country have fundamental rights, and are governed by a social code of conduct enshrined in the constitution, corporate citizens also come under not only a code of conduct, but also norms defined by the government, on behalf of the citizens of a country. In short, every corporate citizen, while its ultimate aim may be to generate economic surplus, has to benefit society as a whole. So they have to elicit the support of citizens, and the government, by establishing how they are benefiting society to grow and flourish. To do this, they have to create awareness of their mission, and the values with which they will conduct their business. This is the first reason for corporate communications as a professional practice.

Secondly, in competitive economies, and particularly in developing, tightly regulated economies, how a company is viewed can make the difference between success and failure. There have been many cases where lack of popular support and goodwill have led to companies being nationalised, or regulated out of existence. Air India's nationalisation, and subsequent decline from being one of the world's best airlines, is an example. Then there are companies whose products or services are deemed inimicable for

(contd.)

Box 9.2 (contd.)

the good of society, and have to diversify into areas considered desirable for society or perish. Having diversified, they have to communicate their achievements to win appreciation for the contribution they are making to society.

An example of such a company in India is ITC Limited. A company that was primarily a cigarettes giant, certainly not good for society, successfully diversified into: hotels to boost tourism and earn foreign exchange; edible oils to reduce the import bill; paper for the same reason, and now is spearheading eChoupals for the development of farmers using the Internet. More importantly, ITC has consistently communicated these achievements, to generate goodwill despite its traditional lines of businesses.

Another reason why corporate communications maybe essential for business strategy is when a company is in a nascent industry not easily understood or supported by government. Such was the case with Sify Limited, India's leader in Internet, networking and eCommerce services. Sify consistently communicated the importance of the Internet and networks to the government and the public, to become accepted as mainstream. In fact, in just five years, Sify has entered the consciousness of people strongly enough to be declared a 'Super Brand'! More importantly, the government, businesses and people now recognise and accept the importance of the Internet as a medium of communications and business.

As recognition of the importance and role of corporate communications spreads, it will not remain the sole responsibility of the corporate communications head. Rather, the CEO and the top management of every organization will become key communicators for their companies, working towards a common goal aimed at eliciting the goodwill of the societies they operate in. Only then can we truly say that the practice of corporate communications has come of age.

The Sify corporate brand towers over its two brand families: the corporate service brands and the consumer service brands. The lesser known, but dominant business-to-business brands are Sify Enterprise Solutions and Sify e-learning. Among the Sify 'consumer' brands are Sify Online, Sify Broadband and Sify iWay. Each of these offers you a unique view of the digitized business vision that surges through the Sify juggernaut, as it grows every moment of its 24/7/365 existence. In terms of communication strategy, the Sify brand and its core messages reach out to both internal and external audiences. The internal audiences include employees who are referred to as associates, while Sify's broad external audiences in the public domain include customers, stakeholders, investors, the government, the media, financial markets, opinion makers, pressure groups and potential employees. But the Sify experience tells us, the first significant initiative in the new era organization should begin with a very innovative internal communications campaign.

Fig. 9.6: The Sify Brand Family

In February 2001, a 400 strong team from seven offices scattered over Chennai moved into their new hi-tech 1,00,000 square foot office at Tidel Park. The man with the onerous challenge on his hands was David Appasamy, the Corporate Communications Chief at Sify Limited. His brief was clear. Within weeks, the entire Sify team had to get used to their new workspace, and more importantly, settle into a new way of working: the 'creation of an internal culture' that would come to be known as the 'Sify Way'.

This was particularly daunting, as associates tended to be intimidated by the size and world-class interiors of the new office. Worse, they tended to bunch together with the people they had worked with in the individual offices they came from, and did not mix with the associates from other offices and businesses. In the weeks that followed, a slew of contests inviting the Sify team to get to know the office were unleashed. In one memorable contest, Sify professionals were invited to name different parts of the sprawling workspace. This meant that every one of them got a chance to visit and christen important parts of the office. And, in time, the names became the basis of an organizational map that led to the various departments in the organization, complete with street signs!

Soon, strangers within the organization become affable co-workers. In the years since, a slew of company events, each more imaginative than the other, continue to be initiated, to build a vibrant internal culture. These include a denim day, *golgappa* eating contests, a regatta winning rowing team, a treasure hunt—on the intranet and off it, quiz competitions, an ethnic day, all thought up and executed by a volunteer team of young associates called the 'Fundoos'! The Fundoos run these fun-at-work programmes called the 'Work FUNdas' series, culminating in a fun event for associates and their families every December. As David points out: 'While Sify and its mission statement form the basis of everything that goes on in our workspace, having a fun filled work place keeps everyone operating at high energy and creative levels'.

Fig 9.7: The Sify Corporate Website and Information Portal

In the years since, the circle of internal communications has grown. For instance, the Sify Intranet has become a significant form of internal communication within the organization. Every month, all the members of the Sify team receive a copy of Sify Pulse—an e-zine with updates on all that's happening at Sify. Furthermore, a quarterly print magazine *Out of the Box* not only provides Sify information to its team, but adds value to their personal lives and families with health tips, quizzes, travel advisories, book reviews and profiles of Sify associates. Every Sify team member receives a new screensaver featuring a theme every month. The other internal audiences include the investors and stakeholders. Here, David Appasamy defines a stakeholder as anyone who is affected by the reputation and performance of the company. Sify's corporate citizenship role is played out in significant initiatives like 'Alambana' through which Sify extends its expertise to reach out to society's less privileged members. No lip service, here. The spouses of Sify associates manage Alambana and reach out to educate children from families that have scarcely imagined the power of Information Technology and the Internet to transform lives.

As India's largest network and e-Commerce services company, Sify has to address many audience groups in the public domain, the most important of these being its customers. The term 'customer' in the Sify context can range from an individual using a Sify Internet access account, to a corporate client investing in Sify's business services for sophisticated connectivity services like 'Virtual Private Networks', that keep his company communicating real time and running ERP systems such as SAP. While the marketing groups in each of these service sub-brands work on integrated marketing communications for their services, the Sify corporate communications team works at building the corporate brand through strategic messages and information to Sify's external audiences. This has resulted in the constant reinforcement of the company brand, and quicker decision making that has given Sify its competitive edge. No wonder Sify was selected as a 'Super Brand' in just five years of its operation!

Investor audiences across the Sify corporation are provided with timely, updated information on the company's progress in the stock markets. Investor meetings cover new ground in reaching out to institutional and potential investors. As this case study was being written in 2003, Sify crossed the Rubicon of corporate growth—it broke even in the fifth year of its operations. This financial milestone was a remarkable achievement. It came a mere two years after the dotcom crash of 2001. Most importantly, Sify's corporate environment gives you the opportunity to watch the awesome processes of Corporatization, Digitization and Globalization work hand-in-hand to create the definitive 21st century corporation with a winning culture—all aimed at making the Internet work for you.

In the Long Run

In his Four Quartets, quoted at the beginning of chapter 6, T. S. Elliot reminds us that our most significant journeys are the ones that return us to the places that we know best. The moment of reckoning is their rediscovery—for the first time. In that sense, this book began with the 21st century Corporate, explored the evolving facets of corporate communications, sought out its domains of influence, highlighted its advertising and public relations components, plugged into the traditional and new media, stopping by at businesses and non-profit organizations to make its way to the ground zero of corporate communications deployment: companies and corporations.

Here, we first established the distinction between these two kinds of organizations. Corporate communications for a company was studied in the light of its real-time application in the Royal Enfield Company, an established leader in one of the world's largest two-wheeler markets. The company reworked and reinvented its way back into market prominence. Its teams reached out to customer-bases, understood their aspirations and apprehensions. And then, in a remarkable corporate turn-around, Royal Enfield began its cruise on the home stretch to market leadership.

The cornerstones of corporate communications strategy were firmly in place, as Royal Enfield revived its flagging fortunes. In its recent history, we first saw its internal makeover, and then a revival of its brand. In doing so, the company keenly built its audiences through its concerted brand strategy. In India, the Royal Enfield resurgence has redefined the biker experience in terms of the leisure and power segments. Globally, it continues to foster and network with global communities of Enfield aficionados. It wisely chose to market its cruiser-Thunderbird in India, while its classic models were revamped for the foreign markets. At the time of writing this chapter, the first of the international power bikes was making its entry into the Indian markets. How Royal Enfield will strategize with its first real challenger on the horizon will make for gripping corporate history.

Then came Sify Limited. And, its unrestricted deployment of corporate communications strategy in its global offices. The Satyam Infoway juggernaut is a key example of new era Indian corporations that are establishing key brand images in the globalized markets of the 21st century. The corporation opened up the possibilities of the Internet age for corporate and customer-bases across India. Its integrated end-to-end solutions and range of products and services spanned the spectrum of the Internet: Connectivity, Content, Commerce and Community. Taking the cue from its mission statement, Sify Limited has harnessed the unlimited potential of the Internet by leveraging it with Indian knowledge resources. Over its seven-year existence, we watched Sify re-invent itself to address new market opportunities, explore new business territory and, importantly, to chart new ground in its market survival-turned-success. We watched vibrant and responsive processes of Corporatization, Digitization and Globalization synergies make Sify a definitive 21st century Corporate. The last words on the subject definitely belong to the folks at www.brightpr.com: 'The game remains the same, it's just the size and shape of the pitch that's changed.' That truth is reflected in leadership on India's verdant highways as on the information superhighway. Either way, you know it when you see it.

Signposts

- Corporate communications is a long-term strategic initiative usually created within a company to communicate its brand and core messages.
- It proceeds from the core of the company—its senior management—in a credible and informative way to impact internal and external audiences.
- Corporate communications is an evolved response to the dynamic communications need of the 21st century Corporate.
- In the final analysis, all corporate communications strategy works its way to the following three processes: Creating an identity, building your brand, and managing its reputation.

Corporate-Initiative

This is the moment of truth. And, it occurs in the B2B realm. Everything that you know about corporate communications is being put to test, as you take on an assignment to head the corporate communications section of a BPO (Business Process Outsourcing) corporation. Briefly, the multi-billion dollar BPO realm is a sunrise sector for India in the decade to come. There are four stages of evolution for organizations in the BPO realm. In the order of importance, they are call centres, BPO companies, BSP (Business Services Provisioning) companies and virtual enterprises. The first three organizations have already established themselves with remarkable success. Typically, the working of a corporation in the BPO realm would involve approaching potential client-companies, corporations and conglomerates, with a view to getting their processes outsourced, enabling them to cut costs and concentrate on core competencies.

The desired organization is the virtual enterprise, where entire organizations work online, outsourcing peripheral work processes to players in the BPO realm. This way, they exhibit a complete focus on their competency areas. In the light of this chapter's learnings, how would you strategize for a globalized BPO corporation's communications approach? Would it be centralized to ensure complete consistency with the brand vision or will the strategy be decentralized to allow country offices to build their own versions of brands in dynamic market environments that they are familiar with? One way to approach this decision is to create a three part corporate advertising campaign that could be adapted to diverse business cultures. Use this campaign as the basis to explain how you would communicate the corporate's brand to its internal and external audiences. Finally, as a point of reference, compare this Corporate-Initiative with the Communication-Initiative of the second chapter. How much has your perception of corporate communications changed since? And, how do you think it will evolve from this point? The answers will mark the first of the milestones on your journey as a corporate communicator.

🔲🔲🔲🔲🔲🔲

Sources

Publications

Blair, M., Armstrong, R. and Murphy, M. (2003). *The 360 Degree Brand in Asia: Creating More Effective Marketing Communications.* John Wiley & Sons (Asia) Pte Ltd, Singapore.

Collins, J.C. and Porras, J.I. (2000). *Built to Last.* Random House Business Books, London.

Croteau, D. and Hoynes, W. (2001). *The Business of Media: Corporate Media and the Public Interest.* Pine Forge Press, Thousand Oaks.

Jute, Andre. (1996). *Grids: The Structure of Graphic Design.* RotoVision SA, Switzerland.

Kitchen, Philip J. and Schultz, Don E. (2001). *Raising the Corporate Umbrella: Corporate Communications in the 21st Century.* Palgrave, New York.

Periodicals

Fernandez, Joseph. (June 2000). 'Corporate Communications', *Business Mandate*, Chennai.
Kamath, Vinay. (12th September 2002). 'The Enfield Resurgence', *Catalyst, The Hindu Business Line*, Chennai.
Navin, Puja. (2nd December 2002). 'Winning Solutions: Public Relations', *Excel—The New Indian Express*.

Online References

http://www.royalenfield.com
http://www.sifycorp.com
http://www.sifycorp.com
http://www.brightpr. com

Interviews

Ashish Joshi
Product Development Manager
Royal Enfield, Chennai

Chaitanya Prakash
Genesis PR, Chennai

David Appasamy,
General Manager—Corporate Communications,
Sify Corporation, Chennai

Girish Mylandla
Motorcycle Expeditionist, Chennai

Rajesh Jambotkar
Management Professional
Boston, USA

S. Varun
Motorcycle Expeditionist, Chennai

Vernon Dias
D'Zine Garage, Mumbai

10 The Corporate Communicator and You: From Signposts to Milestones

For all that has been—thanks,
To all that shall be—yes!

—Dag Hammarskjold, the UN Secretary-General

A ripple is the oldest idea in the universe. And, every known school of thought celebrates its existence. Every action, every move in this universe makes a difference. It affects and influences everything else around it. Nowhere do you find this better exemplified than in the gentle oriental art of Tai Chi. For three decades now, Tai Chi has stepped into the global spotlight with its gentle swirl of philosophy and well-being. Its circular 'Yin-Yang' symbol has become one of the most popular icons of our age. In popular culture, Tai Chi's flowing movements have come to symbolize a lifestyle that is serene, centred and supremely balanced. Tai Chi, in its various forms, is inspired by Nature.

In its basic form, Tai Chi resembles a classical dance—in slow motion. Once your attention is caught by its graceful, arc-like movements, you reflect Nature's tranquil movements. In the Tai Chi 'Small Wave' form, you simulate the flight of a butterfly, gently part the silky mane of a wild horse, and spread the mystic wings of the eagle within you. Every move you make is slow, rhythmic and totally centred. And, its silken movements make you keenly aware of the world around you. In ending, you acknowledge your 'Oneness with the Universe' with a subtle bow, followed by the traditional 'Sun-Moon Fist Salute'. But do not let these smooth and flowing movements deceive you. For beyond them, lies a shrewd martial art. In its combat form, Tai Chi is a series of quicksilver moves that can disarm the most unsuspecting opponent.

In the mysterious orient, Asia's martial arts were borne of spiritual traditions that thrived in its monasteries. In those turbulent times, the quest for spirituality went hand-in-and with the tested ability to survive. This was the age of the warrior-monk. Asia today celebrates the lives of these enlightened, formidable men who held their own ground, while holding forth on their philosophy, simply known as the Way.

Interestingly, Tai Chi's history has a touch of India to it. It is influenced by Shaolin Kungfu, a legacy of Bodhidharma, the Indian warrior-monk who journeyed to the Shaolin Temple. In its full form, Tai Chi Chuan means the 'Supreme Ultimate Fist' and, is rooted in the Chinese philosophy of Tao (or the Way), which dates back to as early as 122 BC. To picture Tai Chi's origins, you need to look no further than the sweeping images of 'Crouching Tiger, Hidden Dragon'—the celluloid epic that swept the Oscars in 2001. The film is set in the breathtaking Wu Dan monastery in northern China, where Tai Chi was born, grew and evolved from China's Taoist tradition into one of the world's most respected systems for meditation, exercize and self-defense.

So, what does old world Tai Chi have to do with new era corporate communications? Everything—if you really think about it. Tai Chi has rapidly become a metaphor for corporate life. It holds tremendous potential as a strategy tool and team motivator for modern corporates. Of particular interest is the 'Qi-Gong' or meditative exercises that precede any form of Tai Chi. And, at the end of the Qi-Gong set, you are invited to take the energy that the Universe offers you, by means of a circular gesture with your hands. And, having become a source of life-giving energy, you are then urged to share it. In doing so, you imagine yourself as the source of Chi—or vital energy, sharing it in ripples that spread to the outermost realms of the universe.

In his book, *The Tao of Leadership*, Robert Heider (1995, p. 35) dwells on this powerful facet of the Taoist thought:

> Ground yourself in the single principle so that your behaviour is wholesome and effective...Your behaviour influences others through a ripple effect. A ripple effect works because everyone influences everyone else. Powerful people are powerful influences...the ripple effect spreads through the cosmos. Remember that your influence begins with you and ripples outward. So be sure that your influence is both potent and wholesome.

From the perspective of the internal and external audiences of a corporate, Tai Chi offers time-honoured insights for a globalized age.

Now, imagine a team of corporate professionals who are learning to perform a Tai Chi sequence in unison. In time, each team member grows to realize that his or her individual moves (or, corporate skills) contributes through planned strategy to the overall movement of the team (or, corporate mission). The synergy realized by the team in the Tai Chi form can then be effectively translated into corporate reality. Beyond team dynamics, Tai Chi's principles of balance, centredness and focus are key contributions to any corporate team's longevity in a change-driven world. Again, a Company's vision is the core of its enterprise. Its message is spread in 'ripples' that begin with the inner circle of influence—the internal audiences—and then reach out to the outer circle of influence—the external audience.

The application of Tai Chi and, through them, Taoist management priniciples has only started being explored by companies and organizations in India recently. In the brand context, we discovered an uncanny resemblance between Tai Chi's outlook and Ogilvy's 360 degree branding practice. Corporate thinkers today view market strategy as a enhanced form of corporate warfare. Here, today's corporate strategizes for forays into an intensely competitive global enviroment (through market strategy) and builds its presence as a formidable long-term player (through corporate communications). Today in India, you will find the principles of this gentle martial art of Asia's warrior-monks applied to organizations as diverse as the American Consulate, the MRF Pace Foundation, Indian Oil, National Institute of Port Management and the Krishnamurti Foundation of India. As these organizations have discovered, there is explosive potential in this apparently gentle approach. All of this fits in with the modern accepted view of corporate communications, congruously. Tai Chi's ripple effect principle, in other words, is a cornerstone of modern corporate communications theory. And, a key to understanding how you can nurture the corporate communicator in you.

The Nostradamus Effect

Of the billions of species on Earth only one life-form ever worries about the future. Or, theorizes about it. And, Nostradamus, the 16th century French seer was the highest evidence of that very human preoccupation. Still, it is this quest that distinguishes mankind from the evolutionary scale—a living sense of the future. We choose to begin this chapter with that living sense of the future with three insights that are expected to revolutionize the new era.

In *The 360 Degree Brand in Asia*, its authors peer into the future, terming the new era—the 'Pacific Century'. They begin by placing the 21st century in a historic perspective. They observe that historians view the 19th century as 'the European Century' and the 20th Century as 'one that belonged to America'. They stress that 21st century will be the 'Pacific Century'. And, for good reason. About 65 percent of the world's population will be living in Asia. Also, 65 percent of the world's wealth is located in the 'Pacific Rim' countries (Japan, Korea, Taiwan, etc.). After the European Union, the Asian nations will emerge as 'the political, economic and cultural powerhouse of the world'.

Speaking at the time the dotcoms boom was at its crest in the 1990s, Louis Gerstner, then head of IBM spoke of the famous 'second wave'. It was his view that the first dotcom boom was only a sign of things to come. In the second wave, Gerstner foresaw traditional businesses incorporating digital technology to empower their business growth. This, according to Gerstner, was when the true potential of the computer revolution would be unleashed. In the first chapter, we discovered, the 21st century Corporate, is being empowered by the dynamic processes of Corporatization, Digitization and Globalization. We also watched businesses become companies that grew in corporations that have now established themselves as conglomerates. From the looks of it, that 'second wave' has begun.

Third, the 21st century's first sunrise sector—biotechnology is here. A nascent science, biotechnology is all set to impact sectors like agriculture, chemicals, health care, industry, pharmaceuticals and environment. In India, it has already grown into a Rs 1,000 billion industry with about 800 companies, 60 percent of which are in the pharmaceutical and health industry sector. And, India is an emerging hub with its seven agro-climatic zones, 19 major crops and spread of more than 5,000 plant species.

Biotechnology, of course, is the application and use of genetic engineering techniques in a wide spread of fields. It is multi-disciplinary in nature and draws heavily from basic sciences like genetics, microbiology, biochemistry, molecular biology, cell and tissue culture. In addition, there are other important spin-offs like bio-informatics, enzyme manufacture and medical devices. Unlike information technology however, biotech, as it is popularly known, relies on a trained and knowledge-intensive workforce that is backed by sophisticated infrastructure. Typical professional specializations here range from research and development to production and marketing. As Satish Khanna observes in *The Value Builder:*

> Even biotechnology is becoming linked with information technology as it is all about DNA-encoded information. It will be essential for each business to align its corporate DNA with the new emerging economy...Each age or wave in the past has had a very significant impact on the evolution of our civilisation, the way our ancestors lived and the way they conducted business. Each new age had a higher impact than the previous one and the current information and knowledge age is no exception...The foundation of the fifth wave is

advanced biotechnology, bio-informatics, advanced Internet applications and the like.

(Khanna, 2000, p.9)

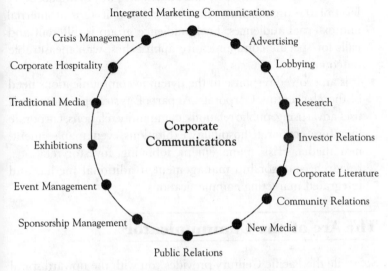

Fig. 10.1: The Corporate Commmunications Universe

And, what does all of this translate into for the crporate cmmunicator of the 21st century? To begin with, the entry of the corporate sector into biotechnology and its related fields brings in the need for an integrated marketing communications approach. This effectively means that corporate communicators in the decade ahead have their task clearly cut out for them. Biotechnology for the corporate communicator, translates into strategizing for corporates, building their image and market presence with a new set of internal and external audiences. In all of this, the triune processes of Corporatization, Digitization and Globalization will continue their ongoing revolution with their emphasis on market success, product and service quality, backed by research and development. Corporate communications will continue to evolve around its core nature, as articulated in the second chapter:

• It is a long-term strategic initiative created within a company to communicate its corporate brand and core messages. In a triune process for corporates, it creates an identity, builds its brand and manages its reputation.

- It proceeds from the top management of the company—its senior management—in a credible and informative way to impact every level of the organization. In a larger sense, it aims at internal and external audiences. Each audience group is different and calls for specific communicative approaches, with measurable outcomes.
- It is an evolved response to the dynamic communications need of the 21st century Corporate. As part of its strategic armoury, it uses advertising, public relations, community relations, corporate literature, corporate hospitality, exhibitions, event management, new media, crisis management, lobbying, investor relations, research, sponsorship management, traditional media, and integrated marketing communications.

The Arc of the Communicator

So, while the Pacific Century provides you with the upward spiral of career challenge, the next best thing to do is to strategize for your own career as a corporate communicator. That is precisely what this chapter sets out to do, which is also reason enough for this chapter to be titled: 'From Signposts to Milestones'. In charting the course of your career, it always helps to look at it, in terms of a time-specific model. The average corporate professional has about three productive decades ahead of him or her.

The average person's career graph usually takes off in their mid twenties and continues till their mid fifties. Our productive work life generally spans an outer limit of 7300 days, spread across the three most productive decades of our life. One often hears that a person's twenties are meant for learning, and the thirties for earning! This aphorism holds true for the career of a corporate communicator. In terms of organisational growth, the first decade is your living decade—where you learn the ropes of the business that you are in. The second decade tests your ability to climb the corporate ladder, one in which the efforts of your initial years have

Box 10.1
A Corporate Communicator—The Organization's Catalyst of Change

Dr Emma Gonsalvez heads Emmaus, a Chennai-based HRD consultancy. For over a decade now, she and her team have led corporates and non-profit organizations to this realization. Energy (or human potential within work environments) is tapped through encounters leading to an overall empowerment. Here is her profile of the corporate communicator of the 21st century:

A Corporate Communicator to me, is an organization's most powerful catalyst of change. He or she is an all-rounder, who takes up many communicative roles within the every day buzz of the work environment. An all rounder in every sense of the word, a corporate communicator is a people's person, an assertive personality and an information hub.

In my view, the model that I have found most appropriate for a Corporate Communicator is the globally popular Corporate 'DISC' Personality Factor Profile (PFP) Geier and Downey (1992). Here, every individual is assessed in terms of four parameters: Dominance (Leader), Influencing (Communicator), Stabilising (Supporter) & Cautious (Corrector). In this light, a Corporate Communicator exhibits the following traits:

A Leader with a high dominance factor in a one-to-one interaction, while being powerfully directive in a group situation.

A Communicator, being an influencer in a one-to-one interaction, and an interactive person in any group situation.

A Supporter, who is a stabilising presence in a one-to-one interaction, while being supportive within a corporate group.

A Corrector, who is cautious in one-to-one interaction, and corrective within a group situation. This last quality is a natural evolution for the first three for a Corporate Communicator.

In the 21st century Corporate, the key to any communication is Assertiveness—as opposed to forced aggressiveness or practiced passivity. Long, long, after the most passive communication has petered out and the most aggressive market strategy has lost its steam, the assertive Corporate Communicator will hold the key to long term corporate growth.

began to pay. The rise to the top of the corporate communications ladder is a fairly quick one.

As a corporate communicator you are the quintessential organization insider. You are its communications catalyst of growth. Your expertise will be reflected in its growth. Your ambit of work will reflect its scope of expansion. In other words, your career growth will be reflected in its corporate growth. For that reason, you have access to your corporate's inner circle. In a larger sense, being the hub of corporate interaction within company ranks, your view will always be seen as a representative of the pulse of the company.

Picture yourself at a meeting of the Board of Directors, early in the financial year. Here, you are called to make a strategy presentation for the corporate communications division. You will need to present your initiative, its range of activity as well as the progress that you will make over the course of the next 12 months. There is also the possibility that you may join an organization that has the more traditional public relations or advertising divisions. The viable choice here would be to go with the flow of events. The best option here would be to add impetus to the living need of the corporate and enhance its working with the enunciation of principles to a corporate communications strategy. A communications strategy, as Arup Kavan of Ogilvy Public Relations Worldwide pointed out in the fourth chapter, needs to be built around the corporate's market plan.

So, today, an empowered advertising or brand management department could enhance its brand-building exercise with corporate communications strategy, by looking beyond customers to communicate with the many audiences that exist outside the markets. Again, a public relations department always adds impetus to its strategy by incorporating in its efforts, the corporate communications understanding of the company as a brand to be built. In an intensely competitive market environment, a corporate communicator would do well to follow the tradition of Asia's warrior-monks. His/her greatest weapon is the assertive deployment of a communications strategy that builds his/her corporate's image. In short, when it comes to corporate communications, it always helps to see the company in terms of a brand whose image needs to be communicated both to internal and external organizations.

From Education to Expertise

At every level of the corporate world, professionals are rated on the parameters of knowledge, aptitude and commitment to their workplace. Like all other professional specializations, corporate communications too bases its approach on three broad parameters—the three 'E's of the corporate communicator. In the order of accomplishment, they are:

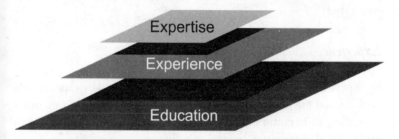

Fig. 10.2: The Three Tiers of a Corporate Career

Education

In the real world, education is always a first point of reference for guaging a corporate professional. And, so it is for the corporate communicator. Education is a broad reference to the evolving body of academic knowledge and information that you possess. It is seen as the first integral step to your current professional position. Corporate communications draws its insights from a collective body of knowledge sourced from the media realms of advertising, journalism and public relations. It also draws from corporate disciplines like business management, marketing and psychology. Added to this, is a real-time understanding of the working of print, audio-visual and digital technologies.

There are no degrees or specializations in corporate communications as yet. Ideally, a corporate degree with a specialization in advertising, marketing or public relations is a good start. Like all professional callings, however, the emphasis remains on a lifelong quest for learning. (So, don't be surprised to find yourself getting acquainted with the essentials of nanotechnology or some similar geek-friendly knowledge area, a good decade after you have passed out of college!)

Many corporate communicators that we know make it a point to learn one new thing every year to keep their spirit of learning alive and vibrant. One year, it could be flower arrangement, the next, it might be Tae Bo and the third it may be horse riding. Having made a case for education, I must also add that some of the world's best media icons revel in their minimal education—or the lack of it altogether!

Experience

By experience, is meant the broad span of time spent in a specialized professional environment. In time, it takes precedence over one's education to become one's most valued professional asset. One's professional experience begins as a signpost going onto notch up milestones of achievement, as one progresses through one's career. Ironically enough, the best corporate communicators are professionals who have spent time in the traditional conduits of the media, particularly advertising and journalism. For this reason, it makes good sense to begin one's career, with a stint in a quality media organization—be it advertising, journalism or public relations.

A stint in any of these industries will give one an invaluable insight into the ways that they think, function and operate, an invaluable advantage in the age of multi-tasking. Remember when you plot the trajectory of your career as a corporate communicator, that you will comes across its more traditional avatars. These too are an invaluable sources of work experience. They include positions such as a public affairs manager, public relations officer, media liaison officer, community relations manager, special events coordinator, publicity officer, political adviser, media adviser and lastly, a lobbyist or advocate. Experience, in whatever form you receive it, is an invaluable career asset and leads the development of your expertise—which is the third 'E' of your professional career as a corporate communicator.

Expertise

In our view, expertise is always a nurtured career competency that is born of one's aptitude, abilities. Playing catalyst to it are one's education and expertise. When your corporate needs to communicate, how do you drive that process? At this moment of truth, your expertise will provide the answer. It is that unique skill set that empowers you to deploy a corporate communications strategy—powerful and with results. Born of the synergy between your education and experience, your expertise will decide the kind of corporate communicator you are and even the choice of organization that you work for.

Typically here, you might be an masterful organizer with experience as an event manager. This could directly translate into a memorable annual general meeting for your company every year. The kind that everyone looks forward to even in a bad year. If you are a media person, you will focus on communication initiatives, a competing website, a dynamic Intranet, a new newsletter that wins industry awards every year—and, in fact, the envy of your journalistic colleagues! Your expertise could make you an industry representative, representing apex associations of your sector or vertical. In the final analysis expertise calls for the deepest kind of self-knowledge. Towards that end, you might want to ask yourself these questions when deciding on a career as a corporate communicator:

Am I a people's person? Do I develop contacts, relationships and networks steadily? Am I recognized as an assertive and reliable person to deal with? Most importantly, how do I work in a team to achieve common goals?

Am I a communicator? Beyond organizational interactive and influencing skills, do I speak and write with exceptional clarity?

Am I a strategist? Do I have a pulse on the corporate environment? Am I able to identify causes of problems, analyze future trends and predict their consequences? Can I multi-task in a dynamic environment with a cast iron reputation for keeping timelines?

Am I an analyst? Does my enquiring mind embrace the world of information and data around me to provide me with key insights into the corporate world, current affairs and global trends? How attentive am I to the small details, while overseeing the big picture?

You can, if you wish, rate yourself on a scale of one to three, on the above questions. A score of two or more on at least three questions broadly indicates that you are good material for a corporate communicator. A more thorough indicator is the Corporate DISC Personality Factor Test. Always remember that it is expertise—the third parameter for judging a communicator—that will put the spotlight on your career as a corporate communicator. It is here that the years of qualifying, the months of training and the hours of strategizing will come to their moment of truth.

Box 10.2
Communication—An Exclusive Management Function

Geraldine Lazaro has worked in Human Resource Development since the mid 1990s. For over a decade now, her experience in HRD has spanned organizations as diverse as Maxworth Orchards and Fountainhead Communications. She focusses on helping companies and organizations to realize their objectives using HR tools that empower entire workforces. Geraldine shares her view of the future corporate communicator:

In common practice in the HR field, the quest for a corporate communicator often forms the most challenging part of our job. And, there is good reason for this fact of corporate life. A communicator is, in a sense, the lifeline for a company or organization. He or she is the centralized channel of communication inside and outside an organization. In the networked era, this has meant more power—and added responsibilities—for communication professionals, that corporates are seeking out today.

In my own work, corporate communicators should take up the communication of a brand as a 'management function'. By this, I mean the communication of the brand is no longer a standalone

(contd.)

Box 10.2 (contd.)

function of an aggressive brand manager or a visible PR functionary. In this scenario, a Corporate Communicator becomes one who can see the 'big' picture—a company's brand vision—and realize communication goals that lead to the dynamic fulfillment of its corporate objectives.

A Corporate Communicator is the management's co-strategist, present at every step of the company's strategy-sessions for the future. The periodical corporate advertising campaign or quarterly press conference are a thing of the past. Today, we find that detailed communication plans are drawn up, encompassing corporate advertising, public relations, event management, internal communications—even initiatives centred around corporate citizenship.

All of this means that corporate communicators have moved from being 'specialist' to being 'generalist'. Their core expertise has moved from knowledge of a single media-driven field like advertising or public relations to the definitively powerful realm of brand communication. So, what does this mean for Corporate Communicators of our new era organizations? It simply translates into a radical change of perspective. Corporate Communicators must view themselves as management professionals who are delivering on communication goals that fulfill brand objectives.

Fast forward to the real-time world of the 21st century Corporate. Here, in the midst of its labyrinthine working, you will find that every corporate has a 'living need', when it comes to communication. All too often, you will find that that you are asked to make a split-second decision on how a particular message will be communicated. The bigger the corporate, the more complex its communications strategy, which is why it helps to see your career as a corporate communicator in three unfolding roles:

The Corporate Strategist

Two decades ago, in the more predictable 20th century, a company that wished to create a 'corporate image' had it relatively easier. A single dimension advertising and public relations campaign, run in the print and audio-visual media did the trick. Markets, and corporate thinking, were customer-centric. One 'consistent' approach suited all audiences. Not anymore. The Ogilvy Group Worldwide puts the new era perspective in focus, when it speaks of 'influencing the influencers'. As a new era corporate communicator, you work to create an identity, build the brand and manage its reputation. You are your corporate's trusted brand builder. You brainstorm with its inner circle, understand its vision, internalize it. As a corporate strategist, you will 'preserve the core and stimulate progress', creating a powerful corporate communications initiative that is layered on its long-term strategy.

Here, you will need to strategize, by defining goals in terms of the company's brand vision, identify internal and external audiences and create its communications strategy. The three stages of creating an identity, building the brand and managing its reputation call for different approaches in a corporate communicator. At the heart of these different approaches, lies strategy, the phased implementation of a communications plan. The step beyond this involves the research and evaluation component. Here, you get to implement the strategy, while addressing its opportunities and problems. In the age of accountability, when a strategy is completed, the corporate communicator analyzes its results. He evaluates the strategy for its planning, implementation, and effectiveness. The corporate strategist is the first of the roles that you play as a corporate communicator in the new era.

The Consummate Communicator

The second key role that you can look ahead to, is that of a consummate communicator. Towards this end, you will use every possible means to communicate with the audiences of your corporate. In doing so, you will become the assertive voice as well as the hub of organizational information. To every level of your organization, particularly the senior management, you will represent the pulse of the organization, its instant opinion source. Your job position would entail gathering information from every valid source within the corporate and outside it. When it comes to the establishment of the corporate as a brand, it involves developing and maintaining the corporate's identity through corporate advertising and public relations initiatives. The difference is that here the corporate's brand and reputation is presented rather than its products or services.

An extension of this responsibility is co-ordinating with external advertising and public relations agencies in other regions, states or countries to maintain consistency in the brand message. Again, you will find that you have an array of communication tools at your command. For instance, you will find that the media technologies are a key tool of the information spread. In time, you will become familiar with the production of corporate articles, brochures, newsletters, speeches, video, audio and multimedia scripts, product information, technical journals, shareholder reports, and myriad other forms of corporate communication. A special reference to media relations—you will establish and run systems for the dissemination of corporate information to appropriate print, audio-visual and digital media: newspapers, magazines, periodicals, websites, broadcast channels as well as general and trade publication editors. A rapport with the media is central to any corporate communications strategy. In your role as a consummate communicator, everybody, and we mean everybody in your organization, will look at you as a hub of trusted information.

The Organizational Catalyst

As the Corporate DISC test insight points out (see Box 10.1) a good corporate communicator brings a unique combination of aptitude and skills for his/her job. In him or her, you will find the qualities of leadership, influence, team work and being proactively corrective where necessary. For these reasons, the corporate communicator is seen as an organizational catalyst in the work environment. He or she is seen as the prime catalyst of change in the corporate, responsible for attuning its internal and external audiences to the directions of future change. In this role, you will find the communicator seeking out appropriate platforms of

Fig. 10.3: A Corporate Communicator's Organizational Roles

interaction with the diverse audiences. This will require skill in one-to-one communication as well as experience in one-to-many communication.

A subset of this role is taking centrestage as a master of ceremonies, preparation of speeches for others and ensuring the smooth conduct of a corporate's interactive functioning. This is a role that spans the gamut of corporate activity—from organizing conferences, exhibitions to product/service/facility launches. To build goodwill, consider hosting corporate events such as company conventions, contest and award programmes, tours and even special get-togethers for opinion-makers or a special interest group. In effect, it could be an special event or platform used to create attention and gain the acceptance of a corporate audience. Your role as an Organizational Catalyst is an integral step for your corporates long-term growth.

Parting Thoughts

In its fullest sense, this book has made a journey that has come full circle. It began its saga by looking at the sweeping processes of

Corporatization, Digitization and Globalization. These processes were typical of the sweeping change that characterized the last quarter of the 20th century—and they had an enormous impact on our corporate planet. In its conceptual flow, the book unveiled the 21st century Corporate in the first chapter, leading you to the logical evolution of the present-day corporate communicator in this chapter. It was a conceptual journey that began with the world of today's corporate, covering new theoretical ground in the emerging realm of corporate communications, and new audiences. It then took an in-depth look at the worlds of advertising and public relations, while delving into the technology areas of the traditional and digital media.

And, once these basic foundations of the subject were laid, there was the real-time application of corporate communications strategy for every manner of organization—businesses, non-profit organizations, companies and corporations. The last chapter has afforded you a look into the signposts of the immediate future, allowing you an anticipation of the broad trends that will typify the first decade of the 21st century. We looked at sunrise sectors like biotechnology, bio-informatics and nanotechnology, all of which are digitally driven.

It is clear that corporate communications is today an indispensable strategic tool for organizational growth. Applied with a sure-fire market strategy, it is a potent catalyst of market leadership. Look closely enough at the top corporates in India and across the world, and you will notice the application of a powerful corporate communications initiative. In today's intensively aggressive market arena, a corporate communicator is always an assertive, frontline strategist in the ranks of corporate warfare. Further, we have asserted that the more traditional fields of advertising and public relations are reinventing themselves to become strategic avatars of corporate communicators. We have looked at the qualities and facets of the corporate communicator as a corporate strategist, an organizational catalyst, a consummate communicator, a 'specialized' generalist and the quintessential network person. And, we spoke of the charmed 7,300 days over which your career graph must make its gradual rise to corporate prominence.

As time will prove, corporate communications is a potent catalyst of change and growth for the times that we live in. As you read these lines, its principles are being powerfully applied to every kind of organization, with the objective of tapping its full growth potential. As a strategy, it is quietly effective, while being powerfully assertive with its singular emphasis on steadily building corporate presence in the long term. In that respect, it draws its unlikely inspiration from the likes of Tai Chi, and other spiritual traditions. From the ripples of corporate communications initiative to riding the crest of corporate growth, it all zeroes in on the core qualities of the corporate communicator in you. It's your turn now.

Signposts

- The corporate communicator is the emerging media professional of the 21st century—an empowered media avatar, who draws on the established disciplines of advertising, journalism and public relations to strategize for building the images of corporates and organizations of the future.
- Education, for the corporate communicator in you, is the evolving body of academic knowledge and practical training that leads to your current organizational position. Ideally, a corporate degree with a specialization in advertising, marketing or public relations makes for a good start.
- Experience refers to the sum total of your work experience garnered over a period of time. It makes good sense to begin your career, with a stint in a quality media organization—be it in advertising, journalism or public relations.
- Expertise is your nurtured career competency—a unique skillset born of your aptitude, abilities and driven by your education and expertise. In the final analysis, it is your expertise as a corporate communicator that will put the spotlight on your career.
- As the corporate communicator of the new era corporate, you will fulfill your potential in three key roles: a corporate strategist, a consummate communicator, and an organisational catalyst.

New Era-Initiative

This one should interest you the most. It derives its inspiration from that time-tested tool of research: the experiential. To elaborate, the experiential is a scientific research term used for a set of findings or perceptions derived from the experience. It bases its projections for the future on results based on past and present findings. In our settings, the time has come to move from the signposts of the present to look ahead to the milestones of the future.

Imagine for a moment, that an entire decade has passed since you read this book. Given that it is the best of all possible worlds, you are now where you have always wanted to be. And, you are a corporate communicator. You planned your future, and you have arrived. In other words, where will you be exactly 3650 days from today?

Will you handle the corporate communications division of a biotechnology consortium for the Asia-Pacific Region in a south east Asian capital? Or, will you handle the communications division of an India-based NGO that oversees afforestation programmes in the wastelands of the Indian subcontinent? Or, very simply, are you a corporate communicator-turned-entrepreneur, running the day-to-day operations of a corporate communications firm that handles the dynamic accounts of the five top corporates in your city? You decide.

Most importantly, what are the realities of the future that you live in? When you gaze into this emerging picture of the future, what do you see? Is the world a radically different one from the one you used to know in the early years of the 21st century? What about the organization you work in, and its diverse audiences? Here, we are talking about the inner and outer circles of influence and interaction in corporate communications strategy. In other words, it is time now to write your own chapter. In 1000 vibrant words, paint your picture of the future. And, trust us, when we tell you that one day, 5 years or 10 years from now, this document of yours will be recognized as an eye-opener, and, it just might reveal the 21st century seer in you. So, share it with us at **median@vsnl.net**.

Sources

Publications

Blair, M., Armstrong, R. and Murphy, M. (2003). *The 360 Degree Brand in Asia: Creating More Effective Marketing Communications.* John Wiley & Sons (Asia) Pte Ltd, Singapore.
Collins, J.C. and Porras, J.I. (2000). *Built to Last.* Random House Business Books, London.
Croteau, D. and Hoynes, W. (2001). *The Business of Media: Corporate Media and the Public Interest*, Pine Forge Press, Thousand Oaks.
Kitchen, Philip J. and Schultz, Don E. (2001). *Raising the Corporate Umbrella: Corporate Communications in the 21st Century.* Palgrave, New York.

Periodicals

Fernandez, Joseph. (June 2000). 'Corporate Communications', *Business Mandate*, Chennai.
———— (April 2002). 'The Flow of Excellence', *The Hindu Business Line—Life*, Chennai.
Ramakrishnan, Anupama. (2nd December 2002). *Looking Up: BT Gets Set to Roll. Excel—The New Indian Express.*
Navin, Puja. (2nd December 2002). 'Winning Solutions: Public Relations', *Excel—The New Indian Express.*

Websites

www.medianonline.com
www.tai-chi.com
www.taichichuanforliving.com.

Further Reading

Geier, J.G. and Downey, D.E. (1992). The Personality Factor Profile, Geier Learning Systems, Minneapolis, USA.

Gunaratne, S.A.(Ed.) (2000). *Handbook of the Media in Asia.* Sage Publications, New Delhi.

Khanna, Satish. (2000). *The Future Manager: A Value Builder for Tomorrow's Organisation.* Tata McGraw-Hill, New Delhi.

Heider, Robert. (1995). *The Tao of Leadership.* Bantam New Age Books, California.

Valles, Carlos J. (1999). *Life in Seven Words.* Gujurat Sahitya Prakash, Ahmedabad.

Interviews

Arup Kavan
Managing Partner
Ogilvy PR Worldwide, Chennai

Dr Emma Gonsalvez
Emmaus HRD Consultancy, Chennai

George Kuriyan
Founder-Instructor
Vajra Warrior Arts, Chennai

Geraldine Lazaro,
HRD Professional, Chennai

Index